THE
FAMILY
FRIEND

For my wife and son

THE
FAMILY
FRIEND

MATT LOWE

EBURY
PRESS

1 3 5 7 9 10 8 6 4 2

Published in 2007 by Ebury Press, an imprint of Ebury Publishing

Ebury Publishing is a division of the Random House Group

The Random House Group Limited Reg. No. 954009

Addresses for companies within the Random House Group
can be found at www.randomhouse.co.uk

A CIP catalogue record for this book is available from the British Library.

The Random House Group Limited makes every effort to ensure that
the papers used in our books are made from trees that have been legally
sourced from well-managed and credibly certified forests. Our paper
procurement policy can be found on www.randomhouse.co.uk

Typeset by seagulls.net

Printed and bound in Great Britain by Mackays

ISBN 9780091912253

This book is substantially a work of non-fiction based on the life, experiences
and recollections of the author. In some limited cases names of people, places,
dates, sequences or the detail of events have been changed to protect the privacy
of others. The author has warranted to the publishers that, except in such minor
respects not affecting the substantial accuracy of the work, the contents of this
book are true. Whilst the publishers have taken care to explore and check where
reasonably possible, they have not verified all the information in this book
and do not warrant its veracity in all respects.

'If, from inside the *Lager*, a message could have seeped out to free men, it would have been this: take care not to suffer in your own homes what is inflicted on us here.'

PRIMO LEVI

~ Prologue ~

'Hi! What's your name?'

I'd pulled myself up against the railings and was looking down at a rough grey sea, waves breaking on the empty patch of sand below me. Twisting round, I saw a man standing a few yards away, grinning, a large camera in his hand.

'Matthew.'

I looked past him to check that Gracey was where I'd left her, sitting on one of the benches on the green.

'Matthew, good. What have you been up to today? Not really beach weather, is it?'

'We've been shopping.'

'Shopping, eh? Well, you'd be doing me a real favour if you let me take your picture. It's my job to take photographs, and I have to take dozens or else I get told off. Would you help me out, let me take one of you?'

I nodded.

'Great. I'll make sure it's a good one. Just relax. Hold it there, then.'

I stood while the man backed up a few steps and crouched down. The camera made a clicking noise.

'There, that'll make a good holiday snap – you can show your friends back home.'

'We're not on holiday, actually.' Having walked up behind

the man, Gracey was correcting him in the posh voice she put on for strangers – no sign of her usual warm Norfolk accent. 'We live here.'

'It'll still be a nice picture.'

The man scribbled something on a pad, tore off a slip and handed it to Gracey. With his untidy, long brown hair he looked a bit like a scarecrow. I was sure that was one reason why she was so unfriendly towards him.

'You can collect the picture from the photo booth by the main steps.'

'I doubt if we will.' Gracey seemed to disapprove.

The man grinned at me. 'Bye, then.'

Gracey took my hand and we walked on up past the war memorial towards home.

A few days later we were established in our usual place in front of the central steps on Shorefleet's fine sandy beach. The weather had turned again. My mother was stretched out on a bright blue beach towel with her eyes closed. She loved the sun. We'd pestered her for money for a trampoline ride, and again for candy floss. Knowing that we'd get no more treats, we concentrated on the free distractions all around us. With my big sister Ella I'd already gone up near the pier to stroke the donkeys, patting their prickly heads and leaping back when they stamped or shook. We knew them well – we sometimes went up to the paddock near our house where they were kept and fed them. And we'd been down to the sea. The water was cold and murky grey, but that hadn't deterred us from splashing in the tame waves before spending an age digging out an intricate system of canals and castles in the wet sand. We'd been clamouring for our sandwiches since finishing our candy floss, but we'd been made to wait until Daddy joined us during his lunch break from the bookshop. When he arrived we stayed close by, listening while he told Mummy funny stories about the customers. We didn't let him rest. When he lay down, my little sister Joanna and I climbed on top of his chest, urging him to pick us up by our ankles, higher and higher until we lost our balance and ended up sprawled in the sand or collapsed back onto his warm, heaving body.

Too soon, he left to return to the shop. The good weather had brought with it holiday-makers and day-trippers who filled the beach almost to bursting point and who also filled the town; this was the bookshop's busiest time of year.

The tide was retreating, and the rocks that extended out to sea on either end of the bay had been exposed. I went off on my own with a bucket, returning with three tiny crabs and some winkles. My brother Peter told me I'd have to take them back to the water or else they would die. Mummy intervened: 'Peter's right, but you don't have to do it yet. Just look after them carefully.'

I pushed the bucket into the sand so it wouldn't fall over and bent down to study the dead-still creatures cowering at the bottom.

'Hello, Elizabeth.'

We all turned round to look. It was the man with the camera.

'Hello, Jeremy. You playing beach photographer again? When are you going to get a proper job?'

'It's better than hiring out deckchairs, I can tell you. Is David coming down today?'

'He's been and gone. Some people have to work for a living, you know,' Mum teased.

Jeremy caught sight of me.

'Hey, it's you – I didn't realise you were a Lowe! I'll smuggle a copy of your photo out and bring it down later. It's a great little picture.'

Jeremy sat down, wrapping his camera up in his shirt and laying it carefully in Joanna's pushchair. He was thin, and each time he laughed his ribs stuck out. He'd taken off his thick cord trousers and sat talking in his swimming costume. He had a curved mouth, a narrow, pointed nose and the same scruffy hair that Mum referred to later as a haystack. He had a habit of pushing the hair up on the sides of his head as if he was afraid of it falling down. He spoke loudly and had a laugh like a bark.

'The day's glorious, isn't it?' Mum's question was directed at Jeremy, but he didn't answer. Perhaps he didn't hear, perhaps he didn't think it was a question that needed answering. But an answer came. Without warning, an inky-grey storm cloud burst over the beach. It caught everyone unawares, having crept up from behind the town and suddenly appearing above the chalk cliffs. It was brilliant: thousands of sun-worshippers, us among them, rose as one in a frenzy, packing towels, pushing books and magazines into bags, squealing as shirts stuck cold to bodies, shouting and dashing across the soft sand for the steps.

~ 1 ~

The streetlights threw their ugly luminescence through the curtains, giving no clue as to the time. I lay in bed, agitated, my body refusing to be still. I tried to soothe my restlessness to the rhythm of my wife's even breathing. But her serenity presented itself as a rebuke. I groped amongst the debris on the bedside table for my watch. Twenty past three. I'd probably lain awake for an hour already. As quietly as I could, I pulled back the duvet.

'Where are you going? What time is it?' Carmen's voice indicated that my efforts not to disturb her had been in vain yet again.

'I'm going to make myself a drink. It's just after three.'

'Come on, love, try and sleep. You can put the light on and read here if you need to.'

'I will, in a bit.'

Switching on the downstairs lights, I took in my surroundings – so familiar yet today so devoid of sense. Just things: cooker, tables, pictures on the wall, piles of paper. I splashed myself as I filled the kettle and jumped back onto the floorboard that creaked. Even the house seemed to be fighting me. I glanced up at the diagonal crack that had appeared across the kitchen wall earlier that year. If I had the money, I thought, I'd underpin the whole house. Fill it in with concrete. Make it solid.

It was a relief to be alone when you couldn't stop thinking and every thought stank. At least in the middle of the night there was no pressure to be agreeable. Of course, I'd pay for it in the morning. At any other time a Henry James novel would have lulled me back to sleep, but I was in no mood to read. Concentrating had been difficult for a couple of months, since some time before Christmas. Christmas: at least that was over. I remembered the relief at getting through the shopping. And then the comments as I did my best to muck in: 'You not feeling yourself, Matt?'; 'You're not very talkative, Matt … anything up?' The week in Majorca feeling dreadful, trying not to spoil another holiday for Carmen and failing.

I sat at the kitchen table. The previous morning I'd lost my temper. I'd lost my sense of proportion, that's what Carmen had implied. Yet I'd felt so incensed and couldn't understand how everyone else was behaving so calmly. I'd walked into the kitchen; Carmen had been pouring the tea. It must have been eight o'clock, because the news was being read on the radio: 'Later today, Tony Blair will give a speech in his Sedgefield constituency, outlining again his reasons for going to war in Iraq. He will acknowledge that that decision has left lasting and deep divisions in the country, but he will insist that his was the responsible course of action, protecting British interests and world peace ….' I'd taken one stride over to the radio and snapped at the 'off' button.

'Love, I was listening to that.'

I'd started shouting: 'He's the fucking terrorist. I can't bear hearing it. What kind of mad place do we live in: how do people sit in Radio 4's studio reporting this stuff without laughing? We shit on the Third World for a couple of hundred years and don't like it when they've had enough of it. "Pre-emptive attacks", destroy the UN … the bastards go and rip up the rules just because it suits them. And it does my head in when they pretend they're inspired by moral principles. Every BBC journalist should be instructed to break out into uncontrollable giggles every time Blair opens his mouth.'

'I agree with you, but you can't let it get to you like this.'

'Why not? He's killed tens of thousands of people, and he's getting away with it. I can't stand it. Pay the fucking licence fee, and have lies and poison with your shredded wheat.'

Carmen had put her arms round my neck. 'What's wrong?'

'What do you mean? The world's full of crap, that's what's wrong.'

'You can tell me, you know. You're depressed again. You're not sleeping properly.'

'I'm fine.'

To avoid further questions I'd gone upstairs. Now, holding my mug in my hands, I was still trying to hold in my rage. I was poisoned with hate and utterly powerless. At the same time I knew Carmen was right: I was going crazy. But, I told myself, I didn't need to tell her, not yet anyway. It would wear off. If I talked to her she would worry. She'd be full of questions I wouldn't know how to answer, and that would just make things worse.

It had begun in small ways. I was tired all the time, a deep fatigue that left my arms and legs heavy and cumbersome. Despite that, I spent hours awake each night, my mind racing. Getting through the business of everyday life seemed a chore, an imposition. I started to resent any request that intruded on my time, anything that demanded an effort. I seethed with frustration, tried to hide it, became short-tempered, and then annoyed and anxious if Carmen commented on it. It was a damage-limitation exercise: a war raged inside me, with its own battle fronts and torture chambers. Like the warmongers, I was trying to present a semblance of normality.

Work had helped keep me sane, but that was no longer the case. As a residential social worker, I helped to look after a group of adolescents too disturbed to manage in foster placements. It had been the right job for me: it gave me a sense of being useful, of feeling good inside. The kids' stories were horrific, so bad they couldn't talk or think about what had happened to them. Instead they were impelled to re-enact the damage, on one another, on the staff, on themselves. Now I fought off the critical, self-loathing voice inside that told me I was incompetent and that everyone knew it. I tried to push away my growing fear of the young people I was meant to be helping; they, I was sure, could tell instantly that I was just going through the motions.

When I arrived at work that morning, bleary-eyed from too little sleep, the residents were still upstairs and the staffroom was humming with a furious energy. There were several groups deep in heated conversation. All I could pick up was their anger, their determination and the anticipation of a fight. It turned out that there had been an incident during the night and the night team were keen to pass their rage and dismay on to their fresh-faced replacements. One of the young boys, Martin, had broken into the director's office. He had forced open the filing cabinet containing the personnel files and had been taunting the staff with details of their salaries and home addresses. Martin aroused strong feelings in the staff team. Some liked him and believed he was 'workable'. Some didn't and regarded him as a con artist, exploiting staff and dedicated only to monopolising staff attention. Now the split was even more apparent, with Martin's allies very much on the defensive.

When Lillian, the deputy director, came in behind me, the noise subsided. We arranged ourselves for our meeting, but for a long moment nobody spoke. It was Cynthia who finally began:

'I know I'm not just speaking for myself when I say that I'm absolutely disgusted. I can't express how enraged I feel. Martin's a dangerous psychopath. How can I feel safe at work when he knows where I live? We can't possibly pretend that we have the capacity to help him. He's a dangerous influence on the others. He gets to know the most vulnerable things about the other children without giving anything away himself, and then he exploits them. I don't understand why we're not taking more decisive action. If it was one of the other boys, there would have been hell to pay by now.'

Cynthia and I had worked well together for several years, but we were on opposite sides of the fence when it came to Martin. After several other colleagues had joined in the call for his exclusion, Heather, a soft-spoken trainee psychotherapist who had only recently joined the organisation, tried to introduce a different point of view. 'I had a meeting with Martin yesterday evening, and he was talking about his relationship with his uncle. I've written an account for his file. He wasn't being explicit, but he seemed to want to tell me that his uncle had abused him.'

A hostile groan emanated from the back of the room. This threw Heather, as it was intended to do, and when she carried on it was with the pleading tone of one who didn't expect to be listened to seriously. 'I was sure that was what he was getting at. I agree that we need to be clear about boundaries, but I also think he's at a critical point and that he needs sensitive handling. I'd like to offer him some additional sessions.'

Looking round, I could see that most of those present were openly scornful. Ryan spoke next. He had worked at the home for longer than anyone else, and his voice, with its confident Irish accent, carried weight. 'I don't care about all that now. For one thing, I'm not sure we should take his disclosures at face value.

He knows how to work the system, that's for sure. And this latest incident puts him beyond the pale. I'm going to be making a complaint if management expects us to go on working when our personal information is freely available to the children.'

The meeting was going badly. We worked with the expectation that a damaged child would use members of staff to 'project' poisonous or perverse aspects of themselves onto. They hit out or raged or made accusations, and we were there to take this behaviour as a communication, telling us something of what they had been through. It was our job to allow that to happen without rejecting them, without pushing the poison back.

And it often worked. Over and over again children arrived accompanied by a chorus of despair: their own, that of their social workers and family members and, as we read their files, ours too. And then, over the weeks and months, we'd see their yearning for love reassert itself. In tiny ways at first and often accompanied by the most challenging outbursts, testing everyone's patience and tolerance, fighting to prove that they didn't need to be cared for and that they didn't deserve to be loved. Sometimes their destructive side won out, but sometimes, at least, we moved forward, and it would seem possible that they might struggle towards a future that was not just about hurting and being hurt. That was how it was supposed to work. But now and then the poison worked too well, and the staff would unite to reject a child outright. This was what was happening at the meeting.

I had kept in the background. At first I'd struggled to feel a part of what was going on, to care about the outcome. Gradually that changed: I started to feel the group's hostility as if it were directed at me. When Martin was judged, I felt defensive. As the opinion that we should end his placement gained momentum, I felt increasingly oppressed and alone. Then Cynthia made another contribution. 'In my relationship with Martin, I sense that the fundamental issue goes back to an early maternal failure. I see this burglary as an envious attack on us because we offer the opportunity of something good. He's hell-bent on destruction. I agree that we need to review the decision to keep him.'

At this, my sense of isolation and despair became urgent. I tried to catch Heather's attention, to see how she was responding. I found myself wanting to scream out in Martin's defence. But being uncomfortable at the strength of my reaction didn't hold me back. I stood up. 'What's got into you? Who the hell are you to doubt his story? What bloody theory is it that leads you to prioritise his relationship with his mother and doubt his attempt to tell us about his being hurt by his uncle? Where's he going to go? What's going to happen to him? Don't you care?'

I was dismayed to find my voice cracking. Ashamed, I looked down at my hands and sat down. It seemed that I'd unwittingly exposed something about myself. I fought in vain to regain my composure, disconnected completely from what was going on around me. I vaguely heard the deputy director rebuke me for my aggressive tone.

I would probably have taken the same line at any other time, but I wouldn't have been shouting and I wouldn't have had tears rolling down my face. Later I would think of how, by reading through our files, Martin had defiled us in the same way that he had been defiled, that he had found a way of getting us to feel the outrage he couldn't feel on his own behalf. But that was later. At this point I was too upset to think. Unable to stop the tears, I levered myself out of my chair, mumbled an apology and fled from the room. I sat in another office alone while I calmed down. Half an hour later, I went to the admin section and handed in my notice.

*

'You resigned?' Carmen sounded anxious.

'Yeah.' The line went quiet for a while. 'Do you mind?'

'No, I don't think so. We'll manage.' She became reassuring. 'When you need to, I know you'll find work, something closer to home, I hope, and with fewer evenings. I'm glad, really. But how are you?'

'Yeah, OK, fine. Relieved. It's going to be difficult saying goodbye to the kids.'

'We'll talk tonight, then. Lots of love.'

*

We talked late that evening. Carmen drew me down onto the sofa and told me it was quite clear that I wasn't fine. She put her arms around me.

'We've been through this often enough, haven't we? It doesn't help that you try to hide it. It just creates this awful silence between us.'

The pressure behind my ribs grew too strong, my eyes stung, and I looked away, blinking. What had gone wrong? Why couldn't I shake this off? The past was bothering me again: images, situations, questions. All coloured by bleakness, by regret. I knew the game was up. 'I'm sorry. I can't help it. I don't want to cause more problems. You've got enough to worry about without me going funny again. But I can't …'

'It's all right. It's always easier for me when we talk about it.'

For a long time I just cried while Carmen held me. It was such a relief. When I was cried out, we talked. I told her about how I didn't feel a part of my own life any more. I told her how worried I was that she'd run out of patience, give up on me. She smiled at that, and held me closer and told me how stupid I was. But still I felt afraid: I watched her expression carefully for meanings that contradicted her words. I glossed over my preoccupation with death. Nor did I share with her the full force of the self-destructive thoughts that intruded as I did my work, cooked dinner, helped our son with his homework.

At the same time the sense of release was palpable. It now seemed silly not to have spoken before. My fears, it seemed, were groundless: Carmen was caring and concerned, not disappointed or critical. I told her that I'd been considering going back into therapy. She thought that was a good idea and brushed aside my worries about the cost.

Why had it happened? Why hadn't I stopped it? Why hadn't I told anyone? A pianist was playing Mozart on the television. The musician's head filled the screen. I watched his concentration, his commitment, his self-belief. This man didn't worry that everyone thought he was a fraud like I did. I wished I could change. But how could I change when it felt as if I was living in the past all over again?

~ 2 ~

Home was 8 Bayview Road, a minute's walk from the chalk and flint cliffs that surround Shorefleet. We lived in an Edwardian semi: a long lounge made out of two rooms knocked into one, a 'living room' where we ate and, attached to that, a kitchen. Upstairs, the bathroom and the bedrooms, mine at the very top of the house. There was a front yard, an untidy overgrown patch with a path running round the side of the house. The back door led out through a lean-to into a tiny back yard – worn grass, clothes-line, a gate to the alley. This was the centre of my world, a world that extended to the end of the alley at the back and, at the front, along the pavement on either side of our house, past the Spencers and the Lamberts to the left, in the other direction the Carters and the Biggses. Further afield were other safe spots: the bookshop where my dad worked, the beach and the pier, and the High Street where I went shopping with Mummy. And there was Nanny Langton's bright and colourful bungalow not far away, and Nanny Lowe's drab and smoky flat in London.

Towering over everything were the gigantic figures of my mum and dad. Other people had kindly faces and eyes that warmed me, but their eyes meant home. To be wrapped up snug in my own bed was a pale imitation of being mixed up with them in theirs, a comfortable exile only, an outpost. On waking I'd head straight for their room and face the dilemma of choosing which side to slide in on. They each had their own smell, the one tart, the other sweet. Daddy lay on his side and breathed on you, while Mummy lay on her back; her hair fell across the pillow and tickled. Once the decision had been made, I'd lie there as the light strengthened, a limb gently laid against the warm skin of my sleeping parent while my eyes wandered over the plaster fruit on the ceiling rose, the carvings around the door of Mum's heavy wooden wardrobe, the pattern of the wallpaper.

My parents were called David and Elizabeth. As well as my sisters Ella and Joanna, I had a brother, Peter. Boy girl boy girl. The symmetry extended to our ages: eight, six, four, two. I think we all felt incredibly fortunate to be part of this particular family.

The conviction that it was special didn't mean liking everyone in it, not all of the time anyway. Home provided security from whatever lay beyond, but within it could be a place of struggle and competition, carrying the real and immediate threat of feeling excluded, of being pierced through by hatred and hurt. My sisters got in the way a good deal, occupying Mummy and Daddy, and I found this difficult. Nor were the children all treated the same, which was almost unbearable. The elder two were given privileges denied to the younger pair, which meant that I suffered the indignity of sharing baths and bedtimes with Joanna, the baby of the house and the one who got in the way the most. At times I felt closest to our black cat, Fifi, whom I considered to be mine and who, I was convinced, shared this assumption.

Gracey belonged to my world too. Gracey and Joanna had arrived at the same time, though by different routes. My dad had put an advertisement for a home help in the bookshop window when Joanna was born. Gracey had come in the next day to offer her services. It was as difficult imagining a world without Gracey as it was one without Joanna. It was more pleasant thinking of a world without Joanna.

Gracey wasn't quite Mary Poppins. She was shorter than most adults, wore horn-rimmed glasses and had a big mole on her upper lip. Her hair was stringy and stuck up. But she was beautiful inside, and the beauty shone through her eyes. She couldn't hide her feelings, and she liked giving hugs and cuddles. I liked to hear her tell about the time she had to chase me up the road to get me to wash my face, something I could barely remember. Gracey was at the house every weekday morning just after we got up, helping with the breakfast things while Dad prepared to leave for work and Mum organised the older children for school. Gracey had a husband called George who would drop in for coffee after completing his round as a postman. He had a singing accent and came from Wales, where he'd been a miner. George was quiet, but he said a lot with his face, his mobile chin and his lined eyes, and it was always good.

It was great being one of the gang of untidy and easygoing kids who spread chaos throughout the three floors of the house in Bayview Road. I looked up to my brother, who was the serious one and was pleasing Mummy and Daddy by doing well at school. I felt closest to my older sister, Ella, who looked after me and told me stories. Ella struggled at school, and struggled at home having her long hair brushed and plaited in the morning, and she clashed with Gracey, who thought she was big enough to tidy up her own bedroom. She sometimes shouted at the adults, which was really shocking. But she always watched out for me. I didn't take any more notice of Joanna than I had to. Having an adult to oneself was a rare treat. My earliest memories were all of times when I'd found myself on my own with one or both parents.

At home I could be a show-off: I was always finding ways to make people laugh. I learnt how to wiggle my ears, and I'd tease and tickle my brother and sisters. Daddy would challenge me to hold my head under the cold tap in the bath, or offer me a reward if I could turn my head around 180 degrees. But I also earned the reputation of being a bad loser – for getting upset and angry if things didn't go my way.

Our downstairs was always chock-a-block with books. We children quickly understood that they were precious. In fact, books were not far behind people in status and value. A constant stream of boxes passed through the house. We had shiny new books that smelt clean and were given plastic covers before being sent off to schools and libraries. And old books that smelt nasty and which sent out a cloud of dust when Daddy picked them up and snapped the covers shut with a bang. There were books that were too big and heavy for us to pick up, like the one Daddy would get down off the bookshelf which was full of coloured drawings of poisonous snakes, and which he said was worth a lot of money. He had a small collection of special finds that would be taken out and pored over from time to time, and an assortment of stories about how they'd been found and bargained for. Books were self-evidently magical, miraculous and worthy, in the way that gold must have been, or silk, in days gone by.

I was already discovering the weird and wonderful ways in which books could change the way you felt, leaving you sad or frightened, and then sometimes so relieved. We were read to every night before going to sleep, so each day would have at its close the prospect of reliving a favourite tale – of Rapunzel, or perhaps of Rumpelstiltskin – made safe by the reassuring presence of one of my parents. At the same time books would take my parents away. Dad had to be at the shop six days a week – seven in the summer, when he stayed open till late. And when he was home, more often than not he would spend the evening pricing up second-hand books he'd bought or covering new ones before packing them for delivery. Mum would usually help him if she hadn't cleared away a corner of the living-room table so that she could spread out the cash-books, which were her particular area of expertise.

*

Starting school was a step I'd longed for. I wanted to join the big children in their smart clothes and shiny shoes; I didn't want to be left behind any more. That first day I was ready early, but nobody else seemed to be. Ella was screaming as Gracey plaited her hair. Peter couldn't find the football that he *had* to take with him. Joanna was still in her high chair eating. I stood grinning by the door. I noticed Gracey turn towards me with an odd look on her face. Then I was kissing Mummy goodbye and walking out into the street, my older siblings arguing about whose turn it was to sit beside the driver.

'Be a good boy,' Mum called after me. To Dad I heard her add her ritual farewell: 'Good hunting. See you at tea-time.'

We sang 'My Bonnie Lies Over the Ocean' as we drove first towards Peter's junior school, Daddy's voice louder than the rest. I remember picturing a Victorian lady walking along the clifftop in a gale, bent against the wind and clutching at her bonnet just too late to avoid it being swept away, up into the air and out above the white-crested waves. We dropped Peter at his school, then Ella and I were taken on to St Cuthbert's Infant School. Ella held my hand in the playground. We walked over and waited near the double doors where there were lots of mothers standing, some alone looking serious, some in pairs talking, while their children – the new first years – hung around their ankles. A lady emerged from the blue doors and rang a golden bell. 'Would all the new boys and girls follow me, please. Say goodbye now and come along with me. Your mothers will be back to pick you up later.'

Ella pushed me forward, and I found myself jostled along with a large group of strange children. I turned and saw her smile. She'd already told me that she would come and find me at break time. And I knew that Mummy would be there to pick us up at the end of the day.

The group was herded along a corridor and then off into a large room with high ceilings and tall windows framed by painted metal bars. Amongst a jumble of chairs and small tables were some longer benches holding boxes of crayons and piles of paper cut into large squares. Within a few minutes we were all drawing. All except a blond-haired boy with frightened eyes who cried loudly and continuously. The other children glanced up at him from time to time and avoided looking at one another.

I knew why he was crying. It made me think of home. I wanted to be back with Gracey, and I wasn't and Joanna was. I'd heard Mum and Dad making arrangements for the day, and knew that when Gracey had finished her housework she was going to take Joanna back home with her. If I hadn't been at school I'd have been going too. I pictured Gracey taking Joanna into the bakery on the way to her flat and pointing to the cakes and telling her to choose the one she wanted for pudding. I stopped paint-ing and looked around. I felt alone, and the room – its wooden chairs, its shiny white-painted walls and the mass of strange, noisy people – felt cold and hard. The blond boy was still crying, his wails getting louder and more urgent despite the efforts of the two teachers to calm him down and interest him in what the rest of us were doing. Suddenly the door opened, and one of the ladies who had been standing in the yard earlier came in and scooped the crying child into her arms and disappeared. I felt my stomach tighten. The grown-ups were bending over one of the tables talking to one another. I looked down at my paper and the scribble pattern I'd started, decided I didn't like it, turned the paper over and began to draw a lightship.

By the time I found Mummy standing by the gate, things had changed. After a while the large group had been divided into two, the first group staying in the classroom with Miss Woodcock, a tall, mousy, soft-spoken lady with a warm smile set in a long face and thick brown tights worn under a heavy long skirt. The rest, including me, were taken across the playground with Miss Olivier to a classroom that stood on its own. Miss Olivier had a fierce voice, pointed spectacles and sharp, shiny black shoes. But I'd found a friend in the boy who'd been sat next to me as we were arranged alphabetically: Alex Jeffreys. I thought we were very much alike. Alex was my height with light brown hair and freckles. Our friendship was properly sealed at lunchtime. I'd always like my food, but Alex didn't. So I had two lunches.

When she came to collect me, I gave Mummy several large sheets covered with my artistic efforts.

'Very nice. And did you make some new friends?'

I told her about Alex. And as we walked over the footbridge by the station I tried to describe Miss Olivier. At tea-time that night I had to tell all the same stuff to Daddy. I wanted to, of course.

'I can't believe it. Three of them at school already. I'll be collecting my pension soon. It feels like only yesterday that you were born, Matthew.'

I made the effort to imagine that time: Peter and Ella would have been around, but no me. And no Joanna. It didn't seem possible.

'We were in the flat above the shop then, of course. It was when we knew you were on the way that we realised we'd have to move.'

Ella wanted to know more. 'Was it a dark flat? Like Nanny's?'

'A bit. Not so tidy. And more cramped. But we had a wonderful view over the bay.'

'So Ella was the youngest then? Before me.' I was working things out.

Mummy answered, 'That's right. We got into a bit of a pickle the night you were born. You were a couple of days overdue, and the midwife came round to see what was going on. She decided that nothing was likely to happen during the night. But around eleven o' clock I realised that you were getting ready to come out.'

'I was inside your tummy.' This was a statement rather than a question, although I hardly believed it could have been true. The idea itself felt wrong, and I quickly let it go.

'Daddy rang the midwife, who didn't arrive until nearly midnight. She was a lovely old soul. She said that the doctor had had a hard day and we should do our best not to disturb him. Peter and Ella had both been born in hospital, and we said we thought the doctor should come, but the midwife said that with Daddy's help everything would be fine.'

'So I was the only one born at home.' Something in Mummy's tone suggested that being born at home was better than being born in a hospital.

'You were the first to be born at home: Joanna was born here. Anyway, the midwife told Daddy what to do – boil up lots of water, organise towels, tell me when I had to push – and we got on perfectly well, didn't we, darling?'

'It was some night,' Dad raised his eyes to the ceiling. 'I wasn't very pleased about it at first, but we did a brilliant job. Not many dads get to be involved like that. And you two were fast asleep in the other bedroom, not realising that you'd wake up the next morning with a baby brother.'

'Just the three of us,' I muttered inaudibly, eyes fixed on my toast and Marmite.

'And the next morning I took you two out for a walk on the beach to give Mummy and Matthew a bit of a rest, but that didn't work out as planned, did it, because you, you little monkey' – Daddy squeezed Ella's ear – 'chose to go swimming! I'd met a customer walking his dog and we were chatting away, and I turned round and there you were up to your neck in the water – in March! So we had to get home pronto, give you a hot bath and hope you hadn't caught pneumonia!'

*

The end of that first school week, like every Friday, was bath night for me and Joanna. This particular evening I ran up the stairs after tea and was already jumping about naked as Mummy put the plug in and began to fill the tub. Then she fetched Joanna and sat her on her lap to undress her.

'You'll miss school tomorrow.' Mum always talked so as to let us know that school was something to look forward to.

'How many days is it before I go again, Mummy?'

'Tomorrow is Saturday, then there's Sunday, and school opens again on Monday.'

'That's a long time.'

'Not so sure about that. Here – put these things, and your pants and socks, in the washing basket, would you.'

When I came back, Joanna was sitting in the shallow bath.

'Come on, in you get.'

As I climbed in, the telephone rang downstairs.

'I'll be back in a minute.'

Joanna splashed the water with her short arms. I picked up a rubber duck and squeezed out the air so that it filled with water, then squeezed it again, directing the flow over Joanna's back. She laughed.

'Ha, ha, I can wee on you too! Look at me, I'm doing a wee-wee on your head!' I stood behind my little sister and directed a flow of wee into her hair. I'd discovered a new game!

Joanna turned and saw the stream of warm liquid dance over her shoulders and into her short curls. She beamed and chuckled and splashed her hands into the water again and again. I heard Mum humming as she came back up the stairs, and as she walked into the room I proudly announced, 'Look, Mummy, I did a wee-wee on Joanna's head!'

Mum froze momentarily. Then bent over the bath, smelling the air. 'Whatever did you think you were doing? You disgusting child! Get out! Upstairs! She's your sister, for God's sake. How could you?'

The tirade rang in my ears; both of us were crying by now, Joanna more loudly than me. Too crushed to protest, I just snivelled and sniffed. There were times when I knew I'd done something naughty, like when I teased Joanna when we were alone, but this time I'd been misunderstood. I wanted to explain that it had only been a game. I hadn't hurt her! She'd liked it. What had begun as a triumph of inventiveness had turned out a disaster. I was hauled out of the bath by a furious woman holding me at arm's length, who then threw a towel at me and pushed me through the door.

Grizzling quietly, I made my way up the stairs to my bedroom and lay on my top bunk feeling that the whole world had been spoiled, and that it was my fault. I put my hand between my legs and held myself. My willy – Mummy called it my bottom – was a comfort, though it seemed a complicated thing. I remembered discovering how lovely it was to hold myself. We'd been visiting relatives, and I'd been curious to watch a distant cousin, a little older than me, holding his bottom while lying in front of the television. And I copied him. And then Mrs Biggs had caught me and her son, Brian, in their outside toilet showing one another what our willies could do: I could pull the skin right back on mine, but the skin on Brian's got stuck. Mrs Biggs was cross and said that if she ever found us in there together again, she'd tell my mother and I wouldn't be allowed to play with Brian any more. So perhaps it was bad or dirty.

The next morning I was the first to get downstairs and put the kettle on the stove. I filled the pot as I'd learnt to do from watching Peter and Ella. Both my parents were still asleep as I put the tray on the floor and pushed open the door. The room was already filled with a wondrous golden light, the morning sun being filtered through the bright yellow curtains and reflected off the bedspread. The scene felt overpowering to me. The bath incident was not mentioned again, and although I never forgot it I was relieved that when Mummy opened her eyes and saw me holding her mug of tea, she gave me one of her best smiles ever.

*

Christmas 1964 was the first holiday I was to remember clearly. Not the events of the day – the opening of stockings or the big meal, Dad lighting the brandy around the pudding or Nanny Langton playing the piano. What I remembered took place in the early hours of Christmas morning, while the rest of the house was fast asleep.

I woke as I sometimes did, needing to go to the toilet. The bedroom was never completely dark as Joanna liked to have the curtains left open, so the streetlamps could throw their ghostly light into the room. I lay on my bunk, blankets pulled tightly around my neck, and tried to ignore the pressure, knowing that it was bitterly cold outside. But in the end I just had to go. My foot felt for the ladder, and I climbed down to the floor. I grabbed my dressing gown from the back of the door, found my slippers and was soon edging my way along the landing past Ella's bedroom and down the stairs, careful to avoid the steps that creaked too loudly.

After relieving myself I hesitated and then descended purposefully to the ground floor. I was excited: for me the night was over. And it was warmer downstairs, thanks to the newly installed storage heaters. I wanted to look at the Christmas tree, then find a toy. I pushed open the door to the front room: it looked magical. By the lights on the tree I could see that the piles of books had been cleared away. The ceiling roses were joined to the corners of the room by the paper chains that Ella and I had helped Mum make from packets of coloured paper strips. Bought decorations hung along the walls. There were balloons pinned at intervals along the picture rail. In the middle of the bay window stood the tree which Dad had brought in a few days before, complaining bitterly about the price and generally behaving as if the whole business of Christmas was a terrible waste of time and money. But now it was a blaze of colour and wrapped chocolates. I considered picking off a bag of chocolate money. I knew I wasn't supposed to, not without permission. Then my attention shifted. In the middle of the floor was a shiny, bright red tricycle. It had large wheels with real tyres, a bell and a boot covered by a tin lid. It was beautiful. I knew it wasn't intended for me, but I couldn't, didn't want to, stop myself from touching this, the greatest of all toys before anyone else got their hands on it. Fearful of discovery, I grasped the handlebars and turned them gently to the left, then to the right. I felt the soft saddle, and then quietly placed my feet on the pedals so that I could stand astride the machine and move it quietly forwards. I sat back on the saddle and rode the bike around the room.

I climbed the stairs again with a heavy soul, with a deep sense of having done wrong. Guilt for having seen the bike before I was supposed to have done, guilt for having ridden it when it was intended for someone else, envy of whoever that was, and grief at having to give up something that wasn't really mine in the first place. I lay in bed feeling deeply miserable, dreading the morning to come.

When the whole family were allowed into the front room, I was shaking. Peter's voice rose above the others: 'Who's that bike for?'

There was an unbearable silence.

'That's for Matt.'

I didn't hear at first, and when it sank in I responded in a way that Mum couldn't have understood: I burst into tears. It was several minutes before I could be consoled. From then on, that red tricycle and I were inseparable.

Once I'd mastered the technique of riding the bike and the weather had got warmer, I was allowed to take Dad's lunch to him at work. Mum would wrap up the sandwiches, put them in a bag with a flask and place the bag in the bike's big boot. She would show me across the road onto the clifftop promenade and I'd make my way round the coast, past the war memorial to the small green opposite the bookshop. I wasn't allowed to cross Clarion Street until Dad came out and checked that it was safe. This was the routine until, one day, just as I came past Jubilee Gardens, a policeman called out to me. I was interrogated as to my destination and the purpose of my journey, and then escorted to the red telephone boxes in Grantham Square. Here the policeman telephoned the bookshop, confirmed that I was indeed expected with my delivery and then scolded Dad for letting a child of such an age out onto the streets on his own. The family thought this hilarious, but I didn't deliver lunch to Dad for a long time after that.

*

An age later – a bright spring morning – I was with my next-door neighbour, Brian, hurrying along the same clifftop route. We didn't want to be late. Passing by the war memorial we took in the view of the bay and pier: nothing in particular to detain us. But it did seem wondrous in the clear sunshine, a sea of sparkling jewels too bright for us to look at without screwing up our eyes. We hastened on. Our destination was the Carlton cinema: it was Saturday morning. Halfway up Market Street we joined the queue and were soon in the auditorium whose hundred or so seats were rapidly filling with boys and girls. Brian called out to friends from his school and began a conversation with the boy sitting next to him, a stranger to us both. They shared a joke I didn't understand, and then showed one another their collections of football cards. I watched a pair of identical twins, identically presented, walk side by side down the aisle and sit down near the front.

'Can you remember what happened last week?' Brian asked, turning back to me. I correctly guessed what the question referred to.

'Dick Barton was taken prisoner. He was trapped in a sinking ship.'

'Oh yeah, he was after those diamond smugglers who'd kidnapped that woman, thinking she knew where the treasure had been hidden. I think.'

Before the Dick Barton serial came three cartoons. My favourite was always Woody Woodpecker.

It was getting on for noon when we emerged back into the sunlight. We turned down towards the pier, taking our time before going home for lunch. After leaning over the railings to watch the waves slap up lazily at the concrete overhang, we climbed down the spiral staircase onto the soft sand. Brian picked up a short piece of planking that was half hidden in a bank of seaweed and threw it into the water. We searched for pieces of chalk and had a contest to see who would hit the floating target first.

'Look at this one – a real skimmer,' I called out. But after I'd thrown the almost perfect disc, I wished I hadn't drawn attention to it, as it only bounced twice before sinking.

'I'll skim with this one.' Brian held out a stone that wasn't a skimmer at all, but I knew that he'd still be able to make it bounce along on top of the water. We counted – seven jumps!

'What are you doing after lunch?' Brian asked.

'Nothing.'

'Why don't you come over, then?'

'OK.'

We walked across the beach to the main steps but took a detour to Clarion Street to drop in on Dad. The town was busier now, with shoppers and weekenders crowding the narrow pavements. Brian hung about outside while I went up the steps into the shop.

I loved the shop because Daddy loved it. Because it was Daddy's realm. He worked, as Mum would say, 'all the hours God sends'. Dad would half jokingly and completely seriously insist that he was running a public service, and the family all bought into that idea. The shop was to be classed alongside the hospital, the post office and, of course, the library, not thought of as in the same league as Woolworth's, W.H. Smith's and the butcher's.

It was a small space crammed to the ceiling. The shelves near the top carried old books so dusty you couldn't read their titles. Over and over again, you'd hear people remark with surprise at the number of books they'd find on walking through the doorway and react with wonder when Dad could find the very thing they were after. The shop was not tidy, but Dad knew where everything was, while at home he would be hard pressed to find anything. I would listen as he responded with dignity and knowledge to each enquiry. He was not at all like the man who ran the post office in Marlborough Place, who smiled all the time and seemed grateful to every customer. Dad's voice was proud, and sometimes I thought he was being rude. I could pick up the edge that would creep into his voice when he felt his time was being wasted, or the slight contempt that would show when a customer asked about a book of which he disapproved.

Dad was deep in serious conversation with a customer, and I held back by the children's books until they had finished. 'Mummy said to come here to get my pocket money.'

'Hello, Matthew.' Dad responded, with a touch of surprise and a real show of pleasure. There was a quality to my father that I often encountered in the bookshop though seldom elsewhere, something that spoke of complete satisfaction and ease. I often came to the shop, where, despite the fact that Dad was always complaining about being busy and never seemed to stop moving, he also gave me the sense of being completely present.

'Where have you been?'

'The pictures with Brian. We're on our way back now.'

'Good. Yes. Hurry back because there's a visitor there who'll be pleased to see you again. Do you remember Jeremy? He's just arrived back from the Continent. Having lunch with Mummy. Go on, now.'

'Can I have my pocket money too?'

'Oh yes, shouldn't forget that, should we. Don't spend it all at once.' Dad reached back to the till, took nine pennies and handed them to me.

Brian and I were talking about the slow-worms he'd found in his garden as we walked up the back alley, kicking the loose stones and pulling at the weeds that flourished beside the brick walls which hid the small yards on either side. At the end of the alleyway we reached our back garden, and with a brief 'See ya later, then,' Brian climbed over the wooden fence while I walked through our shed and into the kitchen. I immediately heard voices coming from the living room, Mum's and a man's, and I hesitated for a long moment trying to identify the second speaker's voice. I couldn't; nor did I recognise him when the pair came into view. They were sitting at opposite ends of the dining table with empty mugs in front of them. Mum's face lit up at seeing me. I was wondering where my brother and two sisters had got to and why they weren't here to dilute the ordeal of being introduced to another stranger.

'Hello, darling. You remember Jeremy, don't you? He's been telling me about his time in France and Switzerland. Come and tell him what you've been up to while I pull some lunch together.'

Jeremy had turned and smiled while my mother was talking. 'I've been hearing about you. Elizabeth tells me that you're interested in dinosaurs.'

I wasn't sure what to do. I liked to hear that I'd been talked about, but I knew well enough that adults didn't really want to talk to children properly, and I wasn't going to be made to feel stupid by responding as if I believed this one did.

'Can I have a drink, Mummy?'

'Of course you can; you know where to find it.'

When I came back with a glass of milk, Jeremy asked if I remembered him, saying that he'd only been away just over a year. I shook my head.

'Isn't that your toy cupboard?' he asked, pointing to the corner of the room. 'Perhaps there's something new in there you could show me.'

I put my glass down and went to the cupboard door, on
which I leaned my weight to counteract the pressure on the catch
so that I could reach up and put it to one side. Pulling the door
back revealed four shelves packed with things to play with: teddy
bears and dolls, an old metal railway set that worked, another
newer plastic one that didn't, wooden blocks that when set out
correctly created a large picture of people in old-fashioned
clothes. A dozen or so cars. Books, of course, and things to
throw; a cricket set, skittles, a tin spinning top. Paint boxes and
thick pads filled with crude outline drawings, many of them half
painted in. A few toys fell out onto the floor. Jeremy was already
on his knees sifting through the debris, as I searched through the
shelves for the rubber dinosaurs I'd been given some weeks
before. I picked up the battered red tin spinning top that
hummed, and considered getting out the equally battered metal
tracks with the wind-up engines.

'Does this work?' Jeremy held up a balsa-wood aeroplane.

'You need the other bit to launch it. There it is.' I showed
Jeremy a strip of plastic with a large elastic band attached at one end.

'You show me.'

I took the plane. 'You do it like this,' I said seriously, as I tried
to attach the rubber band to a spur of wood that jutted out of
the plane's undercarriage and then take hold of the tail fin and
pull it back, as I'd seen Peter do. Each time I almost managed it,
the band lost its hold on the spur.

'How about we try it together?'

I was relieved to be rescued. I felt Jeremy's large and rather
cold hands close over my own and steadily complete the manoeuvre. Together we pulled the plane back, Jeremy raised his left
hand, holding the front of the launcher to aim the plane up into
the air, and then we let go.

'Wooo!' Jeremy let out a loud whoop as the plane soared up and through the living-room door into the kitchen, where Mum was bending down in front of the fridge. She shouted, 'What was that?' as the projectile clattered into a pile of saucepans.

Neither of the culprits answered; we were both laughing too much.

'Can we do it again?'

I was surprised that Jeremy had asked the question, and surprised again when he got up and retrieved the plane ready for a second go.

'Why don't you do that in the garden?' Mum suggested. Jeremy looked over to see if I approved of the idea, and together we went outside. The gap between our house and Brian's formed a long passage, with high walls each side, that was ideal for flying planes – or throwing darts, or kicking balls – and Jeremy and I used it to aim the balsa-wood plane so that it would fly the longest distance possible. I quickly picked up the way Jeremy held the launcher and plane so that contact between the two was not broken, and I was soon able to fly it on my own. I was enjoying myself. There was something different about Jeremy that meant I had no need to worry about whether he was having fun too. I didn't have to plead to get him to do it again, and again, and again; if anything he seemed to have more energy than I had for the game. I knew that whenever I played with adults – even if they seemed to be enjoying themselves – they would want to stop long before me, and I'd learned to play always anticipating a weary 'That's enough for now'. But it seemed to be Jeremy who was most disappointed when Mum called us in for some food.

After lunch Jeremy announced that it was time for snakes and ladders. While we were playing at one end of the front room, Mum put on a record and sat at the other end with her head bent over some large red books, humming along to some of the songs. Snakes and ladders was followed by pairs. I won both games. Then we returned to the toy cupboard and found the dinosaur models while I told Jeremy what dinosaurs ate, and then acted out an encounter between a tyrannosaurus rex and a brontosaurus in a swamp.

None of this would have been possible if 'the others' had been around, and I was pleased to find that they wouldn't be back until the end of the afternoon. Even the talk at the table had been exciting, as Jeremy mixed conversation with Mum that I couldn't fathom with funny stories about losing his luggage on a train and getting a lift with a lorry driver who was drunk. He played the part of the inebriated man talking in a foreign accent, causing both Mummy and me to laugh out loud. I felt very comfortable. Mum was evidently enjoying herself too, and I heard her say how pleased she was to see Jeremy back 'safe and sound'.

Only as I sat in the bath that evening did I remember that I'd said I'd go to Brian's that afternoon. I hadn't given my neighbour a second thought.

'Never mind,' said Mummy. 'You can make it up to him tomorrow.'

*

Visiting Bayview Road frequently, Jeremy quickly became an established part of Lowe family life. Keeping my ears open, I soon picked up his story: as a bright schoolboy he had been a frequent customer at the bookshop, one of those who would get into conversation with Dad about art and literature. The rest of the family had met him doing his holiday job as a beach photographer. So he had become a friend of my parents before leaving for a year abroad. On his return the relationship deepened, and from exotic and eccentric visitor he was transformed into an insider, representative of a kind of intermediate generation. He occasionally helped Dad out, working evenings in the bookshop. He brought fresh vegetables from his mother's allotment and helped Mum cook them. We children were thrilled to have this unpredictable and effervescent force swirling around us. I felt safe with him: he was strong, and while I was getting too heavy for other adults to pick up, he would be happy to lift me up onto his shoulders, and dance and buck and frighten me as we made our way to and from the beach. From time to time he babysat while Mum and Dad went out, but he wasn't the same as the other babysitters, who would wearily dragoon us through the rituals of teethbrushing and changing for bed so that they could enjoy as much of the evening as possible in peace. There would be games and stories and staying up late, and even going to bed was made fun.

When Jeremy came to eat, we children would love to watch him talking to our parents. He always made them laugh. If he wasn't imitating drunken foreigners he would mimic chimpanzees, or aeroplanes coming down to land, or other characters from a story he was telling. Mum and Dad seemed to like him equally. Mum began to make a sherry trifle every time she knew he was coming, which turned into every Sunday, with less predictable visits during the week. They would talk about clothes and food, things Dad didn't talk about very much. And Jeremy would talk to Dad about books, politics and art. We could tell how much Dad liked it when they disagreed strongly with one another, and how that made Mum a little anxious.

So there was no resistance from any quarter when Jeremy offered to take all the Lowe children out for an adventure. If there was any surprise that an intelligent 20-year-old would choose to spend his day off hitched up with three children aged five, seven and nine – it was agreed that Joanna was too young –

Mum did not linger on the subject. Jeremy was, after all, stepping gallantly into the breach – she'd been explaining how Dad worked every Sunday, and her plans to spend the day on the beach with the family had been turned upside down because Nanny Langton was ill and needed her help.

'Are you sure you can manage that many?' she asked. I held my breath, fearful that I was going to be lumped together with Joanna again and miss out.

'We'll have an adventure. Can I take them to Claystone Bay? I used to cycle past there on the way to school, and it's a brilliant place for adventures.'

'What about lunch? I'll be cooking dinner at some point.'

'We could take a picnic and be back here for a meal in the evening.'

'They're quite a handful, you know.'

'If there's any real trouble, I can just bring them home, can't I? We can all muck in together. I'm sure it'll be all right. They'll have a great time.'

We were ready and waiting when Jeremy arrived at nine thirty the following morning. He was carrying a large haversack and wore heavy desert boots, tight, worn, sand-coloured trousers and a checked shirt. He greeted us all, but I felt sure that I'd been given a particular nod and wink that confirmed me in the secret position of being a special friend, the one who'd brought this Jeremy person into the family properly.

It was a treat just to be riding on the open-top bus that ran round the coast and finished up at Claystone Bay. Ella sat on Jeremy's lap while Peter and I sat in front of them. It was a new scenario for all of us. Peter was used to being the eldest, but the way Jeremy was it didn't feel as if we were a group of children being taken out by a grown-up. As Jeremy didn't act like the one in charge, Peter wasn't put out at all. There were no arguments like the ones that happened at tea-time at home over who was going to be given the round end of a piece of toast and who was going to have the square end, the kind that tried Dad's patience so much.

There were no cliffs at Claystone Bay. Instead, a low bluff had formed of packed clay and loose mud, dotted with scrub and bushes which concealed a maze of pathways and shallow caves. Above the slope were grass verges, and stretching out before it at low tide was a vast expanse of flat mud that would be covered by shallow dirty-brown seawater twice a day. The only other people who seemed to be visiting the bay were walking far out onto the mud, digging for worms. After we'd established a kind of headquarters in one of the shallow caves and Jeremy had hidden his backpack under a nearby bush, the plans for our big game were discussed.

We knew how to play It, but we were accustomed to doing so in the confines of the playground or the house. To play over such a vast expanse of wilderness was something else. Jeremy took the lead role while the rest of us scattered. Peter launched off into the bush. Ella took my hand and together we two went slowly around the dusty paths looking for a suitable hideout. A few minutes passed before a blood-curdling Tarzan scream was heard, followed by Jeremy's voice calling out, 'I'm going to get you, don't you think you hide from me. Haaaaaa!' I looked at Ella, whose eyes were wide open; both of us broke into poorly concealed giggles, which we quickly muffled but which kept returning as we attempted to keep our hiding place a secret. Heavy footsteps sounded along a path a few feet below, and then lighter steps, which we took to be Peter's, scurrying back in the other direction overhead, back towards our base. Then there was quiet.

'Gaaaaaaaaaaaaaaat you, you can't get away from ME!' Jeremy's head appeared where we'd least expected it, coming down from above, followed by the rest of his body landing heavily across the exit to our hiding place. He quickly crouched down, arms out wide as if to block any possibility of escape. With a terrifying face he growled, 'Which one will it be then, hey? You – I think – there!' With that he landed a heavy hand on Ella's arm and charged off again. We children had been rooted to the spot from the moment of Jeremy's surprise arrival, and it took several moments after his departure before we broke free. I ran off in the same direction as Jeremy, while Ella remained behind counting out loud to ten before joining in pursuit.

All of us were exhausted when Jeremy called a halt to the game and gathered us together at HQ. He hauled out his rucksack and produced two packets of sausages, a frying pan, a couple of forks and two bottles of cream soda. The next task was to collect dry driftwood. I brought back handfuls, Peter huge armfuls, and Jeremy showed us how to lean the wood in a wigwam arrangement over some screwed-up pieces of newspaper. Peter was given the task of setting the paper alight.

Later, as we blew on our scalding sausages wrapped in foil, a tired group of children sat silently on an outcrop of rock where the mudflats began. The mud was the alluvial deposit of the River Minton, which Jeremy pointed out meandering its way towards the open sea in the distance. There was a light, warm breeze coming in across the estuary. I didn't have much sense of direction, and if I'd been told that Shorefleet was the town we could just make out on a headland to the right, I would have believed it. In fact I tended to believe whatever I was told, something my elder siblings had discovered and often played on to everyone's delight but my own. The strangeness of the place, though – it was a kind of beach, but nothing like the sandy, peopled beaches we knew – impressed itself upon us. Peter started talking to Jeremy about a book he was reading, and I heard the phrase 'Secret Seven' a number of times. Ella interrupted to ask if Jeremy had any tomato sauce in his bag and then stated with a definiteness that impressed me that this was the kind of beach that Stig in the Dump would have lived in. A debate ensued about whether Stig would have had enough food and water to live on.

Jeremy told us to find some drier mud to rub into our hands to get rid of the sausage grease, and then suggested that we might go and see the old Nordic stone decorated with indecipherable runes and preserved as a tourist attraction halfway back to the road. Peter challenged the others to a race and ran on ahead. He was standing by the monument when the rest of us caught up with him.

'Let's imagine we're Vikings,' suggested Jeremy. 'We'd have come here across the sea to attack Shorefleet and burn down the houses. And we'd steal all the gold and silver we could find, and fridges and TV sets, and bring them back here to put aboard the ship, ready to set sail back to Denmark.'

'What did they do to the people?' asked Ella.

'Killed them, of course,' Peter answered, regaining the upper hand.

'Or took them as slaves,' Jeremy added.

'What does that mean?' I asked.

'You'll learn about it at school one day,' answered Ella, in a knowing tone.

'No school if you're a Viking', declared Jeremy.

'I like school.' I was feeling less than enthusiastic about Vikings.

'Let's go and play hide-and-seek back at the beach.'

So we walked back down towards the shore and the twisting pathways and hideouts that had thrilled us all before lunch. As we walked, Jeremy pointed to the horizon in the hazy sunshine, a faint line that separated the shimmering grey of the sea from the colourless sky. 'You can see the curve of the earth's surface, if you look carefully.'

'Where?'

'There. Look: start over there on the left, and follow the horizon right across – it's not flat, is it? It's curved. And that's because the earth, as we all know, is round.'

We were quiet as we scanned the view. I tried hard to understand what I was meant to be doing and, as I couldn't see any curves out to sea, assumed that I'd misunderstood the task. I was glad when Jeremy lost interest in the shape of the earth and instead picked up a gnarled bend of whitened driftwood that he placed inside his rucksack.

*

After that he took us out fairly often, sometimes back to Claystone Bay – a place that was already special to us all – or to play hide-and-seek all over Shorefleet town, from the railway station to the main bay and pier. Sometime in the weeks that followed, Jeremy and I went out on our own, walking around the coast at low tide, east of the pier through Highcliffe Bay, round to Coastguards Peak and then into Whalebone Cove. At the headland dividing the bays was a magnificent arch that, Jeremy explained, had been caused by the waves eating relentlessly into the soft chalk. Soon, he said, the arch would collapse, and all that would be left would be something called a stack, standing alone in the sea.

I'd been looking at the layers of flints that could be seen at intervals in the cliff face. 'How did they get flints in there like that?'

'Nobody put them there. These cliffs were once underwater and were built up over millions of years out of the shells of sea creatures. Something must have happened at certain times that caused flints to be formed on the surface and then covered up by more chalk, but I'm not sure what it was. It all happened so long ago, even before the dinosaurs.'

We trudged along the sand. Jeremy pointed out a series of small, dark openings in the cliff at the far end of the bay. 'You see those small caves? There's a tunnel behind them, joining them up and then coming out at the top. We can't go up all the way because it comes out in someone's garden, but we can explore some way up.' He explained that the tunnel had been built by smugglers and pirates way back in the lawless past, a passage to carry up the contraband they wanted to get into the country without the king's customs officers knowing.

There was no easy way into the tunnel, as the entrance was as high as Jeremy himself. Below this there were footholds, but they were too far apart for someone my size. So Jeremy picked me up and held me above his head. 'Get hold of that bit sticking out there, and put your feet on that level bit. You there? Sure? I'm going to let go now, so just stay still. Now I'm going to climb round you and pull you up from the top. There, we're there – now we can go on up. It's all right, I'm with you. It's a bit dark, but see the light up there, that's the opening we could make out from the beach.'

I held Jeremy's hand all the more firmly as we edged up the smooth chalk slope towards the light. Here the outlook was scary – we could see out across sand to the sea, but the path was at its narrowest and on one side gave way to a steep fall towards the cliff face. We continued upwards again to the next opening. Here there was a wide platform where we could safely sit and look out at the even more impressive view.

Jeremy was playful, as he always was. Catching hold of me firmly around the waist, he picked me up and stretched out his arms towards the cave's mouth. 'What if I tickle you, eh!'

We had played the tickling game before. I began by pushing my fingers under Jeremy's chin and, as he ducked his face away, tried to squeeze his tummy. Jeremy did likewise, gently gripping my knee in a way that sent me sprawling back onto the chalk floor, trying desperately to keep my legs clear. I tried to control my giggles so as to resume my attack. Only this time he lightly pinched me between my legs, through my trousers. I pushed my hands down to loosen his grip, but he placed his hand there again. I squirmed. 'No, not there, it hurts.'

'Does it, are you sure?' Jeremy resumed tickling my knees, sending me into paroxysms of laughter again, and then pinched me through my trousers again.

I moved back, not playing any more. 'I don't like that.'

'OK, just a game. We won't play like that again.' And we didn't.

We retraced our steps across Whalebone Cove and then turned up a steep and slippery gap in the cliff. This, said Jeremy, had been cut through the chalk in early Victorian times as a slipway for the local lifeboat. A landslide had left a gaping hole halfway down the slope: it would have been impossible now to use to launch a boat. We emerged at the top near the ruins of a small fort. We climbed through the wire fence, and Jeremy helped me through one of the windows. 'This was built to protect the beach from a landing by the Spanish Armada.'

'The what?'

And Jeremy explained all about the fleet sent to invade England, and how it was destroyed, leaving wrecks filled with treasure all around the coast.

*

Sometime after this, something terrible happened. My parents' bedroom, until then a source of light and wonder and warm, odorous bodies and itchy hair and funny-smelling breath, became a place of danger and confusion. For a while Mum had earned extra money by taking in paying guests on a bed-and-breakfast basis. The children had to be moved around to accommodate them, and (before the shed was converted to take bunk beds) I was sleeping in a small single bed in Mum and Dad's bedroom. One night I'd been fast asleep but had been awakened by the sound of my parents' raised voices. I lay listening, absolutely still. Facing the wall, I could comprehend nothing but could feel the hatred and violence of the words that jabbed into my mind and chest like arrows. I heard the voice of my father – the quiet, tolerant and easygoing hero of my waking hours – rise in demonic tones, while my mother seemed crushed, defeated, imploring. I made every effort not to move a muscle. Eventually the noise subsided and calm reigned again. In the morning I couldn't discern anything unusual; the world, it seemed, had returned to normal. But the scene was repeated the following night, and for what seemed like an endless stream of nights. The final time I found myself waking up facing my parents' bed, and now I saw the violence of Dad's behaviour as well as heard the raging, boiling, storming of the words that foamed from his mouth. Dad had got up from the bed and was pacing around the room; Mum whispered hoarsely, 'Quiet! You'll wake Matthew.' Dad, instead, strode over to her wardrobe and started pulling out her clothes. I recognised the dress that had been his birthday present to her. Now he started tearing at her things, ripping them apart and throwing them aside, all the time cursing and swearing. My eyes darted from this appalling scene to the even more disastrous vision of Mummy's enraged and distraught face, unrecognisable in the gloomy light.

I woke with a tummy ache. The atmosphere around the breakfast table was tight and cold. I didn't consider how my brother and sisters felt. It didn't occur to me to ask. This could not be spoken about. Dad stood over me and poured boiled milk onto my Ready Brek for me to stir in, but this morning there was no pleasure in the ritual. I absentmindedly helped myself to sugar: one spoonful, and then another, and then a third.

'How much bloody sugar do you need, then?' Dad shouted into my stunned face. 'Here, see if it's sweet enough for you now!'

I sat transfixed as he picked up the sugar bowl and dumped its entire contents into my porridge.

'Don't take it out on him.' The words that left Mum's mouth were thin and shaky, and I looked up to see what they meant. I had never seen Mum cry, and I wasn't sure if what I saw now should properly be called crying. Her face was held in a tight grip as tears oozed down her face. Her body was racked with sobs that spoke more of a frenzied and ineffectual effort at control than of a clear expression of grief. Dad stormed out of the house.

*

It was a bright spring day, and Joanna and I were playing outside the front gate with a group of children who lived in the same street. Brian was there, along with Stephen Andrews, another neighbour, and Sally, who was the same age as Joanna. The bigger ones were playing Catch across the street and kept the Lowe children happy by letting us act as ball boys. We all turned as our house front door opened; it was an odd time for our father to appear.

'Come back in, I want to talk to you. It won't take long.' His tone commanded an immediate response. Peter and Ella were already in the front room; more surprisingly, so was a strangely serious-looking Gracey. She didn't say a word but caught my eye as we sat waiting for Dad to speak.

'I don't know how to say this.' His voice was very odd. 'Your mother has gone away.' There was a tense silence and then in a strangulated, high-pitched tone he added, 'She doesn't love me any more.'

We four children watched dumbstruck as Daddy's body heaved up and down. He covered his face with his hands. After a few moments, Gracey suggested that we children follow her into the kitchen and help make some tea. Unsure what to do, we moved past her as she stood in the doorway ushering us through. My world crumbled a little more as I looked into her eyes and saw a reservoir of unspilt tears. There was no reassurance to be found there. I hadn't understood what we'd been told. It didn't make sense. I hadn't really thought much about whether Mummy and Daddy loved one another: they simply *were*. My friend Alex Jeffreys didn't have a father, but this was not something we had talked about. I'd wondered how it came to be, but it had never occurred to me to ask, and his not having a dad became as ordinary as me having one, almost. Mum had 'gone away'. Dad was sobbing. Gracey was in shock. Something terrible seemed to be happening, but what was it? Joanna was quick to start crying, but it was a nudge from Ella as they went down the steps into the living room that set her off, not Daddy's bewildering news.

'Where is Mummy?' Ella summoned up the courage to ask Gracey for some clarification.

'In London. With Lucy and Leo, I think.'

This was good news. It wasn't uncommon for one or the other of our parents to go to London, and we children knew the Kaufmanns well. In the summer Lucy ran a spooky café in Clarion Street, a few doors from the bookshop. They were remote and strict, and so somewhat scary to us Lowe children, but the Kaufmanns were close to our parents.

'When is she coming back?' Peter now sought further information, but this time no answer was forthcoming. We all looked into Gracey's confused face.

'Soon, I hope,' was the best she could manage. At that point Dad came into the room. His eyes were red, but he was more like the Dad we knew, and instinctively we positioned ourselves around him as he sat in his chair.

'Gracey's going to stay and help us manage things here. So I want you to be especially good from now on. Do you understand?'

The four of us nodded our assent.

'Well, do you want to go back out to play?'

Life at 8 Bayview Road entered a weird phase. We children seemed to take our promise to Dad to heart. Ella kept her room tidy; Peter was even more attentive than usual with Joanna; there was no squabbling about who would get the cream of the milk on their cereal. I concentrated on acting as if everything was normal, whatever was actually happening. I went to school, where my behaviour was not perceptibly different from what it had been before. I played with the boys and girls who lived along our street. During one of our excursions we were grouped on the corner of Bayview Road nearest the sea and I announced, as a quite deliberate attempt at impressing my audience, 'My mum's gone away, and I'm never going to see her again.'

It was the first time I'd put this idea into words. I'd spoken the words without, it felt, thinking the thought. I was surprised at what I found myself saying. There was no particular response: if the intention was to inflate my status amongst the children, it had backfired. I quickly forgot it and lost myself in a game of chase.

I adjusted to Gracey being there when I came home from school. Jeremy was often around, and this was reassuring. I would creep down long after bedtime and listen to what was happening in the living room, and I twice fell asleep sitting there on the stairs, lulled by the tones of a conversation between him and my dad. The worst moment, as far as I was concerned, was one weekend afternoon when it was arranged that Jeremy would take Peter and Ella to the pictures. I couldn't stay downstairs as they bustled around getting ready, and sulked instead in my bedroom. When I heard the back door open, I went to the window and watched Jeremy, hand in hand with my older siblings, as they disappeared down the back alley. My stomach lurched and my head caved in with hatred and envy and the impossibility of doing anything about it. The cries rose in my chest – 'Mummy, Mummy, Mummy!' I buried my head in my pillow so that no one would hear, and called out to her until my throat hurt and I couldn't cry any more.

The following day Jeremy seemed to make a special effort to single me out, and the pain – though not the memory – of the previous afternoon was soon erased. I selected a book and asked if he would stay and read me my bedtime story, as he had begun to do on a fairly regular basis.

'Of course. Are you going to listen too, Joanna? There might even be time for two stories. Would you like that?'

Joanna grinned, and together the three of us mounted the stairs.

'Don't forget to wash your teeth,' Dad called.

In the bedroom we undressed and pulled on our night-clothes before climbing quickly under the covers. Jeremy tucked Joanna in, while I launched myself up the ladder to the top bunk. Jeremy placed the two books on the bed beside my head and remained standing. 'Are you ready?'

With his familiar voice, the telling of the first story had its intended effect. Joanna was asleep and I was feeling dozy.

'Are you ready for the second one, then?'

I nodded. I saw Jeremy take up the second book. He looked down. 'Joanna's asleep, so I'll read more quietly.' He touched my forehead, brushing the hair out of my eyes and letting his hand rest on the back of my head before withdrawing it to open the book and smooth down the page.

'*Snow White and the Seven Dwarves*,' he began, then paused. He shifted so that his right forearm lay across the book, keeping it in place. I sensed his other hand finding a way under the covers before feeling it on my leg. Jeremy stroked my leg as he read. His hand moved down to my foot which he held and gently massaged with his thumb. I always enjoyed Jeremy reading: he acted out the parts, put on strange voices and was much scarier than Mum or Dad. They read calmly, expecting me to be lulled quickly to sleep. I started with a laugh when Jeremy screwed his face into an ugly scowl, with one eye closed, to impersonate the wicked queen. The excitement pushed back the fatigue, but the fatigue was the stronger by far, and I was soon asleep.

~ 3 ~

The memory of our parents' separation faded, or at least took on
a dream-like quality. Some details remained vivid, others disappeared. I couldn't remember anything about the time without
Mum. There was the gathering in the front room when Dad had
cried and told us. The next clear image was from the day she
came back. I was never sure how long a period stretched between
those two points.

Dad drove us down to London to the Kaufmanns' house,
where Mum had been staying. I was on tenterhooks: it wasn't
clear what we were going there for. Mum seemed really happy to
see us all again. What with all of the Lowes and the Kaufmanns
and their three children, it was a noisy day. We children all kept
close to our mother. Without knowing how it came about, the
room suddenly cleared and I was alone with her. She reached out
her arms and clutched me close.

'Mummy, will you come home with us today?'

'Would you like that, Matthew?'

'I want you to come home with us.'

'Then of course I will.'

A particular interpretation of this conversation etched itself
on my soul. Mummy was coming back because I wanted her to,
because I had asked her, for me. For the others too, perhaps, a
bit, but in particular because she loved me. At that moment I had

felt something unwind in my stomach and I launched myself at her, burying my face in her dress. I held her hand tight when it came time to leave, and together we walked down the garden towards the beaten-up Bedford van that would take us back to Bayview Road.

Normality returned, or so it seemed. Only later would we notice the way that Dad and Mum never seemed to touch one another, how calm but businesslike their relationship seemed to have become. We would leaf through the old pictures of our parents dancing together and mutter amongst ourselves about how beautiful they looked. Nor did we notice whether or not the adults monitored us, or whether they were relieved at how quickly we seemed to forget, how soon the old atmosphere returned at mealtimes, and how we became mischievous and quarrelsome again. For me everything was right. I didn't need to think about the awful time, and so I didn't. Yet things weren't really the same. There were nights when I would climb into their bed saying that I'd had a bad dream, and days when I'd follow Mum or Gracey about and be reluctant to go to school. One scene felt so real to me that I never really accepted it as a dream. Mum had come into my room and was bending over the bed, telling me that this time it was Dad's turn to leave for ever. I'd been inconsolable and wouldn't sleep on my own that night. In another dream – I assumed that it must have been a dream, as no one ever talked about it – the family had barricaded the living room against robbers who'd broken through the front door and were coming down the hall towards us. Whenever I thought about this, I could see dark shadows through the opaque glass of the living-room door and feel the terror of what would happen if they burst through.

My worries were not helped when I woke to strange voices and, getting up and sitting at the top of the stairs, watched Mum being strapped onto a stretcher by men in white uniforms, and her weak smile as she noticed me before she was wheeled out. Perhaps the other children were there too. Presumably someone came up, helped us back into bed and reassured us that everything was going to be all right. I don't remember. Nobody talked about it, and it wasn't long before I was questioning whether there ever had been an ambulance with a flashing blue light, and men carrying Mum out in the middle of the night.

Something else had changed. I never seemed to stop searching, as if there was something that, once found, would transform everything. The knot in my stomach would reappear from time to time. I would seek Mum out, but I never seemed able to get close enough to her. I sensed the bones more than the flesh. It seemed that I was always watching her across a distance and that there was always a possibility of the gap growing and growing and growing. It was different with Gracey; her hugs felt really enveloping. But I didn't want Gracey's hugs.

So I hung back, no longer taking anything for granted. I took careful note of my parents' behaviour, searching out clues and looking for hints of what lay beneath the surface. This investigation did not diminish them at all. I was fascinated by them. With her shoulder-length curly hair brushed back and falling away from her head, Mum's face was like the women in the book of knitting patterns that she carried everywhere with her: beautiful, yet a face that didn't give much away. Her features were light, perhaps thin, reminding me of pictures of princesses. She never seemed sad. She could be stern and blunt. If one of the children protested against a decision on the grounds that it was unjust, she would reply: 'You're right, the world's not fair. You'd better get used to it.' More typically though, she was energetic and enthusiastic. Things excited her, and she drew out any anticipated pleasure by planning and drawing us into her ideas. She could give anything the feel of an adventure, from baking a cake to redecorating a bedroom. In particular, she made family occasions like Christmas and holidays special. Yet it was also Mum who kept things safe. It was she, we understood, who held an overview, who was concerned about the family's resources, who knew where everything was, who would note when something was supposed to happen and make sure we were prepared for it. It was she who kept the main meal as the central daily event of the household: we knew she'd be disappointed if one of us failed to appear.

Dad was also a striking person. His most distinctive features were his face and his voice. The lines on his face suggested gentleness, depth and laughter; his high forehead and bald dome, strength; and his eyes, sorrow. His voice enchanted us like a musical instrument; to hear it – the other side of an aisle of shelves in the bookshop, or at the dinner table – was to be soothed and charmed. He was funny and liked to make jokes about himself in a way that Mum couldn't quite manage. Where she was precise about practical things, he was vague, and this could feel like a relief from her high standards. He was indifferent to money and often forgot to ask for change where Mum would always remember, to the last halfpenny. It would worry him to appear authoritarian, and he would always justify his actions if questioned. And while Mum enjoyed expounding on history or geography or literature, she liked to avoid too much discord and would only express political views with the kind of imprecision which Dad reserved for the business of daily life. On the philosophical front, Dad relished a debate, and it didn't matter much if his opponent happened to be a guest sharing dinner or a customer in the bookshop.

There was nothing better than those meal-times when we'd get quite hysterical and the volume would get louder and louder, and we could sense that Mum and Dad were enjoying the chaos around them. Peter knew that there was no easier way of getting Ella going than with a bit of lavatory humour: any reference to toilets and she'd be away, hardly able to stay on her seat. On one famous occasion he was waiting outside the toilet, complaining that Ella had been inside too long. We had just finished a meal with Mum's home-made lemon meringue pie. 'There must have been too much pith in the lemon,' quipped Peter. The joke was repeated when they came back down to the table, and then had to be explained to us younger children. Soon everybody was beside themselves, even Mum's eyes watering with laughter.

We children developed interests and skills that distinguished us one from another. Ella could draw and paint, like Nanny Langton. Peter was good at words and figures, like Mum. I loved history, also like Mum. Dad had given me a large set of books that took the reader right into historical events from the point of view of a child: the misery of the son of an unemployed man in the Depression, pawning his radio before he could receive the dole; the fear of a child in a Royalist mansion besieged by Roundheads; a drummer-boy in a regiment of redcoats during the American War of Independence. The pages had colour illustrations, paintings that emphasised the emotions of the moments they dramatised in the faces of the characters. I read them over and over again.

I loved listening to tales about the Lowes and Langtons too. There were stories of bigamists and rogues on both sides of the family. Both my grandfathers had been soldiers in the trenches in the First World War: both had died before I was born, partly it was said from chest conditions they brought back from Ypres. My dad's father had joined the sappers and had spent the war tunnelling under enemy lines with the intention of blowing them up. Nanny Lowe told me how she had married him on the Isle of Wight and how they'd spent their wedding night in a hotel near Victoria Station. There had been a Zeppelin raid which had frightened her terribly, and the next morning she'd returned to being a lady's maid in a big house in the country while her new husband had left by train for France. And when he returned they had to burn all his clothes on the doorstep to get rid of the lice.

When we visited the Isle of Wight – the place my dad's family had come from originally – I would listen to the broad accent of my great-uncle Laurie telling stories of his hard life. He'd rail bitterly against the poverty and unemployment of the thirties, gazing into the distance as if he was once again the young man forced to leave the island to find employment as a steelworker in Glasgow, then losing that job too and having a wife and two daughters to support. He'd been twice bombed out in Ryde town. He could tell me about his brother Ernie, my grandfather, how stubborn he was, and how as a boy he'd been punished for looking up at a portrait of Queen Victoria and calling her a 'bloody bitch'. Visiting Uncle Laurie was a bit like stepping back in time. There was no fridge, and as our visits would take place in summer the milk would quickly sour, and there would always be white bits floating in our tea. Laurie objected strongly to the use of electric light upstairs: you were to undress by the light of the streetlamps, and if you wanted to read, you stayed down in the living room with everyone else.

My own parents had both lived through the Second World War, in London for parts of the Blitz, though spending several years as evacuees. I was always gripped by pictures of children saying goodbye to their parents at the big railway stations, wanting to get inside the minds of the people frozen in the photographs. I wondered how my parents had felt being far from their mums and dads. Dad described being in a house where the family was quite cold and kept the evacuees separate even at meal-times, and how he'd looked in a cupboard one day and found a pile of *Action* magazines, produced by Oswald Mosley's Fascists. Dad's elder brother, Tom Lowe, was already in the army and took part in the disastrous Dieppe Raid and, later, the invasion of Italy. Hearing Dad describe it, I could feel the atmosphere in the kitchen in Earlsfield when a telegram arrived and Nanny Lowe would refuse to touch it, and her husband would have to take it outside and open it while the rest of the family sat waiting. And the relief to find it was a message from Tom telling them when to expect him home on leave. Then there were tiny black-and-white photographs of Dad on-board different ships, looking like a boy and dressed in a white uniform; this was when he was called up in 1946 and spent two years blowing up the mines with which the sea had been littered during the conflict.

All of this gave me the feeling of being connected to the past, of being interwoven with the people around me, even of being able to be in the minds of those I loved in days gone by.

*

Jeremy was brilliant to be with. You couldn't help laughing all the time when you were with him. And he'd become my particular friend. Outings that included Ella and Joanna were increasingly rare. I knew how lucky I was. Jeremy acted like an adult when he was with Mum and Dad, but when we were out he was like one of us. At times I became aware of having to make adjustments in order to keep this special friend: I loved standing in front of Mum while she crouched down and buttoned up my coat, and rubbed cream into my hair before combing it down tidily. I could tell by the look in her eyes that this was how she liked to see me and I hated it when Jeremy ruffled up my hair as soon as we were out of sight, walking down the back alleyway. But if Jeremy preferred me with untidy hair, that was how it would have to be.

I did sometimes feel a different kind of strain. Being with Jeremy was great, and being with the family was great, most of the time. What could be difficult was spending time with Jeremy and the family, together.

'It's Friday! It's five to five! It's *CRACKERJACK*!'

All the Lowe children except Peter were enjoying the end of the school week in front of the 'box'. The room already looked a mess, with coats and bags thrown across chairs or lying on the floor. There was a half-full cup of milk on the coffee table and pages from an old issue of *Bunty* strewn around the sofa.

'Hello, hello.' It was Jeremy. Friday evening visits were unusual: he must have come down from London early for the weekend.

'Hi.' I scanned the room quickly, as if checking that nothing untoward was on view.

'I see you're making the most of your spare time.'

'Just watching TV.'

The small fat man, Peter Glaze, came on screen and said something patently silly, followed by raucous laughter. Jeremy was studying rather than watching it. 'Who could write stuff like that? Though I suppose it's good enough to entertain you lot.'

Peter arrived. 'All work and no play …'

'That's just the point,' insisted Jeremy. 'This isn't play. It's doing nothing and being fed rubbish. There shouldn't be any distinction between work and play.'

'Shut up, will you, I'm watching,' snapped Ella.

Peter was grinning. 'Perhaps you think they should be reading the Bible.'

'Not a bad idea, seeing as none of you have any knowledge of it, and our whole culture is based on it.'

'Come on,' I suggested. 'I'll make some tea.'

We walked out to the kitchen, leaving the girls with Leslie Crowther and his sidekick.

I seemed to have some making up to do, having been discovered wasting my time watching a worthless children's programme. At times it was hard being the kind of person Jeremy seemed to expect me to be. When he stuck to his regular times I'd be prepared. It made me tense when he turned up when I was just being an ordinary schoolboy. I'd come to respect predictability: it suited me when plans were made and kept to. Then there were no surprises, and no need for complicated explanations.

'So, how's your week been? Did they teach you anything at school this week?'

'All right. School's OK. Did you watch *Blue Peter*?'

Our first conversation of the weekend often began like this. Jeremy's answer would, of course, be no, allowing me to explain what interesting facts I'd learnt from the two programmes I'd seen since we'd talked the previous Sunday.

Fifi jumped onto a chair beside Jeremy, who started stroking her. I poured the tea.

'So no news from school, then?'

'I don't know. I came second in a spelling test. I've got to draw a Norman castle.'

'I'll help you if you like.'

I searched my mind for anything else of note that would confirm that I'd used the week profitably.

'We had gypsy tart for pudding at lunchtime today. Alex

made Mrs Regan' – the frightening, ugly and easily provoked dinner lady in charge of the school canteen – 'really angry because he asked if he could have seconds, and she's always cross with him because he hardly ever finishes any of his dinners.'

'Ah, Alex. If he doesn't eat anything, how does he get so fat?'

'He's not fat.' I laughed. 'He only eats baked beans, really.'

'That's why, then.'

The back door opened, and Mum walked in and dumped four shopping bags on the kitchen floor.

'At last. I thought I'd never get back without those bags breaking. Hello, everyone. Is that a fresh pot of tea you've made there? Count me in, I'm dying for a cuppa. Jeremy – are you staying to eat? There's plenty, but you'll have to put up with some pretty basic fare.'

'No thanks, Elizabeth. I'm going to get off in a minute. I said I'd cook for Mother today. I'll pop back later on though, that OK?'

'Of course. Are the others in?'

'Yeah, in the front room,' I told her.

'Enjoying a profitable cultural experience,' added Jeremy.

Mum went through to see the other children.

'Tomorrow morning, how do you feel about getting up really early and helping collect seaweed for the allotment?'

'Yeah, great.' If someone else had proposed it, I'd have said no, but Jeremy had a way of turning any job into a special expedition.

'We could start at seven. You'll have to set your alarm. We can get a couple of loads before breakfast. I thought that later on we might go for a cycle ride. See if we could get down to Lymbridge, maybe.'

'Right. Is Lymbridge a long way?'

'Not so far. We can go by Feston and then cut across the bay.

There's a cycle path across the golf course. Much better than going by road.'

Jeremy had finished his tea. He walked over to the hall door and called out:

'See you later, Elizabeth. Bye, everyone.'

He laid a hand on my head, bent down and kissed me on the lips.

'See you later.'

Later was about half past eight. In the meantime I'd helped Mum prepare the tea and we were almost ready to eat when Dad arrived home. Tea-time was fun. Peter had begun to learn French, and his teacher had written a note in his exercise book complimenting him on his progress.

'How do you say "I live in Shorefleet"?' asked Mum.

'*J'habite à Shorefleet*,' Peter replied.

'Good. How about "I have two sisters and one brother"?'

'Umm. *J'ai deux soeurs et un frère.*'

'I've got one,' I chimed in. 'What's "I walk to the school and then to the shops and then to the park and then to the bus stop and then to the house and then to the bedroom and then ...''?'

Peter had started giggling.

'That's stupid,' declared Ella.

'You can't do it, can you?' I grinned.

It was Ella's turn to help with the washing-up. Under pressure, the rest of us helped carry the tea things into the kitchen and then escaped to the front room. Peter put on a record and sat down to read a book. Joanna asked if I would play pairs. Ella soon joined us, sitting on the settee with a puzzle book. The card game was still in progress when we heard sounds from the kitchen indicating Jeremy's return. We continued our games, half listening through the glass hatch to the conversation taking place around the living-room table. The visitor had distracted our parents. It was now past Joanna's and my bedtime, and no one had called us. We played quietly, hoping our presence would remain undetected.

Mum burst into the front room.

'Are you two still here? Come on, up you go. It's bath night tonight – but it's too late to wash your hair now. Come on, let's see some action.'

Slowly, Joanna and I collected the cards together and prepared to go upstairs.

'Joanna, don't leave your cardie there.'

'I'll sort them out if you like,' offered Jeremy.

'Are you sure? Make sure they wash behind their ears, and Matthew, don't put your pyjamas on until you're properly dry. If you want, you can take a clean towel from the airing cupboard.'

Jeremy supervised the bath while sitting on the washing basket under the bathroom window. He began talking about our proposed outing to Lymbridge the following afternoon. 'We can stop for afternoon tea in Woodenstree and play on the swings by the river. I'll show you where I used to go to school. We might find another badge for your anorak.' My coat was already adorned with badges from places Jeremy had taken me to, and ones he'd brought back for me from places I knew about but hadn't yet visited, like the Tower of London.

'That'll be great.' I was uncomfortable with this conversation. I wished Jeremy could be as aware as I was of how it would sound to Joanna that he was once again giving me treats, that she was not going to be taken too. I wished Jeremy would include her in the conversation. Although I felt this intensely, I seemed unable to find a way of altering the course of events: my thinking took place somewhere remote from the kind of wondering that could easily be translated into speech.

Jeremy continued: 'In Lymbridge we'll have ice creams. There are two castles and an aquarium to visit. And we can go out on Lymbridge Down. We might spot some rabbits.'

'Yeah, great.' I was stuck between wanting to please Jeremy by appearing enthusiastic and wanting to minimise the scale of the treat to avoid upsetting Joanna. 'What did you say we were going to do in the morning?' I knew that the morning plans would appear less exciting to my sister.

'Collect seaweed. You'll need to set your alarm for half past six. I'll do that for you when we go upstairs. We'll meet down by the allotment, as usual, at ten to seven.'

While we were bathing, Mum had placed our pyjamas on the hot-water tank, so they were cosy and warm when we pulled them on. In the bedroom Jeremy was leafing through a story-book. Joanna and I climbed into our bunks and snuggled down to listen.

'Where were we?'

I tried to remember while Joanna answered. 'There was a fat boy that kept falling asleep and he'd been in the garden listening when he shouldn't have been.'

Jeremy was reading us his own version of *The Pickwick Papers*, which he abridged during his train journeys to and from London. 'That's right, found it. Good. OK, are you both ready for the next chapter?'

'Yes.'

Jeremy began. We prepared to be enraptured, amused, frightened and held in great suspense. I hoped we'd hear more about Sam Weller and his father. I had a vivid impression of these two characters, while others in the book seemed less easy to keep a firm grip on and became confused with one another. We both giggled when Jeremy impersonated the female parts.

As he read, Jeremy pushed one hand under the covers and sought out my midriff. He found the opening in my pyjama bottoms and felt for my willy. This he held, and gently squeezed, before applying a slow up-and-down movement that felt nice to me. I lay on my back, with my arms on the pillow above my head, and concentrated on the story. Then the good feeling finished, and the touching became uncomfortable. I pushed Jeremy's hand away and turned over, now almost asleep.

Jeremy brought the story to an end. 'Goodnight, Joanna, goodnight, Matt.' He lay a gentle kiss on my face and turned out the light as he left the room. As he moved along the landing, Joanna called out, 'Ask Mummy to come up and say goodnight.'

~ 4 ~

I closed the back door quietly. I'd dressed and descended the stairs carefully, so as not to wake anyone, though I doubted that I'd avoided disturbing Mum, who was a particularly light sleeper. But I hadn't heard anyone stir. I pulled my bike free of the pile lying against the shed wall and wheeled it out into the garden. The cold air woke me up properly, and now I was glad I'd managed to crawl out of my warm bed. It was still dawn as I cycled along Carisbrooke Road. I shivered, not with the cold so much as in reaction to the eerie atmosphere. Wood pigeons called out from high up in the elms off to the left, the sounds brighter and more distinct than in daytime.

A few minutes later I was parked on the corner of the allotment that ended where a row of cottages began. The farthest cottage away belonged to Mrs Rushton, Jeremy's mother. If Jeremy and I met up early in the morning, I'd wait by the allotment so that she wasn't disturbed. I could see that the light in Jeremy's bedroom was on and knew he wouldn't be long.

I heard Jeremy before I saw him, clomping along the pathway behind the cottages in a pair of rubber boots and thick, half-length black coat. He grinned across at me. 'All ready for a hard morning's work, then?'

'I'm cold.'

'Soon you'll be sweating. Bring your bike down to the shed.'

I followed, pushing the bike down the narrow grass path between the vegetable plots. From the shed, a tumbledown construction made with old planks and a nailed-down flat felt roof, all protected with creosote, Jeremy retrieved two garden forks and a wheelbarrow. Then he lifted my bike over them and pushed it back in through the door. We made our way back to the road.

'Do you want a lift?'

I nodded, although walking would have been warmer. When Jeremy had placed the forks onto the ground, I climbed in, took the forks back and laid them across my lap, and then felt the barrow being picked up from behind and pushed forward, down Blenheim Street towards the beach.

After three loads had been collected I was in my shirtsleeves, panting heavily. My arms ached. It was now a bright morning, though still early, with just a few other enthusiasts visible on the allotments, bending over their lines of onions and potatoes.

'You stay here. I won't be long.' Jeremy disappeared to prepare breakfast while I waited, resting on a box in the shed. Around me was an array of garden equipment: tools, bags of fertiliser, packets of seeds and a few trays for seedlings. And there were other odds and ends, signs of our earlier visits: games of noughts and crosses chalked onto scraps of hardboard, the scores from games of cribbage, offcuts of quality wood we'd used to construct a small table for Jeremy's flat in London. There were some sacks that were sometimes laid out to make lying on the earth floor more comfortable. And a paraffin heater to keep the shed warm.

Jeremy returned and placed a wide bowl of porridge in my hands – real porridge made with oats (rather than the Ready Brek we had at home), and with added milk, and a generous tablespoon of honey forming a golden rim. Breakfast was followed by some vigorous work on the allotment. We had done everything from turning the soil, rubbing the earth ready for planting seeds – peas, beans of different kinds, sprouts, cabbages, lettuces – fertilising, thinning the shoots, weeding, and trenching potato plants. Now, out of season, we were involved in a big project, digging right down and taking out the clay, laying sheets of plastic two feet underground and replacing the good earth on top. What was put back was to be heavily fertilised with the large pile of seaweed sitting a yard or so from the edge of the rectangular hole.

After digging for what seemed like ages, we went up to the cottage. Jeremy made some real coffee: I loved the smell of the beans as they were ground up, but I didn't much enjoy the coffee itself. Mrs Rushton was around, mostly upstairs, but she came down to have coffee with us. I was afraid of her. She seemed elderly but not at all rounded or soft in looks or voice. She was quite short but always upright. I had observed her laugh and sound quite warm, but when she talked in my direction she always seemed severe and disapproving. She struck me as definitely uninterested in small boys, and I was sure she regarded me as more a 'cause of damage' or 'bringer of dirt' than a person. She was posh too, the way she held her blue-and-white china cup, and the correctness and formality in the way she spoke. I was careful not to dunk my biscuits when she was around, as I knew she considered this ill-mannered. Jeremy had told me this and given me various other pieces of advice in an attempt to make my presence less disagreeable to her.

Mrs Rushton was usually active doing something, often preparing to go down and tend the flowers on the allotment, which were her responsibility. 'What are you boys going to do today?'

'Nothing special, Mother. Perhaps a bike ride later.'

It still shocked me the way Jeremy called her 'Mother'.

'Is there anything you'd like me to do?'

'There is, actually. We could do with some more paraffin. I'm going up to the shops anyway later, but it would help not to have a heavy load to carry home.' She paused. 'Are you in for dinner this evening?'

'Of course.' Jeremy always ate with his mother on Saturday nights.

'Shall I pick up some fish, then?'

'Lovely. I'll do a cauliflower cheese to go with it. We'll get out of your way now.'

As she pottered, the 'boys' went upstairs to Jeremy's cramped first-floor bedroom. The cottage was small, so the first flight of stairs ended at a tiny landing with the bathroom to the left and Jeremy's room to the right. You had to go through Jeremy's room to get to the door to the second staircase up to two more bedrooms, the front one his mother's, the other belonging to Dorothy, his sister, though she was almost never there. In Jeremy's bedroom there were a table and chair in front of the window, a single bed opposite the door, bookshelves floor to ceiling to the left of the window, and two chests of drawers on the other two sides of the room. The walls were of boards painted a washed light green.

We sat on the bed. I reached for the two packs of cards. Jeremy was teaching me to play canasta, and the packs were still mixed up together from our previous week's game. I proceeded to shuffle them. At each attempt to divide and re-combine them, several cards fell out. I picked those up and inserted them at random. We started to play.

I knew that Jeremy was listening out for the noise of the door that would indicate that Mrs Rushton had left the house. He'd been talking almost continuously, as he usually did. Then the noise came, and he stood up and leaned over the table to look out. He came back to the bed and, without speaking, moved the cards aside. I sat passively. He kissed me on the forehead and cheeks, and then on my mouth: closed-mouth kisses, like the ones that I gave my cat. I was aware of Jeremy's smell, so different from that of Mum and Dad. More chemical, harsher than Dad's, not sweet like Mum's. Inside, I recoiled. Jeremy lay me down and moved his hands down to the top of my shorts. I raised myself slightly and he pulled them down, along with my underpants. By this time he was kneeling on the floor, and I could only see his head and shoulders. He ran his warm hand along my tummy and down my legs to where he'd left the shorts, then up again. He moved my legs apart a little and brushed my sac with his thumb. Then he picked up my willy and pulled the skin down. And then up again. My penis responded, and I watched as its reddened head appeared and disappeared as Jeremy rubbed it. The good feelings were almost dispelled by the way his fingers held me too hard, almost pinching me, and holding the skin down in a way that was uncomfortable. He was clumsier too, I realised, because he was using his left hand. His other hand was busy. I couldn't see, but I knew what he was doing. His body was shaking; his face became contorted. He moved his hand up to grip my jaw and squeeze my mouth, before moving it down again. Reaching some kind of crescendo, he stopped. I hesitated a moment before pulling my shorts up. Jeremy seemed nonplussed, uncomfortable, lowering his head. I saw the strange but now familiar sneer cross his face. He reached for a tissue and turned away, doing up his zip and walking out to the toilet, reaching an arm over his shoulder and pulling at his shirt. Not a word had been spoken. It was impossible to avoid the impression that we'd been doing something deeply distasteful and absolutely not to be talked about. I sat on the bed and waited for the other Jeremy to re-emerge. Then we resumed our game.

Saturday mornings in Shorefleet were always like this now. The pattern varied only in the details – what time we'd meet, whether it was woodworking or gardening or model-making, or helping Jeremy with his accounts or listening to one of Jeremy's stories. The game would change from cribbage to canasta to bezique – later, usually to chess. Frequently, we wouldn't spend time in the cottage at all but would go on cycle rides. As I grew, Jeremy ensured that I had a good-enough bike to wander further and further into the countryside. Wherever else we cycled, we'd always stop off in a transport café on the main road near Applestead. They served tea there in white mugs, with the kind of crusty cheese rolls that I particularly liked. Then we'd go to a clearing in a wood about half a mile away.

*

The task of introducing me to the world had, it seemed, been allocated to Jeremy. There had been one major clash over this that I'd been aware of, a year or two previously. He had talked to me about camping, about how we'd make something to eat with the Gaz stove we often used to make tea at Claystone Bay – we went there alone now – and how we'd climb into sleeping bags as it got dark and wake up with the light coming through the canvas. And how we wouldn't have a bath or running water, and would have to make do like the children in *Swallows and Amazons*. It sounded wonderful, and on the evening in question it was agreed between us that it was time to really do it. Jeremy had gone downstairs to ask my parents. I was surprised to hear raised voices coming from the kitchen: Mum didn't seem to be involved, but Dad sounded angry. I hung over the banisters to try to hear what was going on.

'Of course he can't go camping. What a bloody ridiculous idea! What are we supposed to do for the others while he's galli-vanting with you? You just don't think, do you?' Dad's voice was loud and angry.

Jeremy was replying, but I couldn't make out what he was saying. He would explain, I was sure, make it all right so that everyone was happy again. And then Mum said something. Then Dad's raised voice again: 'You put us in an impossible position, don't you? You excite Matthew with your plans and then come and ask us, rather than doing it the other way round. So if we say no, we're bound to upset him. So we're always to be the bad guys, are we? What is it about you? If I were you, I'd concentrate on getting a life of your own. How do you think you're going to find somebody if you spend all your time with a seven-year-old? Have you thought about that?'

Suddenly Dad burst through the door into the hall and saw me on the stairs. Jeremy followed, looking shaken. I started to cry and shout. 'I want to go! Why can't I go? Why not? I want to go!' The tears streamed, my fists hammered the banister, my nose ran.

Dad looked pained and came up the stairs and picked me up. 'It's OK, it's OK. But you can't have everything you want, you know. It's not fair on the others, for one thing, is it?'

'But it's only for one night. Just once. Please. Please.' I was inconsolable and Dad became exasperated, finally putting me down and calling out to Jeremy, 'You caused this mess, you clear it up.'

And with that, he stormed downstairs again and slammed the living-room door.

I retained vague recollections of that terrible scene but had no idea of its consequences. Whatever had prompted Dad's protest – jealousy, some theory of what might be best for me – it had been nullified by a combination of my distress and Jeremy's quiet persistence. As far as I was aware, Dad never protested again, never stood in Jeremy's way, never asserted a father's right to decide what's best for his son. It had taken a real effort for Dad to do this much: while he loved his children and was proud of them beyond anything, he was uneasy about the exercise of authority and repelled by the idea of being repressive. He had devised and defended a policy of saying yes to everything that was requested of him, unless there were clear reasons why he had to say no. So I seldom sensed any tension between the wishes of my parents and the schemes devised by Jeremy, which, from then on, became ever more ambitious.

Our first outing alone together had been a walk to the windmill beyond Coastguards Peak and then a visit to Auntie's Tea Rooms nearby. I'd walked along the top of a long, low, red-brick wall, holding Jeremy's hand to keep my balance. Alive to the strangeness of being singled out for such a treat, I'd asked that we take back some sweets for the others. But soon such treats became routine. From Coastguards Peak and Claystone Bay we progressed to exploring the Rackham marshes, looking for tadpoles in the dykes, traipsing through woods and cycling out to Lymbridge. From sleeping overnight in a tent on Jeremy's allotment, we went on to camping by a stream in the woods outside Finglebury, cooking new potatoes and green peas picked fresh from the allotment and tasting better than almost any meal I'd been offered before. One November 5th we cycled round the local villages, enjoying the eerie atmosphere and easy camaraderie of Bonfire Night. When I later read Thomas Hardy's *Return of the Native*, I was reminded of that ride. We set up our tent beneath the walls of a medieval church standing on a knoll all alone. Jeremy told me that it had once been at the centre of a villlage, but that everyone had died or fled during the Black Death.

In the early mornings we'd sometimes meet on the beach at St Mary's Gap and try to shoot seagulls with catapults. Other times we'd leave for one of our cycle rides north into the countryside, often passing through Lisson, where there was another café with crusty cheese rolls on offer. And the stories continued: the Arthur Ransome books, *The Royal Escape* by Georgette Heyer, *Tom Sawyer* and *Huckleberry Finn*, *Flight of the Doves* ... He introduced me to serious music and literature, taught me how to draw maps, showed me carpentry skills, tried to interest me in foreign languages. He talked to me about science, history, and astronomy. Often I didn't understand, but I was flattered that he thought I was a worthwhile companion and pupil. I was conscious of being offered something different and good, and I was grateful. Feeling the cold on my face as I walked down to the beach at first light, or sitting miles from anywhere, cooking sausages over a wood fire. Experiencing intense fear as we were chased by a man and a barking dog out of an orchard where we'd been stealing apples. At the orchard's boundary, Jeremy had wrapped me in his coat and thrown me over the fence into the nettles on the other side, then leapt clear himself. Another time we'd climbed up an almost sheer cliff, that rose above the waves breaking on the rocks below. It had been horribly frightening, and a passer-by on the clifftop path had called down, asking if he should call the rescue services. I was almost paralysed with fear and the stranger's suggestion felt eminently sensible, but Jeremy shouted that we were fine. And eventually we did reach the top. These things gave me thrills of a kind that would certainly have been prohibited on family outings. I was having a childhood filled with adventures. It was life like it was described in storybooks.

Brian, next door, was rather put to one side, as were my other friendships in the street. I almost never met up with school-friends outside the playground. They had things going on that I wasn't a part of, and I had a life they knew nothing about. It had become second nature for me to keep the weekends clear, as I knew I'd be with Jeremy. Brian would drop in during the week. One evening he stayed to tea and, after we'd eaten, he came up and sat on the washing basket while I had a bath. We were nattering about guns and about how to save up to buy an FN rifle – actually, I knew I wouldn't be allowed to have one, as toy guns were not encouraged in the Lowe household. Without warning, Jeremy walked in. I knew instantly that he was angry at finding Brian there. Jeremy didn't like Brian, full stop.

'All right, Brian, you can go home now.'

'What are you talking about? I'm playing with Matt.'

'Matt, you are not able to play any more now, are you.' This was a statement, calling for confirmation, rather than a question. 'Come on, you heard what I said.'

Jeremy had gripped Brian by the shoulders and was pushing him past the bath and out onto the landing. Brian continued to protest – by now out of my sight – and then suddenly burst into tears and ran down the stairs, slamming the front door behind him. Jeremy came back into the bathroom, grinning. 'Saw him off, all right. You didn't expect me today, did you! There was nothing for me to do at work this week so I thought there was no point hanging around. Have you finished in there yet?'

I nodded and Jeremy held out his hands. I raised my own and was lifted out, held in the air for a few moments to let the worst of the water run off my body, and then placed on his lap. He picked up a towel and started drying me. It was different from the way Mum did it. She'd hold the big towel open while I stood up and would expect me to step out of the bath to be wrapped up completely. Then she'd give me some vigorous rubs and encourage me to get on and dry myself. As Jeremy dried me, there was a knock at the front door and then the sound of Mrs Biggs – Brian's mother – shouting, 'Where is he? I want to speak to him now. I don't care, go and get him, I know he's in there.'

Jeremy hesitated, then put me down. 'I'll be back in a minute.'

I listened while Mrs Biggs gave Jeremy an earful about never laying a finger on her son again or she would get the police onto him. Jeremy tried to sound apologetic.

~ 5 ~

It took me a long time to find some serious help. In some ways I'd been programmed to despise exactly the kind of support that I've regarded, since I found it, as a lifeline. Jeremy had been sneering about any kind of professional input: to him, social workers and psychologists were agents of a conforming and coercive society, like prison warders. I'd been exposed to Dad's attitude too, which was that there was no such thing as a mental health problem, only self-indulgence and feebleness of character. In his view, the true road to health lay in sinking one's individual neuroses into the struggle for social change. So it took a crisis to get me to see a proper therapist. Once there, though, it was a revelation. Not an instant cure, not by any means. But a catalyst and a turning point.

I was in my late twenties, but I hadn't grown up. On the surface everything was fine – it looked like I was making good. A good first degree, then research at Coventry. From there to teaching in Ghana, then a job in overseas development in London. In Jayne I had a beautiful and loving partner. We'd been together eight years. But we were exact opposites. She was life-loving, open, full of mischief and solid. I was joyless, secretive, controlling and brittle.

Inside, I was crumbling. Jayne shored me up, but I resented my dependence on her. That we seemed so well suited made the recurring difficulties all the more distressing. I wasn't her equal, and I was convinced that it was only by pretending to be other than I was that I could keep her interested in me. The strain of this dissimulation wore me down. Being with Jayne was the best thing that had happened to me, but I never felt safe. She seemed to sense that something was wrong and, it seemed to me, sought reassurances that I could never provide.

The difficulty at this particular point involved another woman, but she wasn't important. Some weeks earlier I'd been unfaithful with a temp I'd met at the office. She'd only stayed a week. We'd had sex twice: there was neither the wish nor the opportunity for anything more. Yet the secret had gnawed at me. Convinced that it was this that was spoiling whatever chance there might be of an honest relationship with Jayne, I confessed and found myself inflicting horrible pain on the woman I loved. I'd also presented her with a tangible reason for giving up on me, and this time it seemed as though she would call it a day. In real danger of losing her, I put everything I had into persuading her to stay. This was a crystallisation, a recognisable emergency, but as it cleared, I understood that my cheating hadn't been the essential cause, and that getting over it would leave us just as we had been. We'd been through this routine several times before. Both losing Jayne and returning to normal seemed intolerable.

On the morning in question, I narrowly avoided making a spectacle of myself amongst the commuters travelling in to Charing Cross, but once inside the office the lid came off. Colleagues arrived to find me lying on the floor of the meeting room, sobbing uncontrollably. Marie, who had once warned me that constantly putting myself down was weakening my position on the team, came in and sat with me, her hand on my shoulder. I eventually calmed myself but continued to hide in shame.

Without looking at her I abruptly got up and went to the bath-room to wash my face. I was joined by Luis, who asked how I was.

'OK. I'm OK.'

'I don't think so.' His warm, accented English conveyed real care and concern.

'I'll be all right. Things aren't easy at the moment.'

'It's not just today, is it, Matt? I don't know what it's about, but it's been obvious that things haven't been OK for a while.'

I didn't reply.

'I know somebody who talks to people in trouble. She's pretty busy, but I could give her a ring and see if she has any suggestions.'

'Yeah, that might be an idea. Yeah. Thanks.' I felt I'd reached the end of something and didn't know if any kind of future was possible. I felt I'd tried everything. However ridiculous the idea of talking to a shrink was, I was up for it.

Later in the afternoon, Luis passed me a slip of paper with a name and telephone number. 'My friend has given me the number of one of her colleagues. She's expecting your call. I don't know her myself. Good luck.'

And so I found myself, in the upstairs room of a community centre in Peckham, sitting awkwardly opposite Caroline. I was wondering what to expect; she gave me some direction. 'I know nothing about you, except that there have been some difficulties at work and that you think it might be helpful to talk about them. Today we have an hour and a quarter to see whether or not we want to work together. We can spend some time at the end think-ing about that, and about practical arrangements if we are to meet again.'

I didn't know where to start. 'Look, I don't believe in this stuff, that it's all to do with your childhood and all that. I'm in a mess, but talking about it is not going to make any difference. I said I'd see you because I'm finished. I'm frightened. I can't manage any more. I don't think you can help me. I'd have said yes to anything.'

'You're feeling desperate. You say you're frightened?'

'I … I … Sometimes I just don't think I can go on any more.'

'You think about suicide?'

'Sometimes. I can't do it, I know that; there are too many people involved. But it's hard hanging on. Sometimes I just want to be dead.' Tears stung my eyes, and for a while I couldn't speak.

Caroline handed me a box of tissues.

'I'm just bad. Everybody thinks I'm good, but I'm just bad. I work with people who have been imprisoned and tortured, who have lost their homes, who have every reason on earth to feel down. Instead, they're optimistic and active. But I'm not like that. I've had it easy. I come from a lovely family, I had a good childhood, and now look at me.'

'You don't deserve any support because there's nothing awful in your life that explains why you feel the way you do?' She asked me about my current problems and I explained about my betrayal, how the sex had not meant anything but that obviously it was still so hurtful to Jayne.

'So why do you think you told her?'

'I couldn't not tell her. I felt guilty.' It was a struggle to be expected to consider my behaviour and wonder at my motivations. My voice became stronger, and with some energy I began to spit out the thoughts that had been tormenting me. 'I should be beaten up. I should lose my job. Jayne should leave me. I've always known I would end up alone, living on the street. My whole life is a lie, one big lie. I lie all the time. No one knows who I am.'

'So, you were perhaps trying to tell your partner how bad you are?'

'I don't know. Maybe. I've had a good life. All my life people have been good to me. Not like other people who get depressed. I'm the only one in the family who is like this.'

'So it's a mystery why you should find life so hard.'

'Everyone around me is good, and I turn everything bad. My girlfriend is wonderful. All she wants – the only thing she said she needed from me – is that I am honest with her. And I can't be. I'm so scared. I can't live without her. But I make her miserable all the time.'

'You are perhaps worrying that I won't want to work with someone as bad as you. Worrying, perhaps, that you will have to protect me from all that poison inside you.'

Already I'd said more than I'd ever said to anyone else. I'd been monitoring Caroline from the moment we'd met in reception. I found myself drawn to her strange combination of warmth and directness.

'Why don't you tell me something about your life. Something about the family you grew up with.'

I described the family structure, my parents' work, how close they were to one another. 'There's one thing I have to get out of the way. When I was young, a child, I had a relationship with a man. A friend of the family.' I paused.

'A relationship?'

'He thought I was special; he was very loving. It was different, of course, being in a sexual relationship from such a young age.'

'What age would that have been?'

'Probably about five, in some sort of way. But it was a good relationship. He was really caring and tried to help me when I felt down. He was the only person I could really let see how difficult things were for me. I'm like this despite him, not because of him.'

'You don't want me to rush to any conclusions. It's important to you that I see this man as a good influence.'

'He introduced me to literature and music; he took me to all sorts of places. Whatever is good about me is down to him. All the bad stuff is inside me. It won't help me if you decide that this is the cause of my problems. It'd be like letting me off the hook. So I'm not going to talk about it. I don't know what I will talk about, but if you want me to talk about that, then I'm not coming back.'

'You feel deeply that you deserve to be punished. You want to make sure I'm not going to be soft on you.'

'I think you've got to be really harsh – if there's any chance of rooting this thing out.'

By the end of the session I knew that I'd stumbled onto something that I'd been dreaming about for years deep inside. It was astonishing but also the realisation of a powerful wish to be able to speak out loud the thoughts that I'd tried so hard to ignore. They swam about beneath the surface, they were often confusing and self-defeating, but they seemed to have a terrible hold over how I felt and lived. I was curious about who and what I was getting myself into. 'Are you a psychiatrist? Or what?'

'I'm trained as a psychodynamic counsellor.'

The word *counsellor* conjured up an image of my old teacher, Mr Oldham, but what I'd encountered so far was nothing like what he'd have said and done. My expression must have registered my confusion. Caroline went on: 'I would hope to provide a place where you and I can explore together the meanings behind the way you think and feel. In the belief that some of the more important, sometimes the more troublesome, parts of our minds are difficult to access. This might only make sense when you've had an opportunity to experience it for yourself.'

I was shocked when Caroline said directly that she was prepared to work with me. Did that mean that I was really ill? I checked that I had understood, that she felt I was worth her time and energy, that there weren't other people who needed the appointments more than I did. She told me that she could offer to work with me for six months, that we would meet for 50 minutes each week, and that, as I was working, there would be a charge of £10 per session. She offered me a time, and I said I would be there. Then she asked if I would show myself out.

*

I was always early and had to wait. I used the sessions to disgorge so much that had remained half buried or actively suppressed. I talked about Mum and Dad, and about how sad I was to be so distant from them. I told Caroline how I had tried very hard to be the clever son I knew they'd wanted by working diligently at school and university, but how I knew that that was all a lie too, as I was basically slow and unimaginative.

I described my relationships with girls, and the problems I now had with Jayne. How each evening, on the way home from the station, I walked across the lorry park looking up at the lights in the flat windows with a feeling of dread. It seemed to be a fear of being found out, but I didn't know what for. And the feeling of relief each time she was just happy to see me. But how the next day it would be the same all over again.

I heard myself repeatedly lash out at my own failings, my laziness, mediocrity, weakness.

Caroline listened, made occasional comments, and reinforced my first impression of her as being able to withstand an exposure to pain and anger to a degree that I had doubted possible. Not just to survive it, but to stay close to me as I began to open up. I soon felt deeply attached to this slight but power- ful woman who seemed to concentrate on me utterly for the allotted 50 minutes, and who would then, quite abruptly, stop the session and wait for me to leave. The transitions were diffi- cult; the arriving and the leaving. But though the gaps between the sessions seemed long, I held fast to the notion of a thread that connected me to her. The image came to me of a cartoon character being swept along a river towards some rapids and reaching out and clinging onto an overhanging branch just in time to avert disaster.

*

'I wonder if you've noticed how you divide the world so completely into "good" and "bad". You have no complaints about anybody except yourself, as if you have taken everything bad in your life inside.'

I'd worried that Caroline might offer reassurance. Instead, she pointed things out about what I'd said. The implication was that my convictions might be merely a point of view. Beyond that, there was the hint that there might be a reason for seeing things in this particular way. It was as if she was saying: let's wonder why you look at things as you do. She was saying that there was a great deal more I might find out about myself, just by asking questions about the bits I thought I knew.

'You seem to punish yourself severely for the feelings you have. I suppose that you don't have any control over them – none of us do. What we *do* have is some choice about what we do with those feelings: that is what determines whether they become dangerous or destructive.'

I was struck by the wisdom but also the simplicity of her comments. Why hadn't this sort of stuff been taught in school?

Her words did not have a miraculous effect on how I felt, but they encouraged me to think more about what was going on when things got bad, rather than simply to sink under the weight.

'It's interesting,' Caroline said in one meeting, 'that you are angry with so much about the state of the world in general. I'm not saying that there isn't a great deal to be angry about, but perhaps we sometimes focus our anger on something "out there" rather than let ourselves know what or who it is we are truly angry with.'

There it was again: it was clear from her comments that Caroline was interested in my rage, or rather the absence of rage. I didn't feel angry towards the people closest to me, but I understood that to be her point. I might be protecting them out of fear.

'One of the places we can focus our anger is against ourselves, of course. This might be a cause of depression. Certainly, you talk about yourself with intense cruelty.'

*

About a month after we started working together, I mentioned Jeremy again. And again it was to impress on Caroline just how much I had benefited from his interest in me. 'He was a self-educated man. He never went to university like I did, but he seemed able to pick up the essence of any subject. I'm so dull by comparison. He had a spark. He wrote scripts and stories, and then he published some children's books. And he made films. I was so lucky when I think back on it. I worry about him now. He has so much talent, but he doesn't get the recognition he deserves. When I was a child I was really happy, but it got difficult when I was a teenager. It would have been easier if I'd been gay, really, but I'm not, and we fell out over the whole girls' thing. But we've made up since.'

'You make it sound like an ideal friendship. But I suppose that, in reality, relationships are always difficult; there are always complicated feelings involved in being close to someone.'

I heard. And an image came instantly to mind. 'Well, there is one thing that I've always known but never really understood. Every Saturday morning I'd cycle down through the allotments to the cottage where Jeremy lived with his mother. And on the way I'd always hope that he wouldn't be there when I arrived, that he would have been killed during the week.'

'So, perhaps not all of you felt so grateful that Jeremy played such a large part in your life.'

'I know I had other feelings about him. There's an ungrateful side of me that just wanted to be left alone, to be like my brother and sisters.'

'To have an ordinary childhood.'

The words struck like a hammer blow to the head. I reeled and cried out. The notion of an ordinary childhood was so clear and so meaningful. It seemed to suggest being cared for in some wholesome way. Of not having secrets or stomach cramps, or a world inside my head that shut me off from everyone else. I was such a freak; my life had been a mess from beginning to end; there was no hope of getting out of it. Visions of blinding sunshine across the beach at Ryde, the school trip to Paris when I was twelve, being amongst ordinary kids, joking about girls, smoking in secret, reading *Skinhead* and *Suedehead* in the back of the coach, having a laugh. I sat back, my eyes closed. It was like swimming in a pool full of memories, clutching at some, starting back at others. Dad talking about the 1962 missile crisis, how he'd come upstairs and gazed down at us sleeping children, wondering if that night we were all going to die. Why hadn't I stayed close to that love? What had I done? I wanted to reach inside my brain and wash away the stench. I wanted to tear it all up and start again, and I knew I couldn't, that there would never be a second chance. I struggled to keep the feelings from bursting through my ribcage. I thought I might be sick. I looked into the therapist's face and found her eyes still there, on me, unblinking and accepting.

'What am I going to do?'

Caroline said nothing, but her expression conveyed a conviction that this was survivable, that together we could bear whatever there was to be borne.

*

During another session, Caroline said, 'You came to feel responsible, or at least as responsible as Jeremy, for the sexual abuse. But you were just a little boy.'

There was a long silence. I was taking in her use of a term that had recently appeared in the papers a lot. A doctor in Cleveland had identified a number of children who had, she thought, been sexually assaulted, and this had caused an uproar. People took sides and an investigation had been launched. I'd followed the story and read the attacks on the doctor involved. I had wanted to write her a letter, something supportive, though I didn't know quite what or why. I'd never associated the term 'sexual abuse' with myself.

'That term wasn't around then, was it? I don't remember ever hearing it. There were dirty old men in raincoats exposing themselves in playgrounds, that kind of thing. I remember Gracey raving about someone who'd done that in a park near her house, saying they ought to be castrated, or worse. And I remember thinking she was being ridiculous. But I never heard that term, not then.'

There was another silence as I pondered the implications of applying the phrase to my own experience. I rebelled against the idea of letting myself off, of seeing myself as a victim. 'It's not that easy with me, though. I may have been young, but staying with Jeremy was my decision. He didn't force me to do anything.'

'You think that a child of five, or nine, or thirteen, has the capacity to decide for himself to be in a sexual relationship with an adult.' After another silence, Caroline added, 'Children may, perhaps, want to be physically close to adults and behave in ways that adults find seductive. But it is the adult's responsibility to recognise the child's vulnerability, not to exploit it for his or her own pleasure.'

So, now, did it feel right? Is that what had happened to me? The inference was that Jeremy was responsible. I felt as if some great bird had come and picked me out of a smelly sewer and deposited me on a mountain top, a position from which I could begin to see life from a very different point of view. For many years I'd had dreams of being naked in public and covered in shit, but now I envisaged a place where I could be clean and fresh. It was troubling to find that I had based the story of my own life on a series of assumptions I'd hardly been aware of. I was regarded by many as a cynic and thought of myself as a sceptic. I was trained as a historian, someone who reviewed evidence critically and was alive to its general misuse. Someone who distrusted the media and sought to keep at bay common-sense assumptions about the world. But when it came to myself, all these reflective capacities had failed. My beliefs had never been subjected to any procedure of verification. Picking them up and turning them over, as I was doing now, they were being revealed as uniformly groundless, even lethal.

*

Between sessions I thought about little else other than what had come up in the work with Caroline. I hadn't always been a child, or always reluctant. There were times I knew I'd been keen to participate. And I knew I had loved Jeremy and needed him. At times I doubted if I had grounds for viewing myself as a victim, or for believing that anything untoward had been done to me. After all, I could have told my parents, but I hadn't.

'Why didn't I tell anyone? I can't understand that. I could have done, and I chose not to. What does that say about me?'

'You think it means that you were really to blame? Why do you think you didn't tell?'

'I don't know. Shame, I suppose. Didn't want to upset anyone. Didn't want them to see how bad I was. I think I needed Jeremy. I don't understand why, but I was frightened of being without him.'

'There was something he provided you with that you couldn't get in any other way?'

'No, that can't be it. The others didn't need anything extra. Maybe I was just greedy. There was a time' – the tears were flowing again, as they did through most sessions – 'when I started calculating. I was relying on Jeremy to buy me things or to get rich and pay me.' It was clear that I wanted to add to this, and Caroline waited. 'I was a kind of ... prostitute, I think.'

'You seem to have been trying to convince yourself that you were in control, that you had a choice.'

'I believe what I wanted was continued love and support, but the only thing I had to offer in return was sex. I see sex as a way of giving, a way of attracting people, perhaps *the* way. I don't know entirely where I am in a non-sexual relationship. If I was really honest, I'd say that I offer more to people as a physical object, as decoration, as something sexual, even if no sex has taken place, than in any other way. This sounds horribly arrogant. One thing that's been changing since I've been coming here is the way I no longer fear looking my age, growing older, fatter, that I'm not needing to be so arrogant. I no longer maintain eye contact with total strangers in the hope of seeing a reassuring hint of desire lurking there.'

*

I wasn't sure what to make of Caroline. Her reactions repeatedly caught me off guard. Her mindset was completely alien. She was always there on time, always expecting me. I could tell from the things she said that she listened and remembered what we talked about, and even thought further about them, as I did, during the days between our meetings. Against this I sometimes worried that there might be something sinister going on during these sessions. Was I being brainwashed? That's what Jeremy would have said: that I was taking the easy way out. I wondered as well what it was that Caroline got out of working with me and whether I was right to trust her. If I began thinking like this, I quickly checked myself, because it was obvious that Caroline cared about me. She clearly wasn't there for the money. If she wasn't good, then I was entering a kind of hell, so she must be good.

Yet Caroline herself seemed to realise that I had these thoughts. 'I know that you value these sessions and that you work hard to make the most of them. But I wonder if you don't protect me from your anger in the same way that you used to protect Jeremy.'

'Why should I be angry with you?' Her question irritated me. 'You're helping me. You could push me harder sometimes to make sure that I learn as much as possible, that we get to the core of it all. But I have no anger towards you at all.'

'Mmm. Yet we only meet once a week. The sessions are generally very intense. I end them each time, and then you have to wait six days before we can meet again.'

'But that's not your fault, is it? It would be ridiculous for me to be angry about something that neither of us can change. No, you're wrong about that.'

This was a completely new and different kind of relationship to me, and I adamantly rejected any attempt by Caroline to suggest that the complicated feelings I had experienced when close to others might repeat themselves with her.

*

For a while the counselling itself was yet another secret. I needed time to see what it was about before trying to describe it to anyone else. Jayne had stayed with me, while struggling still to come to terms with my infidelity. We were walking on Hampstead Heath; the atmosphere was gentle.

'Do you think we're going to make it?' Jayne asked.

'Of course we shall. I feel more confident now about the future. That perhaps I'm growing up, changing, anyway.'

'In what way?'

'Well, I haven't mentioned it before because I didn't know what it would be like and I didn't want to raise expectations, but I've been seeing a counsellor for the last couple of months.'

'Really? That's brilliant, Matt. I'm so relieved. I wish you'd told me. You're always so secretive. How did you arrange it?'

I explained. I was in two minds about Jayne's enthusiasm: it seemed she might already be explaining my behaviour in terms of some kind of illness. 'I've already changed my ideas about certain things, and I feel bad about it because I know I've refused to listen to you in the past when you were right and it would have been better for both of us if I'd not been so controlling.'

Jayne kissed me and held me close. 'Go on.'

'Well, a lot of it's about Jeremy.'

'Of course it is.'

'Well, you knew it would be, but I didn't. Anyway, it's clear to me now that a lot of difficulties stem from my connection with him. It's terrible, the way I've been seeing it all these years. Do you think it's right to think of it as sexual abuse?'

Jayne was wiping her eyes. 'You couldn't see it, and you wouldn't hear it, and there was nothing anyone could do.'

'I know, I realise that. Crazy. It seems to have so much to do with feeling different and not coping. And perhaps not believing that I deserve to have a good life.'

'It explains a lot, I'm sure of that. So it's important you get as much out of this as possible, and then maybe we can have an easier time of it. If you get well.'

I was uneasy again at the idea of being ill, of getting well. I was and I wasn't. We agreed that our problems were not my fault but the fault of the abuse, and that once that was clear we could look forward to a more harmonious future.

'Look.' I held out my hands to show the signs of growth and healing around my nails.

'That's amazing! I'm so proud of you.'

'I know. I just stopped. Without even thinking about it.'

I'd begun biting my nails years before; I remembered the occasion vividly. I'd been playing football with my brother in Jubilee Gardens, in the fading light of a winter afternoon. The inky clouds were still visible, but the streetlights had already come on. I was in goal. As Peter ran to collect the ball, I put my finger to my mouth and trapped a nail between my teeth. The soft nail gave way, and I was left with a sliver of it. I spat it out. The end of my finger tingled. I studied it, seeing the way the nail was made up of thin layers lying over a soft, white, springy base. A line of blood appeared. It was getting cold, and I put my finger back in my mouth. My teeth sought out another piece of nail that could be detached. Then I had a go at a different finger. I forgot the game until Peter shouted to me, but really I didn't want to be distracted from my discovery. After I had taken off the excess nail on all five fingers of one hand, I found that there was a small flap of loose skin beside my thumbnail. I pulled it off with my teeth. The pain was horrible, but relieving it seemed to require putting the thumb back in my mouth and sucking the blood that had seeped out around the cuticle. I'd found a new way to give myself pleasure – or was it pain? – and I wasn't going to give it up, no matter who said what to me.

Jayne asked me, 'How long are you going to go on having therapy for, then?'

'I've got about four months left.'

'That seems a long time. Are you sure you need that much?'

'We'll see. At the moment it feels really helpful.'

*

'What am I going to say to Jeremy when he comes back?' Jeremy, who'd been abroad for several months, was scheduled to return any day.

'What do you want to say to him?' Caroline put the question back to me.

'Can I kill him?'

'You're asking me to endorse murder?'

I laughed. 'I've been imagining myself doing it. Or tying him up in a chair and torturing him.'

'There's a world of difference between wanting to kill someone and actually killing them.'

'I know. I feel quite comfortable hating him. I can't see how killing him would really change anything. Just get these images floating through my head. But I do have to say something. I can't avoid him; he's stored several suitcases with most of his worldly possessions in our flat. To be honest, I'm frightened. I know it's pathetic. I'm just scared that when I see him everything will collapse again and I'll feel as much in his power as I always have done.'

'You have an image of yourself as a needy child and Jeremy as the adult who has all the power to care for you. You're afraid that that's all there is to you.'

'Even after everything we've learnt here, it still feels like that. But now there's also a me that wants to confront him.'

'What would that involve?'

'What do I want to say to him? Fuck off. FUCK OFF! Will that do?'

'It would be letting him know how you feel.'

'I don't know. It feels so huge. But I know I have to say something. I can't bear the idea of him any more, around me or the family.'

*

'Hello, is that Matt? It's the world's number one jet-setter here, returned from the tropics. Just touched down at Heathrow. How are you?'

'I can't see you. Things have changed.'

'Changed?' Jeremy's voice lost its jaunty tone. 'What do you mean?'

'I don't think of you as the kindly uncle any more, more as the evil witch.' I was annoyed that I sounded so stilted, my choice of words so inept. There was a long pause.

'It's taken you a long time to decide that.'

'Maybe, but that's how it is. All your luggage at the flat, when do you want to collect it? I could bring it to my office tomorrow morning and you could get it from there.'

'That's how it is, eh?'

'That's how it is. Your luggage will be in the lobby at

Grosvenor Court by nine tomorrow morning. You can collect it from there. And I don't want you going near any of my family again.'

I replaced the receiver and sat down. I was shaking uncontrollably.

*

I was back with Caroline.

'Everything feels contaminated. If I listen to music, it seems down to him. The food I cook, the books I've read. He's everywhere.'

'It's difficult not to give him the credit for everything that you are. *You* read the books, *you* listen to the music.'

'Maybe, but I wish there was more of me that seemed to be mine, just mine.'

A silence followed.

'I haven't told you what actually happened, have I? What he did.'

'No, you haven't.' There was a silence. 'Perhaps a part of you would like me to know, to find out if I would turn against you, be disgusted. While another part is too afraid to take the risk.'

'It's too sordid. When I think of it, I have to look away. It's so demeaning.'

*

The sessions became heavier, almost unbearably tense.

'Going through the motions seems more and more difficult, not less. I no longer want to drop hints about killing myself; I want to indulge those fantasies. I want to give up. I want to roll on the floor screaming at work rather than go on feeling that heavy weight and tension. I'd like to let go on the train. I'd like to explode inside my chest, to break free.'

'It's terribly hard, facing yourself in this way.'

'I don't really believe that you're on my side. I know that you can also see the trapped child in Jeremy, whose pain and need to hide it mean that he wasn't really to blame, and isn't to be hated for real – only I'm allowed to hate him because it might do me some good.'

'The notion that Jeremy could also be understood somehow devalues our attempt to understand you?'

'I'd feel more confident you understood if you were revolted by me. Or if I could make you cry – if I could overwhelm you with the waste and the shit and the rest – rather than be so unmoved because you're sure I'm really good and strong and all that.'

'You're saying that I have to reject you as disgusting and useless before you can feel that I understand you enough to help you?'

'I'm sorry – I feel I'm just using you to dump all this shit on. At the same time I want to force you to see it, even more than before. You seem to like me, so I'm not convinced you see the real me. You wouldn't like someone like me. I've not shown you what I'm really like. It's more palatable coming out as a little boy's grief. But now I'd like to force your face into it, to see how endless and bottomless and vile it is.' I paused to calm myself. 'I despair at being close to anyone. I'm in pain – I always was and I always will be. I don't know why I go on. I'm miserable and mad because I'm alone, and it's only here – as a patient – that I find someone I can tell and not be scared of how you're going to take it.'

'I think you're letting me know how unprotected, unsupported and isolated you felt as a child. And how you've been carrying an enormous secret. You seem to have felt the whole experience as if you'd done the seducing. And you've been left shouldering all the pain, distress, disgust and guilt, all accepted as punishment for what you did. You've idealised those around you because you had to, in order to survive, so as not to have to be angry with those whom you needed to protect you. You've convinced yourself that you were loved, not abused.'

After a pause Caroline added, 'You're afraid I might take away your convictions. If through your work here you get closer to feeling how powerless and vulnerable you were, then I become a kind of abuser. And for that you're furious with me.'

'I don't think so,' I smiled back.

*

At various times Caroline touched on the notion that there might be earlier issues that were still hidden, yet to be encountered, circumstances which might explain why I'd been vulnerable to Jeremy's attentions and unable to tell my parents once the abuse had begun. I fended her off. I had taken up fully the idea that what had occurred could be described as abuse. Doing so changed so much; in fact it explained everything. It was like look- ing at the reflection in a spoon and then turning the spoon over. The same items could be located, but the perspective was completely changed. And once the change had been made, there was no turning back. I read books on abuse and its consequences, and recognised my feelings about life, and death, in them.

When we'd been meeting for about four months, Caroline reminded me that our contract had been limited to six months of weekly sessions. She'd occasionally referred to this before. I hated any mention of the ending.

'One question we might want to consider is whether our work has been sufficient to help you cope better in the future, or whether you might benefit from seeking further therapy with someone else, perhaps on a more intensive basis.'

'Why would I want to do that? Everything is sorting itself out now.'

'As it's turned out, we've focused on Jeremy's impact on you. At the moment it feels as if when this is resolved, everything will have been solved.'

'What else is there?'

There was a silence. I found myself thinking about my parents. My father was then recovering from major heart surgery. 'My dad's been up and down since his operation. He seems even more precarious emotionally than physically. Great optimism one moment, giving up entirely the next. We visited him in hospital this weekend. The first evening he was very tense, even at one moment hitting himself in frustration, complaining about being so unrelaxed. The next day I asked if it was his health that was causing the tension, or his addiction to tobacco – he's no longer allowed to smoke. And he said neither, that he thinks he's always been like that, it's part of his person-ality. He said that reading was difficult because books were full of problems and so many of them seemed to relate to him. It was all very different from the image I had of him, the one I think I gave you. Later, I tried to tell my mother the gist of what he'd said, and she flinched visibly. I think she must be very scared, and it comes out as insensitivity. When we visited Dad together, she hardly listened to him, taking those bits she wanted to hear from what he said and ignoring the rest. I felt this must be very frustrating for him, but he's probably used to it and understands the reasons for it. Driving back to London I felt how little I knew them, and also how strange it must be for them, knowing me so little too.'

'Your relationship with your parents is also a source of difficulty for you.'

'Mmmm. Maybe.'

*

'I've got a story I want you to read. It just came out of me while I was sitting by the river, during a lunch break.' It had come to me almost like a dream, clear and complete.

She took the sheet of paper I held out to her and read in silence:

In romantic books the rabbit found stories of green fields and damp forests; indeed his elders assured him that his own early years had been quite idyllic. But the rabbit couldn't remember and had grave doubts. In any case this was hardly surprising: his present environment, in the deep freeze, could hardly have been more different from the dreams of freedom that troubled his endless nights.

This is not to say he was *un*happy. He *could* remember a great deal of life filled with caresses and caring. These were his best memories: of being picked up by large, gentle hands smoothing down his fur, stroking him under the chin while metal wires were attached to his head. The wires irritated and confused the rabbit, but they quickly became synony-mous with the large, loving hands, and he eagerly looked forward to this treatment, which, he was told, was reserved for very special rabbits.

The shocks that followed didn't hurt. The rabbit was simply numbed, 'frozen'. There were side effects – headaches, bad dreams and suicidal fantasies – but the rabbit's brain was not sophisticated enough to make the connection. In the midst of these traumas, he longed only for the return of the large, caressing hands that would calm him.

The long-term effects were more devastating. Although himself unaware of it – his memory of what had gone before was that poor – the shocks, and the growing sense of the rabbit's alienation from his own body, were causing a severe deterioration in his physical condition. The caressing hands smoothed away his fur and skin, leaving the flesh exposed. The rabbit was in continual pain. He thought it was just a passing phase, for he'd been warned of a difficult period that rabbits pass through called adolescence.

It was around this stage that the rabbit discovered the deep freeze. Here he could temporarily escape from the pain. This is not to say that he could feel any real satisfaction there – the only benefit the deep freeze brought was to kill all feeling, and the rabbit was intelligent enough to know that feeling was the only thing that distinguished him from the thoroughly dead. So he would periodically creep out from the deep freeze when no other rabbits were around and warm himself sufficiently to feel his nerve endings tingle. His special treat was to listen to music, for this seemed to bring many senses into play. He sat himself between two large black speakers and turned the volume to full.

The great thing about this orgy of emotion, from the point of view of the rabbit, was that he could keep it all perfectly under control. He loved to turn the music up so loud that the whole room vibrated. His ears hurt; the beat shook his whole body and particularly thundered into his chest. The various instruments sounded like machines of torture – electric knives, curved meat hooks that would tear the flesh and splinter the bone. And just when it all became too true, when his surface flesh had properly thawed and the pain had returned as if the skin had only recently been ripped off, then he would put the music away, control his sobbing and climb back into the deep freeze, where he would rub up against any big chunk of meat and dream of the large, caressing hands, electric wires and freedom.

'It's a terrible story. I wonder what it might mean to you.'

'It's self-evident, isn't it? I think I'm still trying to find ways to represent what was going on. I can't really bear the idea that I was dependent on him, and he had hurt me so much, and yet he was the one I was always going back to for comfort. It's hideous.'

'Mmm. It *is* hideous, and you present it very powerfully in the story. I wonder if there might be another meaning there as well. It could be read as a description of what I'm doing to you now: spending a brief 50 minutes with you, putting you in contact with so much pain, and yet in a way that is also about taking care of you. And then I leave you alone to deal with it.'

*

'There *is* something I can't use you for. I'd like you to know what it feels like being me, how down I can feel. There's no way I can put that into words.'

I'd let myself express a wide range of feelings in my meetings with Caroline. There were times when I'd crouched in the corner covered in my coat, becoming as pathetic and immature as I felt myself to be. I'd opened up, trusted her in a way I'd trusted no one else in my life. As I'd done so, however, my fear of rejection and abandonment became ever greater. I had questions I knew she could not, or would not, answer. Why was she seeing me? What did she get out of it?

During one session I tried to explain the dilemma I felt about her attitude towards me.

'At the beginning you could see I was in trouble, and you wanted to help. If I get well, then you won't want to see me any more. It'll be a waste of your time. But if I stay ill, you'll be pissed off with me for being a bad patient, someone who's spoiling what you're trying to give me. In fact I work hard and I'm making progress, but I know it means that you'll soon be pleased to see the back of me so you can spend the time more profitably with someone else.'

However hard I worked, and whatever progress I made, there remained a deep misery at my core that I longed for her to touch. I felt real despair at the thought that this part of me would have to remain separate and secret for ever. 'Whenever I think of how I would describe it to you, it feels ridiculous, or exaggerated. Like the other day I was out with Jayne and a couple of friends. We'd driven down to Kent and were walking around this village. And there was a point when I felt really good, like there was no side of me that I was hiding. But I hated the atmosphere of the twee shops, so I wandered away on my own and it just happened. Suddenly I was not just alone but isolated, and with a cold pain around my middle, and the only way I could describe it to myself was that a ball of ice had formed around my soul. I imagined telling you that, and it felt so limp and meaningless.'

'It makes me think about Matt the baby and little boy, and how he felt before Jeremy came along.'

'There was nothing wrong before that.'

'It is difficult to look back beyond the abuse. But you're describing something like the feeling of needing a mummy to hold you and understand the bad feelings inside, to relieve you of them.'

'Yes, but that doesn't mean the feelings themselves date from that time, does it?' There was an extended pause. 'I don't blame my parents. It wasn't their fault. But I've been thinking about it, not blaming them but wanting to know what they thought about it at the time. How they understood my relationship with Jeremy. I've told you that he and I were put in the same room on holiday. I've wondered about that for years.'

'You've wondered if they really knew, if they thought that it was all right. You describe thinking about their attitude, but it seems that there's no sense of rage at their failure to protect you.'

I tried, but I could find nowhere inside myself that felt even remotely resentful. I just wanted to be accepted, to belong.

*

Christmas was approaching. There was to be a three-week break in the therapy, and then we were to come back in January for the remaining month's work.

'This is our next-to-last session before the break.'

'Yes, I know. So much has changed. Things with Jayne have improved. I'm managing at work better than before. I'm not nearly so depressed.'

'It sounds as if you might be preparing for the end of therapy rather than for a break.'

It hadn't occurred to me, but I took the idea and thought about it, and it seemed to make a kind of sense.

'Well, I suppose I could end early. I'm feeling better. Not just better, but well. Strong. I can't imagine going back to how I was when I first came to see you. It's been such an experience working with you. I don't think I could ever have done it on my own.'

'You seem to have heard me as suggesting that you should stop.'

'Weren't you? Perhaps you weren't, I'm not sure. But now that we've talked about it, I think maybe it's the best plan. I know that you believe there are lots of things I haven't dealt with yet, my relationship with my parents perhaps, but I'm not sure that's right. We've worked hard on the relationship with Jeremy, and that always seemed to be the main thing to me. Everything flows from getting that into a proper perspective. It's just a question of time, sorting out the consequences of all those awful ideas I used to have about the past. So rather than come back after Christmas and start opening everything up again, I'd prefer to end it now.'

'This is very sudden.'

'But after the holiday there'll be so little time to settle down again. It's hard stopping and starting and then stopping again.'

'This has been an intense and important relationship, and working towards the ending is important too. I wonder if there's a sense in which you're keen to end now so that you won't have to face me ending the counselling, face feeling abandoned and rejected.'

'Maybe. It's true that doesn't sound a very happy prospect. I'd rather walk away when I'm feeling strong than risk you leaving me when I'm not.'

Despite Caroline's entreaties, the discussion turned into a retrospective review of our work together, and what it had meant.

'You could never know how grateful I am for what you've done. For me this has been and always will be totally unique. It's not like the love of one's parents or even one's partner; it could never have been expected or demanded, and that fills me with a sense of well-being. All that mixed with the feeling of being trapped into an absurd, pathetic, laughable, child-like dependence, and knowing it's just a part, a small part, of your work, which will recur endlessly with one client after another. That doesn't make it less important for me. My actual childhood feels a great waste now. I fantasise about you adopting me ... I don't know why I feel so calm and unthreatened by the past now. Either nothing has changed, and it's just a question of time before I start going off the rails again, or I'm freed from all that went before, and the decision to stop the counselling is the right one.'

'I'd like you to come back and see me after the break, so that we can look at that together. Would you do that?'

'Yeah, of course, if you think it's important. But today I'd like us to assume that we are going to end.'

I walked out of the clinic with a lightness bordering on euphoria for, as far as I was concerned, the last time.

~ 6 ~

During 1967 a new idea was raised: instead of Jeremy always coming to Shorefleet, from time to time I could visit him in London. I was eight and big enough to travel on my own. Jeremy would meet me off the train, and together we'd see some of the sights of the big city. It was all agreed. In the middle of the week I received a letter from him spelling out what items I should pack, which train I should catch and where I would be met.

That Friday morning I filled a small suitcase and took it to school with me. I parked it under my desk, occasionally checking that it was still there. I handed a note to my teacher, Mrs Crick, asking permission to leave at half past three so that I could walk to Shorefleet Station in time for the train to Liverpool Street. I felt oddly tall as I walked out of the school gates early, my suitcase swinging at my side. At the station I used the money that Jeremy had left with me for my ticket and walked down onto the empty platform to wait.

In the course of its frequent stops the train filled with older schoolchildren and then emptied them out again. A lot of adults climbed in at Norwich and the train that arrived at Liverpool Street just before six o'clock was crowded. It had grown dark during the journey. I was excited by having to be responsible for myself, and tense at the possibility that something might go wrong. I smiled broadly when I caught sight of Jeremy standing by the ticket gate.

'You made it all right, then.' Jeremy gave me a warm hug and took the case.

'Everything happened just like we said. I read my comic on the train. Look.' I showed him my copy of the *Beano*.

'How many cows has Desperate Dan eaten?'

'I don't know! Where are we going now?'

Liverpool Street Station seemed huge and noisy, and I held Jeremy's hand to be guided through the bustle and noise towards the exit.

'We're going to a pancake restaurant for something to eat. How about that? You can have pancakes to start with, and pancakes for pudding.'

'Wow.' I was only used to having pancakes with sugar and lemon.

'And then we're going to meet Tony at the flat.' Tony came from New Zealand and was a close friend of Jeremy's. They shared a flat near Victoria.

We had our usual conversation relating to whatever had been covered on *Blue Peter* that week. The television provided me with topics of conversation with Jeremy, and Jeremy provided me with ways of impressing my peers at school. As we discussed the programme, Jeremy would show he already knew more about the subject in question than I did.

'Tomorrow we could go ice skating, what do you think?'

'I don't know. I don't think I could do that.' Peter had given me an old pair of roller skates the previous Christmas, and I'd never got the hang of them.

'It's easy. I'll show you. And after that we'll have lunch in a restaurant where you can eat as much as you like. That'll suit you:

you can fill your plate up as many times as you want to.' That seemed highly unlikely, although usually Jeremy meant what he said, however extraordinary it sounded at the time.

We ate at the pancake house and then took a taxi. I remembered the address because it sounded grand; maybe Jeremy said it in such a way as to suggest that it was grand. 'Dorchester Drive, Pimlico.' The flat was impressive to someone used to the room sizes in Edwardian terraces and Victorian cottages at the seaside.

'When will Tony get here?' I asked, before looking round the flat.

'Not until much later, I don't think,' replied Jeremy.

Like Jeremy, Tony was in his mid-twenties. They had been close friends since meeting at art college. In some ways they were very different; Tony dressed well, and though he tried to wear his blond curly hair long, it persisted in looking neat and respectable. Mum and Dad, who met him from time to time when he came down to Shorefleet to stay with Jeremy, were convinced that Tony was the more mature and responsible of the pair. And it was true that he seemed more grown up: he smoked and drove a blue Mini van. The two men had formed a partnership at college that had grown out of their joint leadership of the film club. Jeremy's ambition was to become a film director, while Tony had trained as a set designer. Together they were going to write their own scripts, make films and become rich and famous. Their company was called Outcast Films, and they were working on a film about a family of gypsies.

I'd met Tony a number of times, and I enjoyed being with Jeremy and him together because they seemed to share a clever sense of humour and were always predicting what the other one was going to say. Being around them could sometimes be like participating in an unscripted comedy act, full of surprises, puns and practical jokes.

A record sleeve that I found propped against the skirting board in the lounge caught my eye. I'd just picked it up when Jeremy came back into the room. 'See if you can find Stan Laurel. He's there somewhere.' I studied the cover closely and then read the title out loud: '*Sgt Pepper's Lonely Hearts Club Band*.' The words didn't mean anything to me: a club for lonely hearts?

'Why don't you put it on while I make us some tea.' I had heard of the Beatles and knew some of their lyrics because Dad had added them to the repertoire of songs we sang in the car on the way to school. 'She loves you, yeah yeah yeah!' 'I wanna hold your haaaaaand' and 'If there's anything that you want'. I worked out how to use the turntable and placed the needle carefully on the narrow black edge of the LP. With the music playing we drank our tea; then I helped Jeremy set up camp beds. One song, 'When I'm Sixty-Four', made an instant impression.

I was in bed by the time Tony came back. But I was too excited to sleep. I called out 'Hello', and he came in and asked me whether we'd had a good time at the pancake house. It wasn't long before the three of us were snuggled down, Jeremy and Tony in the two single beds and me in a sleeping bag on the floor. This was so different from being at home.

Tony said, 'Those bastards at the studio are trying to rip me off, claiming they never ordered the bloody photos I made for them in the first place.'

Although I'd picked up that my parents were reassured whenever they thought Tony would be around, as they considered him to be a calming influence on Jeremy, it always seemed to me to be the other way around. Tony *looked* more reliable with his conventional clothes and quiet manner, but Jeremy, who often looked like a scarecrow, would never swear in front of a child.

'That's the world of adults for you,' Jeremy answered. 'Cynical and nasty. You don't realise that yet, do you, Matt? You think that everyone is good and full of life like you are, but they're not. All adults except me—'

'And me,' added Tony.

'—are full of nonsense about their mortgages and their unhappy marriages.'

I wondered about my own parents.

'So you're not to change, Matt. Keep your beautiful mind, and don't let them spoil you and turn you into one of them.'

I was glad it was dark in the room. I didn't know what to think about what they were saying, but it seemed somehow to be directed against my mum and dad. I ventured to defend them. 'My mum and dad are adults, and they're not like that.'

The other two laughed.

'I wanted to kill my dad,' said Tony.

'I still want to kill mine,' said Jeremy. 'Every boy wants to kill his father; Freud said so.'

'Why?' I asked, upset.

'It's just a crazy man's crazy idea. Forget it, Matt.' Jeremy tried to reassure me. That made me feel better, although I didn't forget what the two men had said. They'd meant something by it, though I couldn't grasp what it was. Soon the room fell quiet.

Tony was working on the Saturday and had set an alarm clock that woke us all. Jeremy and I stayed in bed while he got up, turned on the electric heater, showered and dressed. A while later he called round the door to say goodbye. Once he was gone, Jeremy climbed out of bed and pulled on a dressing gown. He reappeared with mugs of tea and sat on the floor. 'First we can have a shower, then we'll get the bus down to the ice rink.' He put his arm around me, and I snuggled against his body.

'Come on, then.' He took off his dressing gown and unzipped my sleeping bag. I knew what was going to happen next.

On the Sunday, the two men took me up the Post Office Tower. Tony had brought me a present to take back home: *Sgt Pepper's Lonely Hearts Club Band*. I felt absolutely spoilt and was sorry to say goodbye to them both at Liverpool Street Station.

*

'Mummy. I've got a tummy ache.'

'Where is it, darling? Point to where it hurts.'

'It's here.'

'Let me put my hand there. Does that feel better? Perhaps you'd like a warm drink. I don't know what's the matter with you. If it's not your tummy, it's your head or your throat.' Mum sounded concerned. I seemed always to be complaining of something. Like the others I'd survived the usual childhood diseases – measles and chicken pox, even mumps. But the rest of the children had gone on to enjoy robust good health. I had sore throats, headaches and stomach upsets, sometimes an unexplained high temperature. Mum had taken me to Dr Whistler, listing my various ailments. The doctor had referred me to a specialist at the hospital who'd recommended that I have my tonsils removed. I hadn't liked being in hospital, despite the promised jelly and ice cream. I was put in a small ward with a quiet and sickly boy to whom I took an instant dislike. After two weeks at home, I returned to school. The minor illnesses returned as well.

'What are we going to do with you?' I liked it when Mum said that. She fetched some white medicine and gave me a teaspoonful. It wasn't as if I was using this tummy ache as an excuse to miss school: if it followed the pattern of the others, I'd be all right in the morning.

*

Little by little, weekend expeditions with Jeremy sealed me off from fully participating in family life. If plans were made for the children, they'd leave me out in the knowledge that I'd be other-wise occupied. I often regretted this, but I didn't say so. My feelings about many things were only dimly registered, particu-larly if they signalled conflict between the people upon whom my world now depended. It was certainly easier to cope with sadness inside than to deal with angry and disappointed people outside. I became used to ignoring urges arising in my own mind, moni-toring others instead to ensure that I was keeping them happy.

The ache to remain at home and simply be with the others was counteracted by two things. First, I really enjoyed the adven-tures that were only open to me as a result of my connection to Jeremy. Second, Jeremy presented me with a deeply negative picture of 'doing nothing'. He implied that the Lowe family was lazy and ordinary, conveying very strongly the idea that I too lived in danger of indulging a thoroughly despicable tendency towards slothfulness. This was described as a kind of sin. Jeremy was not religious; that was not the kind of sin he meant. It was the kind of sin for which there was no forgiveness: to look at oneself and know that one's talents were being wasted. With the added horror of Jeremy seeing the same thing.

For instance, when we cycled past Giovanni's, the ice-cream parlour on the sea front, and saw groups of teenage boys and girls standing apparently aimlessly, Jeremy never failed to use this as an illustration of children gone to the bad. And to wonder, ominously, whether I'd be able to avoid such a miserable outcome when it came to making the choices I'd be facing later. I had to regard myself as lucky that I'd been made aware of these moral distinctions: I didn't think that Peter or Ella had been, so they weren't to blame if they were already going down the wrong track. I could not entirely silence my envy at their unwitting self-indulgence, but guilt, or the avoidance of guilt, helped me resist the wish to be with my siblings as they hung around the house and garden on their days off from school. I didn't like to provoke Jeremy into talking about this, particularly as he hinted from time to time that he also regarded Mum and Dad as having resigned themselves to a narrow vision of life's possibilities. Jeremy, on the other hand, claimed to be living a life free of these limitations, and to be offering me the chance to follow him, if only I chose the right direction. I hated having conversations with him when he accused me of 'taking the easy way out'.

Mum's worries grew as I began wetting my bed on an almost nightly basis. I knew she was anxious by the weariness in her voice each morning. 'I don't understand, Matthew, you used to be dry all the time. You know that you were potty trained at a younger age than all the others.' Mum and Dad, and Gracey, were concerned. From their conversations I gathered that various theories were being considered. Perhaps it was 'just one of those things'. Perhaps they were lucky that only one of the four children wet his bed. It was a question of developing some kind of muscle control, it was about sleeping too deeply, something like that. Regimes were instituted where my evening intake of liquid was monitored, where I was woken late at night and helped in my befuddled state to use the toilet. But nothing worked. While Gracey hung yet another set of sheets to dry in the garden, Mum made a deal with me: 'I'll give you a penny for every night that you're dry.' But that didn't work either.

Mum's and Dad's attitude changed from concern to exasperation. I endeavoured to be good, but will power seemed just as ineffectual. I tried to help by changing the sheets myself, or pulling the wet ones off, using them to dry the plastic sheet that now and for years afterwards travelled with me wherever I went. I'd arrange the blankets in a way that was warm and comfortable enough to go back to sleep.

The sheets could be washed and replaced, but that had no effect on the way it made me feel. Luckily, no one teased me about it. But I knew it was what babies did, and that I was supposed to be a big boy now. Despite the incriminating smell, I'd lie when Jeremy came into my room, claiming that the reason the bed wasn't made was because I'd spilled my drink on it in the morning. At school the classes were divided into four teams, and the children had a rhyme about each one: 'Yellows, Yellows, Smelly Fellows;' 'Reds, Reds, Wet Their Beds.' I was a Red.

If only I could stop having those dreams. They started out differently but always had the same ending. Whatever I was doing, I would come to the realisation that I needed to find a toilet. Everything else would be forgotten in the search – I'd hold myself in regardless of how much pressure there was to wee, until I found myself in front of a toilet. And then I'd let go with tremendous relief and pleasure which would quickly become mixed up with a spreading warmth around my middle. As the warmth turned cold and nasty, I woke, the relief turning once again to exasperated disappointment.

*

It was time for another trip to London: this must have been the sixth or seventh. Jeremy and Tony had moved to a ground-floor flat in Fleet Road. I liked to identify the sights that gradually made the train journey familiar and predictable. One landmark was a large red neon sign, the word TUCS – which stood for the salty cheese biscuits we ate at home – above a town about halfway to London. I'd watch out for the bridge across the Slipway and try not to miss the brief view of Borchester Cathedral. Then there were the gardens and houses that backed onto the track as the train meandered through the darkened suburbs. I could wile away the time trying to see into the lit windows. I'd try to read the names of the suburban stations as the train sailed through without stopping. And then count the white numbers painted on the low brick walls along the side of the railway for the last few miles. Then, at last, as the train ground noisily across a succession of points, a thrilling lurch of metal against metal that seemed to be the train complaining aloud, we were there. Jeremy was always standing just behind the ticket collector to meet me. I'd become used to weekends in London always being special, each time in a different way. There was ice skating, the museums, eating in restaurants, going to posh cinemas to see films that would never come to the theatres at home.

Someone living in the Fleet Road house had a black cat that looked just like Fifi, my cat back in Bayview Road, and Jeremy took a photograph of it on my lap. Jeremy had a human skull, and he dressed up in a sheet with the skull poking out the top to scare me. It was great fun. The special occasion planned for this visit was to go to see the new film of *Oliver Twist*. This was a book that Jeremy had already read out aloud to me, and there were scenes from the story that were vividly etched on my mind. Jeremy had brought the characters – Oliver, Mr Bumble, Fagin and Bill Sykes – to life, and I immediately recognised the figure that towered above Leicester Square of a blond-haired boy in brown rags, holding up a bowl. We had been to a café in the square and ordered toad-in-the-hole, which I had found difficult to eat and Jeremy had denounced as disgusting, not fit for pigs. His saying this to the waitress had made me blush, and I'd pleaded with him to leave.

The film started. I watched the clever way the titles were made, a sequence of brownish drawings depicting scenes and characters from olden times, and then one – of small children labouring in a workhouse – changing colour and coming alive. The previous year Jeremy had taken me to see the stage version. I couldn't remember much about that, except that he'd been cross when I'd been too shy to applaud the cast during the curtain calls.

'It's the way you show your appreciation. They'll think you haven't enjoyed it if you don't clap.'

But I was too self-conscious to do so.

Now there was no live cast to worry about looking at you. I watched and was bewitched. The haunting build-up as the parentless children sang. The tension as Oliver was picked: my heart thumped as this fragile-looking boy was pushed forward to provoke the ire of the terrible Mr Bumble. Who then seemed almost to have a heart as he touched Oliver's shoulder, walking through the snow, offering the boy for sale to the highest bidder. Now Oliver was stuck in a household that didn't treat him like family at all, not even to the extent that his sharing his lot with fellow inmates at the workhouse had done. I sat spellbound, listening to Mark Lester sing with his sad and delicate voice, though Jeremy told me after that it wasn't really Lester who'd sung the song, which seemed a shame. The rest of the film gripped me just as much. I found myself mesmerised by the power of Sykes's glinting eyes and handsome features. I recognised Gracey in Mrs Bedwin, only the woman on screen didn't really ring true. She didn't feel as tough as Gracey, as tough as Oliver would need her to be. And Mr Brownlow was a bit feeble too. I loved the way the film ended, not with the soft luxury of Oliver's new home, nor with Fagin waiting in the condemned cell to be hanged, but with Fagin and the Dodger linking arms and dancing off to new adventures. I could pretend that one day I might be someone like the Dodger, clever and self-sufficient, funny and loyal.

Oliver! became our film. Over the next couple of years we saw it together eight times. Wherever we were, Jeremy would take me to see it, even in Shorefleet's own tiny cinema in Market Street. I was given the record of the songs, and I soon knew every one by heart. We'd sing them together as we cycled through the countryside, or walked along the Thames towpath, or dug up weeds on the allotment. Through his work contacts Jeremy was able to get Mark Lester to sign a record cover. He also bought two denim suits – jeans and jacket – that Lester had worn in another film we'd seen him in. I wore nothing else till I outgrew them.

*

Jeremy seemed to occupy two worlds: the world Mum and Dad lived in, and somewhere else. A kind of Never Land. He never read *Peter Pan* to me, but he was always referring to himself as Peter Pan, and it made sense. Jeremy only pretended to be part of the adult world; adults couldn't see that he was different in the way that I could. Often it seemed that it was my role to play the part of the adult, worrying about the danger of some particular escapade. Like when we went 'scrumping', or when Jeremy would climb up so high in an old tree that I could hardly see him and would shout for him to come down. He sometimes worried Tony too. Once we were all driving in the blue Mini and Jeremy wrote me a cheque for a million pounds. Tony urged him not to sign it, or to sign it and then tear it up, but Jeremy paid no notice. I pinned the cheque onto my bedroom wall, amongst the other memorabilia of our excursions and activities. The world that Jeremy invited me to join was one where there were no real adults at all. Mostly he seemed to hate the world as he found it – I'd sit listening while he described his colleagues at work, their boring marriages and conversation. I dreaded becoming like that.

We were standing outside my dad's bookshop one morning when Jeremy talked with real excitement about something happening in France. 'There's another French revolution happening. The students have taken over the universities and the workers have occupied their factories. People are coming alive. Amazing. The world might change after all. What would that be like, eh? It's like you, and all the other boys and girls at school, going up to the headmaster and all the teachers and telling them that you don't need them any more and that you're not going to let them into the school. And having a big meeting, just the children, and deciding how you're going to run the school on your own. How does that sound? Fun, eh? I doubt they're saying much about *that* on *Blue Peter*. You could play all day and paint the walls red and plant cabbages on the football pitch.'

Events in France were uninteresting to me, but the image of my school as a centre of revolt was quite vivid, and I found it difficult to share Jeremy's enthusiasm for the idea. Mr Tucker, the headmaster, filled me with awe. He was a heavily built man with a round face and large, sad eyes. Some weeks previously, I'd sat spellbound as he had talked of his early career as a teacher in the 1930s, when children would faint from hunger in the playground and the school had to provide breakfast if their families couldn't afford food. I wasn't sure if my fellow pupils had heard him in the same way, but I felt I knew exactly what Mr Tucker was talking about, and my chest tightened and my eyes stung, and I wished that I could be held by this caring giant whom I saw all too fleetingly around the school. I didn't tell Jeremy about this. I told him about nearly everything, but there were some things that needed to be shielded from his sharp intelligence.

While Bayview Road and *Doctor Who* and lifts to school with Dad was the world of family, Jeremy's stories took me somewhere else – to the world of the outlaw. Pirates, the Wild West, highwaymen, a world of children alone, of people on the run. I was shocked one day when I asked him about what it was like in prison only to discover that he had never been there. Not far away, in fact, he'd found people who, he believed, shared his outlook. He and Tony had written a script called *Billy the Meddler*, about a boy from a family that travelled around the countryside, stopping here and there so the adults could work in the fields but never staying long enough to have to worry about school or to own a house. Time was taken up tracking animals and looking for treasure and getting into trouble. This was their film about gypsies. Now they had enough money to begin making it, and they wanted to do it using real gypsies rather than actors.

Jeremy was taking me to meet a group of gypsies whom Tony had located in the countryside. He'd already told me that I was going to be in the film, playing one of the children. We were met off the train by Tony in his Mini. The two men discussed plans for hiring cameras, what Tony had told the gypsy families about the film, and how they imagined the gypsies saw them. Half an hour later, we stopped by a metal swing gate which Jeremy got out to open; from there we headed down a track which ended in a clearing with a group of lorries, trucks and caravans. I regretted that the journey had not gone on longer, and stayed by the Mini as Jeremy and Tony got out and walked towards a group of men standing outside one of the caravans. They seemed to hang back too, although I saw from the way they greeted the newcomers that this wasn't the first time they'd met. There was a fat woman standing in the doorway to one of the caravans, and two small children half hidden by her skirts. One of the men called to her, and she disappeared inside. Gradually others turned up and stood staring, women and children. I felt very much alone, but knew that Jeremy wouldn't let me come to any harm.

The men sat drinking tea. Tony had brought lemonade and throwaway cups which he offered to the children. I found it diffi-cult making out what was being said – the men's accents were strange. I watched the children instead, and they watched me back. One little girl there, with a dirty face and big eyes, smiled at me. The bigger girls kept their distance. The boys were lean and looked tough.

The party broke up suddenly.

'Come on,' Jeremy called, 'the boys are going to show us places we might film in, and we might organise a big game of hide-and-seek – have some fun, eh?'

So the children formed a group around the three foreigners, boys at the front and girls coming up behind. They livened up once they left the camp and were traipsing along the edge of a ploughed field towards some woods. Jeremy became louder and more excited too, though Tony appeared only to speak when he was spoken to. Two of the boys seemed to take the lead, walking one each beside the two adults. Mannie walked alongside Jeremy, and Billy with Tony. Mannie was about six inches taller than I was, with long hair falling over his eyes. He wore lace-up boots, trousers that were too big for him and a bulky jersey with holes in. He looked sharp and seemed to be regarded as the leader by the other children. Billy was much shorter, with large front teeth, freckles and a constant grin. Suddenly Mannie stopped, turned back and let out a long, low whistle. Everyone laughed when, a few moments later, a small black-and-white dog emerged from the undergrowth, snorting loudly.

'His name's Tone. Like yours,' said Mannie to Tony.

We resumed our walk. Another smaller boy came alongside and took my hand. We smiled at one another, though neither of us felt brave enough to say anything.

We walked through the woods, with Mannie and Jeremy deep in conversation about the kind of landscape needed for the film. At one point we all stopped while Jeremy explained to Mannie exactly what a particular scene required, and we set off in another direction. We came to a steep slope rising above a sparsely wooded area with a stream: Jeremy was excited now and wandered about with Tony, talking and holding his fingers arranged in a square up to his eyes. I was stroking Tone the dog, whose tail was wagging excitedly in response.

'Hey Matt, come up here and look at this.'

I didn't welcome being singled out, but I did as I was told. At the top, Jeremy started describing which scene from the story could take place here, how a gang of boys would be chased through the undergrowth and would then half run, half fall down the chalky slope and try to escape their pursuers by splashing through the stream and disappearing into the woods on the other side.

'Mannie says that Tone can belong to your character in the film. That'll make it even more interesting.'

Visits to the gypsies started to take place every weekend. Jeremy and I would meet Tony at the station very early in the morning, so that it was only just getting light when we arrived at the camp. Often the back of the Mini van was loaded with large black boxes holding a movie camera, silver cans of film and other equipment. There was also a tape recorder, though Jeremy had explained that the quality of the sound recording didn't matter as it would be changed later in a studio in London. We returned to the chalk slope and filmed the chase; that day, like all the days when they filmed, was a trial for me, as I was often cold and bored. But there were many other days spent playing games. Jeremy was in his element. On one occasion he started up a tractor that had been left in a field and drove the children around until the machine tipped into a shallow ditch and couldn't be started again. He left a note on the tractor so that the farmer wouldn't blame the gypsies. Another time the children were organised into two teams, one led by Jeremy, the other by Tony, and we played a game of hunter and hunted on a grand scale. By now I was more comfortable with the gypsies, who did their best to include me.

There was one particular day when I felt that I'd successfully lived out the role of gypsy and outlaw. With shirts tied around our waists we'd raided a cherry orchard, and then the children had shown us how they tracked game. Following Tone, who'd found a rabbit's scent, we discovered a warren, blocked as many exits as we could find and then began to dig. A cry went up when the hunted animal was trapped and quickly killed. We went home via Lymbridge, where I walked through the town centre, cherry juice staining my face and chest, my shirt still tied round my waist, carrying a dead rabbit by the legs. 'Straight out of *Lord of the Flies*.' Jeremy's reference was lost on me. But I enjoyed the looks of surprise and horror on the faces of the passers-by.

Then there came a day when we arrived in the early morning to find that the camp was deserted. Jeremy was furious. In fact, over the weeks he seemed to have become more and more disillusioned with the gypsies, and had begun to talk of them as being just the same as everyone else, grasping and vulgar. 'Vulgarity' was one of the worst sins in Jeremy's world. We went around the villages stopping by any likely looking caravans and asking after 'our' gypsies by name. It turned out that they were fruit-picking near Thetford. There were one or two further visits, but as they coincided with the money for the film running out, we stopped going and it remained incomplete. Jeremy told me that Tone had been shot by a farmer for worrying his sheep.

*

'I've got a swimming medal.'

'Oh, that's lovely. What did you have to do to get that?'

I was in the playground talking to the dinner lady. 'I came first in the hundred yards swimming race. I've got a lot of medals at home.' I was lying. It wasn't the first time. I just found myself saying things that came out of nowhere, but always things that made me sound impressive. It was as if I wanted to leave people with a vivid and exciting impression of me, one that they would remember. I think I wanted to be somebody like Jeremy, or maybe just a somebody.

But always, immediately, the lie turned bad. What if someone asked Joanna, who went to the same school, to corroborate my story? Someone might tell my parents that I lied. They wouldn't understand any more than I did, and they'd be cross and disappointed. The others would laugh at me.

And I stole. I hardly counted it stealing, taking the odd shilling from Dad's bedside table, but it was more serious when I stole outside the family. The first time was at Dominic Green's birthday party. There were so many people there, and every one of them had brought Dominic a present. I only took one for myself, a small metal model car that fitted nicely into my pocket. The next day I buried it in the rubbish bin.

The second time I took my friend Alex Jeffreys's collection of Thunderbirds cards. It was the work of a moment. I sat on the bus going home, worrying about what to do with them. Then I concocted a plan: I'd pretend they were mine and make a gift of them to Alex to compensate for his loss. It appeared to go like clockwork. Alex took the cards home; I forgot about it. And then Mrs Jeffreys pulled me over to interrogate me, to tell me that I'd lied and stolen, and made it clear that she was angry. I denied everything but made sure I didn't steal from Alex again.

~ 7 ~

After the fiasco with the gypsies, Jeremy and Tony continued to churn out scripts with dialogue and directions as to the type of shot and camera angle. They dreamed of turning them into films for the big screen. *When Did You Last See Your Father* was set during the English Civil War. At the centre of the action was the interrogation scene depicted in the well-known painting of the same name, where the stern but dull Puritans confront the beautifully attired aristocratic child, vulnerable but stoic, standing proud while his family weep and cower in the background. Only the boy knows that his father is still in the building, hiding in one of the chimneys, and he saves his family and proves his own worth by resolutely keeping his secret safe. For a while this project formed the backdrop to our other activities – the books that Jeremy read to me at bedtime, the castles we visited, the characters we adopted in our games.

Then Jeremy's interest turned to ancient Rome and the story of St Tarcisius. This early Christian boy-saint had been killed after witnessing the martyrdom of Sebastian, a figure who seemed to fascinate Jeremy. I helped while he sewed tunics and togas for us to dress up in, and together we recreated the Roman recipes that he had copied out as part of his research in the British Museum. He started to teach me Latin, and his weekly letters would include new phrases for me to learn. On a cloth Ordnance Survey map Jeremy located the sites of isolated tumuli, and we'd take our bikes on the train to the nearest station, wander into the woods and dig down into likely looking mounds. When we chanced upon a piece of pottery, Jeremy would dance ecstatically at a find that brought his imaginary world tangibly into the present. We also went to a lecture about the villa being excavated at Fishbourne. Cycling down to the Isle of Wight to stay with my uncle, we called in to visit Fishbourne before catching the ferry across The Solent. In London we visited coin shops; soon we had a small collection of our own. My bedroom was taken over by the ephemera of our activities: there was nothing to suggest that I shared the space with Joanna. An alcove in one corner housed a chest of drawers converted to accommodate a museum of Roman coins and pottery, all properly labelled.

Another big adventure was to launch a raid on a Roman castle. We'd been to Henchley several times before, cycling along the St Leonards Road and entering like everyone else by paying for a ticket at the gate, and obeying the rules about where we could and could not climb. This was going to be different. We carried an inflatable dinghy and oars, and took the train to Rackham. From there we walked to the river that ran south of the village, blew up the boat and pushed off. It was fun trying to keep the small boat from running into the bank or getting stuck in the reeds. The flow of the river took us downstream towards the castle ruins. The sun was weakening as we came to the point where the river circles round the hill beneath the granite walls. We moored the boat before climbing the perimeter fence and scrambling up into the castle grounds. They were deserted. This time we could play in the ditches and climb on the walls. We also sifted through the piles of broken pottery that had been left at the back of the museum, seeing if we could find anything interesting. As it began to grow dark, we carried our treasure back down to the boat and pushed off, paddling further downstream to the point where the river was bridged by the main road, near to where we could catch a bus. We were cold and wet but laughing and triumphant. We often reminisced about this 'mission'.

For Jeremy it was not a question of *whether* he would become a great film director but of *when*. His great fear was to turn out like his father. Cuthbert Rushton had been a moderately successful artist. His oils and watercolours decorated the walls of Mrs Rushton's cottage; he'd illustrated many books, drawn election posters, even written a book about astrology. But he'd not been a family man. Much of his life had been spent wandering, paying for his board and lodging with his paintings. Jeremy saw this as his father prostituting his art to sustain an endless pub crawl, typical of the man who was hardly ever at home and who, when he was there, would be drunk. To Jeremy he was the archetypal failure, a grandiose mediocrity, believing himself a genius but achieving nothing. Although Jeremy couldn't see anything positive about his father, he did on a couple of occasions take me to meet him. Rushton Sr reminded me of Fagin – not the Fagin of *Oliver!* but the Fagin of the condemned cell in the original illustrations to Dickens's novel. He was a diminutive man, unkempt and slightly smelly, whose nodding head was half hidden by the collar of a great coat he kept wrapped tightly around his body. I would sit eating ice cream while the two men kept up an awkward conversation about nothing in particular. Then Jeremy and I would leave, and Jeremy would give vent to his hatred and contempt and his determination to succeed where his father had failed.

To realise their ambitions, Jeremy and Tony required serious financial backing. Jeremy approached wealthy producers, major

movie companies and the Children's Film Foundation. His optimism would be only temporarily dented by successive rejections.
Meanwhile he and Tony persevered with their plan to prove their
ability to make films by producing a pilot of their own. They
turned to the idea of an ordinary boy (me), with a passion for
digging for Roman remains, who makes a find in a field belonging to a short-tempered landowner (Jeremy). The working title
was *Matt's Film*.

I felt no compulsion to act. True, I was developing an expertise in dissimulation, playing a part to avoid self-disclosure. But
mine was an artless hiding; I knew I'd be hopeless at any
purposeful putting on of roles. In any case I couldn't separate out
the character I was asked to play in front of the camera from the
view people would form of me in reality. When I was a little older
I was asked to say the lines: 'I'm never going to get married. I'm
going to have servants instead.' I refused. I wasn't going to invite
people to question my normality through anything I might say
on screen. This confusion wasn't helped by Jeremy's insistence
that he wanted me to be myself, to be 'natural'. He told me that
he wanted to capture on film the special little boy only he recognised and appreciated.

Mum was enthusiastic and would talk about me as a future
film star in a way that left me crestfallen and silent. I wanted to
tell her not to talk about it, and hoped in vain that she'd pick up
how uncomfortable I felt every time the filming was mentioned.
I never spoke of it myself, not to siblings and certainly not to
anyone at school. I had once rashly boasted there that I had
gypsy friends, and one boy was still asking me questions about
what they ate and whether I'd tasted hedgehog stew. It was a
mistake I had no intention of repeating.

As the time for filming came closer, Jeremy insisted that my hair could not be cut without his permission. He took charge of my hair from then on. He took me clothes shopping. We bought several identical golden polo-neck jumpers, jeans and desert boots.

When they had saved sufficient funds to hire camera equipment, filming began, though only at weekends. Jeremy and I would leave Shorefleet Station on an early train and be picked up at a small country station by Tony in his Mini. I'd sit in the back with the camera equipment. At first it was just the three of us alone in a field. I enjoyed operating the clapperboard and reading it out: 'Scene four, take two'. The first shots were of me kneeling over a bare patch of ground, scraping the mud from pieces of black earthenware and beginning to see how they fitted together to form a broken pot. As I concentrated on my hobby, the voice of the irate landowner was heard, faintly at first but getting louder and louder. I found it hilarious watching 'Sir Arthur Blowers', with his false moustache, plus fours and ludicrous accent, striding across the field with his shotgun, shouting, 'Hey you! What do you think you're doing? Get off of my land. Do you hear me? Get off.' I couldn't keep a straight face though I was supposed to be surprised and scared, and they had to shoot my reaction several times before I could get it right.

Later we filmed at Black Manor, near Fakenham, and here there was more of an audience. The 'manor', an old timbered cottage, was occupied by Mrs Hogben, a flabby and sour-faced woman, her silent and near-invisible husband and her adolescent sons, who'd been neighbours of the Rushtons in Shorefleet when Jeremy was a boy. He and I would make jokes about the Hogbens, who were posh and, except one of the sons, unfriendly. The cottage overlooked a wide, low valley through which ran a watercourse about two feet deep. Near the point where the stream was bridged was the site of an ancient rubbish tip. Jeremy and I went to the manor to wade through the mud at the bottom of the stream, looking for pottery even when there was no filming to be done. On filming days he would prepare me in a room alone, making sure my clothes were right and spraying my hair so that it would reflect the light better, going over the next scene and quietening my doubts. I found it more difficult with a bigger team: there was a sound engineer called John and a continuity girl called Jennifer, and occasionally other hangers-on as well as the Hogbens. The worst point of all came when we filmed a scene in which I woke up and had to get out of bed dressed only in my underpants. Just like at home, the boy in the film had turned his bedroom into a museum.

I'd often visited Jeremy's workplaces in London – cutting rooms in Soho, dubbing studios in Dean Street. As well as writing, directing and acting in *Matt's Film*, Jeremy was going to edit and dub it. He and I made a cutting-room bench – a long table with rectangular cut-outs hung with white cloth bags for catching the film, with a flat surface in-between for the cutting equipment – and 'bins' for hanging rows of film clippings. Jeremy hired a room in a house, in Lymbridge, belonging to another school friend, Ben, now a solicitor. Ben had a pretty Spanish wife who was usually in the house on her own on Saturdays while her husband, to Jeremy's derisive amusement, played rugby. We went there every weekend for several months. We were never interrupted in the improvised cutting room.

*

I found myself embroiled in a life of secrets. I didn't advertise the plans Jeremy had for my weekends in order to avoid arousing my siblings' curiosity and envy. Experience indicated that this was the kind of thing that would attract their unwanted interest. So I provided information only on a need-to-know basis: the question was what to reveal, not what to conceal.

Peter was a good deal older at a time when age difference counts. Ella was now a teenager and had a busy life of her own. But Joanna was a child, and I still shared a room with her. She couldn't openly object to Jeremy's presence, but she could – and did – show that she felt neglected, and was resentful of the attention and privileges I received. She'd begun to view me as spoilt and the world as unfair and herself as hard done by. I did what I could to minimise the causes for grievance, but there was a limit to how much could be hidden from her. So I became especially wary.

I knew – I'm not sure how – that Jeremy's touching my penis had to be kept a secret. Perhaps it was because Jeremy himself seemed so ashamed, almost revolted, by what he did with me. He never told me to keep it a secret, but his silence spoke volumes. I felt no guilt about touching myself – I rather revelled in what I called my 'bottom business' – and I had no clear misgivings about what Jeremy did to me either. He, after all, was an adult and a friend of the family. For me, the difficulty concerned the allocation of time and the distribution of treats. It was my siblings' envy, not my parents' disgust, which I sought most to control. At school I wanted to appear ordinary, like my friends, not like someone who made films at weekends or was taken to the theatre in London, or on cycle rides into the countryside. These things I worried about, and at times the worry seemed a gruesome burden. It was not easy managing information when so much depended on getting it right.

Gradually, imperceptibly, I came to feel different from everyone else in a particular and painful way. The ever-multiplying anxieties about who knew what, in terms of facts and events, induced a sense of loneliness. My preoccupation was not to be known. I had to be thought of in a positive way all the time, as I couldn't distinguish between people who were being envious and cross about everyday things and people who knew I was bad in some more sinister way. I lived in the space between my family and Jeremy, knowing that each had completely different expectations of me. To be safe, I needed to be loved by both. I felt freer in Jeremy's world, because there I only had to feel guilty about what I might become, whereas with my parents I was unsure how they'd respond to who I already was.

People treated me as an adventurous and privileged child, whose exciting life and unusual experiences boded well for my emergence as a confident and well-rounded young man. I had deceived them. The more successfully I covered up the fact of my confused and mundane self – contrasting myself with Jeremy's colourful and creative character gave me the measure of my own mediocrity – the more isolated and fraudulent I seemed. I'd never done anything for myself. I couldn't have initiated any of the activities to which Jeremy had introduced me. I was completely dependent on him for being able to sustain the picture people had of me.

*

Jeremy was an enthusiastic skater, and when we were in London we often made trips to the skating rinks in Bayswater and Richmond. That winter, conditions became severe enough for him to think of using one of the small lakes behind Lymbridge instead. We took the train out to the village of Rocksford, bleak council houses strung out either side of a straight main road. Even Rocksford looked beautiful that day, under a layer of fine white snow. We found the side road that led down to the lakes nearby. They were frozen solid. Jeremy put on his ice skates. While he glided gracefully along, avoiding clumps of frozen grass and worrying what would happen if the ice cracked, I kept warm by skidding over the ice on my worn soles. We were totally alone in our Siberian landscape. The silence was just occasionally broken by the tortured shriek of a distant crow.

When the time came to leave, we made the long walk across country to the station. It was a Sunday, and Jeremy was travelling back to London. We waited under the station lights. My train back to Shorefleeet arrived first. Before I stepped onboard, Jeremy gave me a hug and a big kiss. I said goodbye and took my seat, and he closed the door. We waved to one another as the train pulled away.

'Is he your father?' The question was posed by an elderly man sitting with his wife in the same compartment.

'No.'

'You shouldn't be kissing a grown man like that.'

I held in a slight panic and turned to look out of the window. I didn't glance round again until I heard the couple get out of the train.

*

In my divided world, family holidays stood out as beacons of simplicity. Away from Shorefleet there were no complications and no need for subterfuges. With both parents and neither a library jacket nor a cash-book in sight I felt complete, as much a part of the family as I ever felt. I could share fully in Mum's excited planning of expeditions, and afterwards be part of the laughter about adventures exclusive to the family, relived around the dining table. Our first holidays abroad were to a small hotel in Le Brusc, near Toulon, recommended by one of Dad's friends. When I opened the shutters of my ground-floor room in the morning, I was hit by the thick smell of pine. From there, I could climb out into the dirt-garden to collect pine cones to give to Mum.

Holidays were always taken in term-time after Easter, so as not to keep Dad away from the shop during 'the season'. We went to Le Brusc twice before spending two holidays in Yugoslavia. The first was at Ika, a village near Opatija. I found a small snake and chased lizards. Peter's football burst so he filled it with stones and gave it a solemn burial at sea, from the end of a small jetty. I discovered a dinar coin in the mouth of an old cannon on the quay, from where we watched the fishing boat set sail at dusk and dock in the early morning to unload its catch. Ika was serene.

When we went to Yugoslavia, we crossed on the car ferry from Dover to Calais in the afternoon and arrived towards evening in Paris, where we had dinner. Once, we made time to go up the Eiffel Tower before eating. Dad then drove through the night and all the next day, so that there was only one overnight stop before reaching the Yugoslav border. The second time we spent the night in Dijon. We ate in the small restaurant attached to the hotel, served by a portly lady with a ruddy face and a full smile. She kept up a lively conversation with Mum, who spoke good French. At one point the lady bent down in front of me and let out an unintelligible stream of words, then put an arm around my bewildered shoulders. Mum was laughing; the woman threw up her hands as if she were giving up and walked off laughing as well.

'What was all that about?' asked Peter.

'She was saying that she would like to keep Matt here for a year. And that she would teach him perfect French and we could pick him up on our holiday next spring. How do you feel about that, Matt?'

'What would she want to keep him for?' cut in Joanna. 'What's in this soup? It tastes horrible.'

I shrugged my shoulders. What was there to say? The woman had gone, the subject had already been forgotten. But looking around at her back I felt a yearning to be close to her. From then on, the name Dijon would conjure up regret, a lost opportunity. I was sure the lady had been serious.

The following year, 1969, the family headed for Yugoslavia again. Jeremy, however, wanted to do some further research on the Tarcisius script and was proposing to take me to Rome. This resolved itself – without my involvement – into an arrangement where he would drive with us to the Yugoslav border and take the coastal ferry from Rijeka to the island of Hvar, where we'd stay for a week. The rest of the family would stay on while Jeremy and I would take another ferry, this time from Split to Bari, on the heel of Italy, and proceed by train to Rome. After a week we'd fly to Paris, take a train to Calais and then the new hovercraft across the Channel.

So that I could travel without my family, Jeremy prepared a document which read:

OUTCAST FILMS LTD

I, DAVID LOWE, OF 8 Bayview Road, Shorefleet, do hereby certify that JEREMY RUSHTON, of 255 Fleet Road, London NW3, a director of OUTCAST FILMS LTD, is the *bona fide* guardian of my son MATT LOWE, for the duration of a script research trip to Rome between April 19th 1969 and April 27th 1969.

I further certify that the above-mentioned JEREMY RUSHTON is a fit person to have charge of my son MATT LOWE, and that he may act *in loco parentis* for the duration of the aforesaid period.

Dad signed at the bottom, and one of his customers acted as a witness.

The journey down went well. We arrived in Paris in time to

go up the Eiffel Tower for a second time, before eating in a nearby restaurant. For the first time I tried some smelly cheese, the kind I'd always scoffed at before, and liked it. When we came out of the restaurant it was dark, and Joanna and I were settled in the back of Dad's Vauxhall Estate, while Jeremy, Peter and Ella remained seated in the middle. We two younger ones had stood waiting in the quiet, cobbled side street while Mum prepared the boot for us to sleep in. Jeremy had bought me a camera before we left, and he took a snap of us as we settled down.

As we made our way through the city, Joanna and I waved and made faces at the drivers of the cars behind, but we were soon lulled to sleep. The following night was spent in Verona, where we played at being gladiators in the amphitheatre while Mum and Dad sat high above the arena as our audience. The next day we arrived at the Yugoslav coast. Jeremy and I were given our own cabin on the steamship *Osijek*.

I lay in my bunk watching Jeremy shave. He'd covered his face with white foam and was dragging the razor across it, leaving regular strips of smooth skin beneath. He finished, threw some water over his face and reached for a towel to dry himself. Then he stood on tiptoe, leaned over towards the mirror, picked up the razor again and shaved the area around his nipples.

'What are you doing?'

'I'm making my body smooth, the way you prefer it.'

'The way *I* prefer it?'

'You once told me that you don't like hairy bodies, so I thought I would be less off-putting to you if I shaved.'

I looked at Jeremy's arms and the backs of his hands, and realised that they too were hairless. What Jeremy had said was confusing. As if he was telling me something about myself that was wrong or that I didn't know anything about. I couldn't imagine ever saying such a thing. I was unaware of having had any feelings about Jeremy's body, and it was difficult to imagine the circumstances in which I would have voiced any I might have had. But then Jeremy often remembered things differently from me. And I was a child, so there were many things I'd forgotten from when I was even younger. Sometimes it was interesting that Jeremy was there to tell me stuff I couldn't recall, but at other times it was horribly disconcerting. I couldn't think of anything to say.

While I shared my family's love of sun, swimming and doing nothing, Jeremy could not remain still when he accompanied the Lowes down to the beach on the first morning. He needed to be entertaining us with stories or games, or imitating different animals. Even so, within a couple of hours he was restless. He proposed a walk along the coastal path, and Peter and I agreed to go with him. The following day he wanted to leave the beach even earlier, and this time only I reluctantly agreed to go along. Each successive day followed the same pattern, so mostly Jeremy and I set off on our own.

There were walls around the town of Hvar, and an old Venetian fort on the hill. We'd already been to the fort as a family, but Jeremy was keen to go again, if only to get away from idling on the sand. As the two of us clambered up the uneven pathways, he spoke at length and with some bitterness about the family's laziness. I felt culpable and resentful, and suggested that my father, who worked so hard, could hardly be considered lazy. But Jeremy assured me that there was something decidedly lazy about Dad, which was disguised or camouflaged by his apparent industry.

Then he changed the subject. 'I've been reading the guidebook, and there's another museum in the town that we haven't found yet. Apparently, it's full of Roman remains, pottery and jewellery, and some coins with the bust of Diocletian.' Diocletian had been emperor at the time that Tarcisius had lived, and I knew a lot about him.

'What's a bust?' I asked.

There was a pause.

'A bust is a representation of the head and shoulders, as in a statue.' Now there was a further pause. 'It is also used to refer to a woman's bosom.' Jeremy's tone told me that I'd asked a bad question, and that he was angry with me. He was saying, I thought, that there was something bad about women, and I felt guilty about this because I knew what the word *bosom* meant, and perhaps I shouldn't have done. More than that, I knew that I felt particularly drawn towards women's bosoms. As we walked on, I tried to think of a way to get back into favour. It was not until we were back in the room we shared at the hotel that I was really sure that Jeremy had forgiven me.

The following day Jeremy bought a blow-up dinghy, much like the one we had in England. We christened her 'Rosemary I', after the aromatic herb that covered the island's craggy scrubland hills. We took the boat to the beach and had fun splashing around and tipping one another out of it. The next morning Jeremy proposed a sea expedition. From Hvar we could see a number of islands, the nearest of which seemed close enough for a strong swimmer and certainly reachable by boat. So he and I pushed off while the rest of the family returned to the beach. The crossing was further than I, certainly, had anticipated. Away from the shore, the sea turned choppy, and as it was still only April the water that splashed over and drenched our clothes was uncomfortably cold. As we neared our destination, a hydrofoil appeared, approaching the harbour. Jeremy pointed out the danger of being overwhelmed by the wash, and as he explained the difference between a hydrofoil and a hovercraft, we pulled urgently on our oars in an attempt to reach land without capsizing. We made it to the island just in time.

We were cold, and our clothes were soaked. But the sun was warm.

'We'd better get these wet things off.' Jeremy pulled his jersey off and unbuttoned his shirt. 'We can be nudists on our deserted island.' He took all his clothes off.

I giggled and copied him. There was something exciting about this. I liked the feel of the warm air on parts of my body that I normally kept covered. It had been a long time since I'd felt comfortable on the beach naked, even though Mum would say I had no reason to be shy and thought it silly to change wrapped in a towel. I'd never seen an adult naked on the beach before. It felt rude. My gaze followed Jeremy's large drooping penis, flopping about as he walked. Without touching it, I could sense a familiar aliveness in my own willy.

We walked across the small island and looked over its only house, deserted and boarded up. The ground rose up at the side of the house, giving us access to the pink-tiled roof. There we hid a half-crown piece under one of the tiles, pledging that one day we'd return and recover our hidden treasure. We worked out the co-ordinates of our hoard – so many tiles from the front, so many from the edge – and tried to commit them to memory.

Then Jeremy proposed that we play hide-and-seek.

'All right. But if I shout, you'll tell me where you are.' I was afraid we might still encounter an angry local.

Jeremy disappeared around a headland while I stood in the dust and counted. The excitement hadn't dissipated; rather it had become more intense. I charged off to find my prey. It took me some time to find him. He made it easier by continuing to move about, letting me follow the sound of footsteps and breaking twigs. Then it was my turn to hide. I ran back towards where we'd left the boat, checking that there were no good hiding places by the deserted house. I found a sunny clearing we hadn't visited before and lay down on the sand. I looked up at the blue sky and felt the vastness of it, the roughness of my back on the earth and the warmth of the sun on my body. My hands crept back towards the centre, to my penis, which I held and stroked. I felt completely alone. I thought about Jeremy's body, and about the two of us naked, standing proud in the sun. I started pulling vigorously and continued for a minute or so before stopping abruptly. I'd heard a noise not far off. I stood up in a panic. My penis shrank, though not as quickly as I wished. I was mortified by the idea that he'd seen me. What I did to myself was completely separate from what Jeremy did to me. I sometimes liked Jeremy touching me, but it wasn't the same. What I did to myself was private, accompanied by thoughts and feelings that no one else knew about. I was sure that Jeremy had no idea that I'd do such a bad thing. I hoped beyond hope that he hadn't seen. Quietly, I ran away from the direction of the noise and found another place to hide. Peering through the trees I saw Jeremy coming, looking about for signs of where I was. When I was finally found, I knew that something *had* changed.

The rest of the day was miserable. There was a pretence of enjoyment between us, as if we were acting with one another, something I'd never experienced with Jeremy before. He sometimes criticised me and that hurt. I would feel particularly stupid when he used the phrase: 'I don't envy you that at all,' which indicated that I'd been excited about something worthless and stupid. Now, I just didn't feel safe; I didn't know what was going on in his mind. Then it occurred to me that my parents might have been able to see me from the beach. As we rowed back, I kept measuring the size of the human specks on Hvar, working out if it would've been possible to tell if we'd been dressed or not. I wondered how I'd face Mum.

Back at the hotel they all seemed to respond normally, and the worst of my fears were calmed, though they never entirely disappeared. They were revived when Mum made a comment that seemed to imply that she knew something more had happened on that island trip than could be openly discussed, but by then I couldn't remember if, on our return, Jeremy had confessed to our naturist experiment.

A couple of days later the family were saying goodbye on the quay in Split, as Jeremy and I made our way up the gangway of the steamship *Tintoretto*.

*

When we disembarked in Italy the following morning, I was shocked to find people in rags begging and muzzled dogs that Jeremy said must be carrying rabies. The train journey north was tedious and stuffy. The carriage was crowded, and many of the passengers were smoking. Jeremy made conversation in Italian with a man who, he explained, was a professor of history at a university in Rome. In broken English the professor spoke to me directly: 'In one week, you learn more in Roma than in many weeks in school classroom. You remember this, OK. You tell your professor.'

In Rome we stayed in a hotel a few steps from the Pantheon. Jeremy took me to the catacombs, the Circus Maximus, the Coliseum, Trajan's Column, the Forum, the baths of Caligula, the Trevi Fountain and the Vatican. We visited a stream of museums in an itinerary packed with educational opportunities. In the museums we took scores of photographs of Roman artefacts and furniture to help Jeremy design the sets for the Tarcisius film. He took my picture in the street named after the boy hero. We visited Roberto, a man with whom Jeremy had worked in London; he took us around the set of a cowboy film that was being made there. After that, Roberto took us to the races.

The days were hot and sunny. The nights were dark. On the first evening in Rome, when we had undressed and Jeremy came over to my bed, I knew what was going to happen. I moved over and he lay down beside me. As usual he reached inside my pyjamas and held me while his face came down close to mine, and his lips brushed my cheeks and mouth. He was naked, and his hard willy pushed into my leg. This was new: he generally kept his body away from mine. I had got hard and I lay back as I always did. Then I felt Jeremy's hand move from my willy to my arm.

'You do it.'

'What?'

'You do it.'

My hand was pushed towards my penis.

'Like you did on the island.'

I froze. Shocked. Jeremy had never spoken about what we did together before. Everything had always taken place in a heavy silence. Now he seemed more confident, more comfortable with himself. I couldn't object; he'd seen me and I had no right to keep secrets from him. He loved me, so it would have been disloyal of me to keep things from him. Yet it didn't feel right. It had been less complicated before.

I held myself. The pleasure took over. My fingers moved back and forth, so much more effectively than when Jeremy did it, while he raised himself up on his knees and worked himself off with a brazenness that was entirely out of character. He climaxed with a low moan, and I watched as a white foamy liquid shot into his cupped hand, some dribbling through onto the bedcovers. Jeremy used his discarded shirt to catch the contents of his palm, and then disappeared into the tiny washroom.

When we woke up the following morning, Jeremy seemed happy again. I had an enjoyable if tiring day sightseeing. In a fancy restaurant that evening, I ate minestrone and was told I was sufficiently grown up now to drink wine mixed with water. I felt great. I half dreaded, half looked forward to returning to the hotel. I assumed that there would be a repeat of the previous evening's events. This time, Jeremy started the touching when I was standing in the half-bath being showered down. He directed the stream of water at my genitals as I played with them. Then he removed his clothes and stepped into the bathtub. He took my small hand and wrapped it around his erection, moving it the way he wanted me to do it. I recoiled at touching a man in this way, but I did what was expected of me. It was so different from mine, massive and veiny. Not only that, but it didn't work in the way that mine worked. There was no loose skin and the end was exposed and bulbous. Touching Jeremy, there was none of that sublime unity between what my hand felt and did, and what I experienced all through my body when I touched myself. Now I could see a look on Jeremy's face that suggested similar feelings coursing through him, but it left me cold. Although this, too, became part of the regular routine, I never liked the feel of Jeremy's penis in my hand.

~ 8 ~

Back in England life continued in its apparently unalterable pattern. I worked hard at school: I loved bringing home stars and high marks to show my parents. I put more emphasis on this as life in other respects became more complicated. As long as the routines of term-time continued, I could just about keep everyone's expectations within bearable limits, and the weekends remained Jeremy's domain. Sundays were better in the winter, as Dad didn't work in the shop. Jeremy would be there, of course, and would join us for a long roast lunch, and then in watching the Sunday afternoon serial. At some point after that he'd leave to spend some time with his mother. I was expected to have a farewell conversation with him on the back doorstep. I always wanted to cut this short, to get back to the others in front of the TV, in front of the fire, but Jeremy wanted to talk and, before he left, to kiss. I'd walk back into the front room blushing and hoping that my absence hadn't engendered any unwanted speculation. But after that it was great: cosy, warm and relaxed.

Then there were five days when there was just me and the family again, when ordinary family things happened. And some extraordinary things. Like the time when Mum and Dad had some special news to give us. We'd had tea. Nanny Langton had come over to eat and was sitting with the adults around the table, while we children had got down and were playing in the front room. I was playing with Peter, who'd lined up a dozen cards against the skirting board. The game was to take turns trying to knock down the upright cards by flicking the rest at them. Joanna was brushing the hair on a big doll that Susan, her friend from across the road, had lent her. Ella was pushing the buttons on the TV set, keeping the volume down low, hoping to catch a glimpse of the banned *Coronation Street*. The adults were making a lot of noise in the living room, loud exclamations followed by howls of laughter, and Joanna knocked on the glass hatch that connected the two rooms. 'What are you laughing about? Come and tell us.'

'We're coming now,' Mum called back, and they soon walked into the room, all looking flushed, and with Mum and Dad looking happier than Nanny Langton.

'Well, tell them,' Mum said.

'Your mother is going to have another baby,' Dad proclaimed, grinning. There was a moment's silence while we checked our parents' faces to see if they were kidding. And then whoops of joy from Ella and Joanna and embarrassed giggles from Peter and me.

'When? When?'

'It's due in mid-February. I went to the doctor today, and everything seems set for then.'

'Oh my God!' exclaimed Ella. 'I can't wait to tell my friends! Is it a boy or a girl?'

'We'll have to wait and see.'

'Nanny isn't sure that having five children is such a good thing,' said Dad.

'I didn't quite say that, David. I just said that I thought you'd finished with all that a long time ago.'

I took a surreptitious glance at Mum's belly. I imagined the act that had resulted in this extraordinary announcement, couldn't really, and pushed my mind to other matters. I started to think about what else would change as a result of a newcomer in the family. 'Where will it sleep?'

'It will have to be the spare room. We've been thinking whether we shall have to move to a bigger house or whether we can make do here.'

'I want it to be a boy,' I announced. 'If he's a boy, can we call him Roger?'

'Roger? Whatever made you think of Roger?'

'You know, Mum. It's Roger the Dodger, isn't it, Matt?' Joanna sounded very knowing.

'I just like the name Roger. Well, can we?'

'We don't know if it will be a boy yet. And if it is, we'll all have to think more about a suitable name.'

'I'm going to call it Roger whether it's a boy or a girl.'

They all laughed. My eyes stung.

'Don't be silly, Matt,' called Joanna. 'Roger can't be a girl's name.'

'I don't care.' I suddenly felt like crying. It was all a bit too much to take in.

On the Friday that followed, I took part in an 18-mile sponsored coast walk in aid of guide dogs for the blind. I went with Alex Jeffreys, whose mother was one of the organisers, and we enjoyed ourselves, at least until the last five miles or so, which were murder. I was given a lift home. The house was empty when I got back. I found a plastic bowl and filled it with warm water, and sat in the living room bathing my sore feet. Soon after that, Jeremy walked up the back path.

'Hello! Suffering, eh? Well, I did tell you, didn't I? You wouldn't have got so badly hurt if you'd had some proper walking boots. Shall I make us some tea? I've just come from a meeting with a rich producer called Carl Foreman. He's been involved in a lot of films – do you remember *The Guns of Navarone?* – he wrote that.' He'd also produced the film on which Jeremy had been working for some months, in the dubbing theatre. 'That film's crap, but so what? The important thing is that he seems really interested in the Roman film. That would be good news, wouldn't it? All that hard work might come to something, after all. How's your week been?'

'Mum's going to have a baby.'

'A baby?' Jeremy wasn't pleased. But I couldn't fathom what his reaction meant. How could he disapprove? Why would it strike him as distasteful?

'Oh, that's wonderful. Is everyone happy about it?' Jeremy was pulling himself together, but I wasn't deceived. Perhaps I'd been wrong to feel so excited: clearly I'd have to hide my anticipation from him.

'It's due in February. Mummy says that we're going to have to be quieter around the house.'

'Umm. Lots of dirty nappies and screaming and dribbling. I'm afraid babies are extremely boring. You can't talk to them, they don't even know you're there for a couple of years.' He seemed angry and dismissive, as if someone had done something bad to him.

I frowned. This wasn't the impression my parents had conveyed. To them a new baby seemed one of the most wonderful things that could possibly happen to anyone. The chasm between the two worlds had revealed itself again.

*

Apart from Tony, Jeremy didn't seem to have adult friends. There was one exception that I met a few times, Robert, who shared with Jeremy an enthusiasm for cycling. Robert would sometimes come with us on cycle rides. He was a tall, muscular man with dark eyes and heavy eyebrows, and said very little, even to the friend that he always brought along with him. These friends changed, but they were always boys a few years older than me. There was Stephen, the son of a farm labourer who lived near Thetford. When we drove over to collect him, I saw the meaning of real poverty for the first time. The family lived in a dilapidated cottage that smelt of damp. There was nothing covering the floor, and almost no possessions or furniture in the living room. Apparently, the house had been flooded the previous winter. Sometimes we picked Stephen up from a nearby children's home. He didn't talk much.

Then there was Andreas, a Greek boy, who lived on an estate near a reservoir in the outer reaches of north-west London. His parents seemed pleased that their son had made such generous friends: Robert had bought him a bike so that the four of us could ride out to Oxford and Stratford together.

A third boy came from a family in south London. When we collected him we had to go in and have a cup of tea. The mother was loud, and there was a man – I don't think it was the father – watching the TV.

'Did you watch that programme last night about rent boys?' The mother was being jolly and sounded quite excited. 'They were giving blow jobs for a fiver a time. Imagine that! I give Gerry one every night. I'd be a bloody millionaire if I charged him that, eh?' And she dissolved into raucous laughter.

*

Jeremy moved again, this time to a cabin on a boat moored at Richmond. To get to it you had to walk along a raised wooden gangway for about 50 yards. Underneath was uneven grass when it was dry, a murky swamp after rain. The other people living on the boat were quite friendly, but we didn't see much of them. Every visit would include at least one trip to Richmond's ice rink, a few hundred yards from the mooring. Jeremy had bought me my own pair of skates. I progressed from the stage of clinging desperately to the railings at the side and developed the skills needed to join the mass of people circling the rink. Jeremy would race round, weaving in and out of the crowd, while I looked on laughing.

In the spring another trip was envisaged. We would see a Buster Keaton film accompanied by someone playing the piano, like they used to with silent films. Jeremy proposed a visit to the British Museum, then swimming and skating. He also wanted to get some Diocletian coins. I packed my case as usual, asking my teacher if he would look after it for the day, and arranged to leave early so I could get to the train on time. Everything went according to plan. Buster Keaton was instantly one of my silent film favourites.

Saturday was hectic. I waited in the Roman galleries of the British Museum while Jeremy had a meeting with someone who worked there, and in the afternoon we fitted in both the skating and the swimming. At Warren Street tube station we tried racing up the 'down' escalator. We had lunch in a café in the Tottenham Court Road.

By the time we got back to the boat, I wasn't feeling well. I wasn't seriously sick, but I could hardly finish the meal Jeremy had prepared before wanting to lie down. In his small cabin there were two beds; I was to sleep in one of them. I fell asleep while he cleared away the dishes.

It was dark when I became aware of him standing over me.

'You're still in your clothes. Come on, let's get your pyjamas on. You'll catch cold if I leave you there. That's it, arms up. And one leg in here, and the other one.'

Drowsy, I did as I was told and climbed under the covers as they were held back for me. I quickly went back to sleep.

Then Jeremy was there again, stroking my head soothingly. 'Are we waking up now? How are we feeling? Eh?'

I felt Jeremy's face against my own, and his hand reaching down inside the covers. Instinctively I turned over, pushing his hand away. The hand pushed down my body and inside my pyjamas from the back. I was awake now and turned round again to face Jeremy. I felt scared; angry and scared. I was sweating. 'No, not now. Let's go to sleep.'

Jeremy didn't answer. Through the gloom I seemed to see a fixed grin on his face. His hands came back; I pushed them away and backed up against the wall.

'Go to sleep. Go away!' I heard the panic in my voice.

'It's all right. We can sleep soon. Just let me be with you for a little while.'

'No, you're frightening me. Just go to sleep.'

I wasn't used to being openly coerced, and had never felt that my express wishes could be disregarded like this. I pulled up my legs and lashed out, catching Jeremy in the chest. He returned to his bed, and I pulled the covers up tight and settled back to sleep.

A little while later Jeremy was there again, pulling the covers down. I pushed him away until he caught my arms and held them both in one fist, while his other hand roamed down my body. I wheeled about to avoid this, twisted my hands free and hit Jeremy in the face.

'Can't you just go to bed now! I'm too tired. Go away!'

Again Jeremy moved away. Able to see now despite the dark, I watched him sitting on the side of his bed. I watched, afraid, as he came back to mine yet again.

'What's the matter, Matt? I'm not going to hurt you. Let me love you a little bit now, then we can sleep properly. How does that sound?'

His words only frightened me more. I was in uncharted territory, alone with a stranger, alone with a maniac. I burst into tears.

'There's no need to be upset. Come on, let me hold you. It's all right, you know.' Jeremy reached out to put his arm around my shoulder, but I punched it away and crouched even further back into the corner. This was horrible. The man I loved and needed had turned peculiar, become a kind of animal. I'd seen him snarl for the first time. I didn't know what to do. I was desperate for us to go back to being friends.

The to-ing and fro-ing seemed to go on for ever, although in the dark I had no way of knowing how long. Eventually it stopped. Jeremy went back to his bed and didn't return. I watched. I listened as his breathing became slower and more rhythmical. After a long time I, too, was able to sleep again.

In the morning I woke first, and lay worrying about what was in store. Light was coming in through the porthole. Jeremy turned over and smiled. 'Shall we take the motor boat upriver, then? Perhaps some porridge first, eh? We could eat it out on deck if it's not too parky.'

I breathed a huge sigh: it was the Jeremy I knew. The aberration was just that, and could be forgotten. Or, if not forgotten, put to one side, relegated to the place where bad dreams were stored.

*

If it had been another child doing these things, then I might have had more of a problem with it. But it was Jeremy. Jeremy was an adult, a man the family looked up to. It couldn't have been wrong; at most it was something that didn't suit me. It seemed reasonable – possible anyway – to think that my parents knew what was happening. They had, after all, arranged for me to share a bedroom with him in Yugoslavia and on another holiday to the Isle of Wight. They knew we went camping, that I stayed many times a year with him in London. What else could that mean? And everyone seemed to regard us as a couple: not only immediate family but aunts and uncles, staff in the bookshop, my parents' friends. They all seemed to regard 'Matt and Jeremy' as an item, like 'Laurel and Hardy' or 'Marks and Spencer'. I knew 'it' had not been talked about openly, but then nobody talked about those kinds of private activities. It was clear from the way Jeremy behaved that he hadn't told his mother, and that he did everything necessary to hide the nature of our relationship from her. But that was not unusual: sex wasn't talked about in our family either. Anyway, it wasn't Jeremy who'd introduced me to that stuff. As a much younger child I'd played doctors and nurses with the neighbours' children, who had enlightened me on how babies were made. And I felt an oh-so-powerful pull from inside me, the part that got excited by the word *bum* in a book title, the bit that led me to search the books passing through the house for explicit and incredible descriptions of what people – though always a man and a woman – did to one another in private. If it made me feel bad, it was because I had given in to desires that perhaps other children didn't have.

Sometimes I imagined there was some terrible secret about me that would explain the strange torn place I found myself in. I heard from Jeremy how Tony had joked to friends in London that I was really Jeremy's son – that he'd had an affair with my mother. I knew that wasn't true. But there had to be something that explained why I was treated differently from the others. I knew they loved me, but maybe they only loved the surface Matt, the one who got good marks at school. Perhaps it was only Jeremy who loved the me underneath.

But 'it' did make me feel bad. 'It' felt too complicated. I had this dream that if 'it' stopped, things would become simple again. I could be loved by Jeremy and my parents: there wouldn't be a secret Matt. I'd be like the others, like my friends at school. If only we could agree to stop touching each other's willies. I kept this opinion to myself for a good while. But the dream became so strong; the solution seemed so easy.

We were on a bicycle ride through the Norfolk countryside a few weeks before my eleventh birthday. It was customary on cycle rides to find a place to stop, a private place, where we wouldn't be disturbed if we lowered our trousers for a few minutes. And for a long time we'd always stopped in a particular clearing in the woods, half a mile from the transport café at Applestead.

'We'll go on this road for another three miles and then turn left towards Applestead.'

'Let's not go there today.'

This was greeted with an extended pause. 'You don't want to go there?'

'I'd like to go another route. Let me look at the map and I'll choose the way this time.'

'I think we need to talk about this, Matt. Perhaps there's something you're trying to tell me?'

'I was thinking … I've been thinking about things …' I stumbled to find the words. 'Perhaps it would be best if we were just friends, like other people.'

Jeremy braked and turned off the road by the gate to a field, where a score of sheep were bent over chewing grass. 'But we're not just friends, are we? We never have been. There's something really special between us. You don't want to stop having that with me, do you?'

'No, of course not. I know we're special. But couldn't we be special and still stop?'

'You don't love me any more. Is that what you are saying?'

I wasn't accustomed to disagreeing with Jeremy, to not rapidly seeing the world as he saw it, and it caused the muscles in my tummy to seize up. 'Of course I love you. I wouldn't stop loving you if we stopped. I just don't want to do that any more.'

'Well, of course, we can be just like ordinary people if that's what you think you want. We wouldn't be the same, though, not the same at all. You don't seem to realise what this would mean. No reason, of course, why you would. But we can try it and see, if that's what you really want.'

My relief at hearing this was short-lived. Jeremy had set his bike back on the road and was cycling away at a pace I couldn't hope to equal. My bike was lying on the ground. I picked it up and got on just as I saw Jeremy disappear round a bend in the road, hundreds of yards away. I was alone. My heart raced, my throat tightened. I tried calling, but no sound came out. There was no strength in my muscles. My legs were shaking and I gave up the attempt at pursuit. I stood beside the road, suddenly aware of the cold and grey all around me. A block that felt like sharp flint formed behind my ribs and interfered with my breathing. I sat down, frozen.

Minutes passed. An age. And then I was saved. There was Jeremy with his familiar loving smile, dismounting and walking over to me with his arms open, picking me up and holding me close.

I snivelled. 'I didn't mean it. I just wasn't sure. I didn't mean it ….' Tears flowed from my eyes.

'It's all right, dear. I love you. Nothing's going to change us, is it? I know you'll have your doubts, that's only natural. It's difficult for people like us. But everything is all right, really. I love you. Nothing will come between us. I'll always be there for you. Don't worry any more.'

The rock began to melt. The relief was so real. I collapsed into Jeremy's arms. Nothing was worth feeling that bad over. I never wanted to feel that bad again.

*

I was with Jeremy in Lymbridge the day the baby arrived. When we got home, Gracey was downstairs and announced in a loud whisper, 'It's a girl. A beautiful little girl. Eight pounds, eight ounces.' This meant nothing to me. Disappointed, I was led upstairs still thinking of how things weren't going to turn out as I had hoped. I hadn't given up on the notion that I'd have a younger brother called Roger. I turned into the spare bedroom and looked over the bars of the wicker crib at the tiny creature that lay sleeping there. And my heart opened. Something immediate and unspeakable overcame me as I took in this being whose fingers, I saw, were barely bigger than my fingernails. Her face was a bit screwed up, but this did nothing to sully what struck me as a vision of beauty. Of vulnerability. Of wonder. I was frightened for her: were babies meant to be this tiny? I felt like crying. I blinked, but then I turned and found my dad watching me from the doorway, grinning. I grinned back.

'She's going to be called Jenny.'

'Lovely. Lovely.'

*

It was approaching the time of my eleven plus exam. The class sat for other tests on a regular basis, and when the big day came, the exam that mattered didn't seem such a big deal. I did my best, as

I always had, and then forgot about it. It wasn't so easy to forget the fact that I was leaving a school that felt so safe, whose teachers liked me, to go to a much bigger school where I'd be amongst the youngest and littlest. A complicated form had arrived in the post for my parents to fill in. It provided a list of local schools and instructions that parents should list their first three preferences. I was alarmed when Dad said that I was going to Greendale Grammar School, and that he was going to put that on the form. There wasn't any question about it, no second or third preference. Dad sounded completely confident, and it troubled me, because for the first time I didn't believe he was as powerful as he seemed to believe.

There was further tension in that Jeremy felt that Greendale Grammar would be a disaster for me. 'Look at them in those ugly green uniforms! I don't know why it is, but private schools are different. Their boys are prettier. State schools drain all the originality and beauty out of children. I dread to think what you'll be like after a year or two there.'

*

It was June 1970. The weather was fine. I cycled under the bridge past the railway station and turned left into Vale Road towards the allotments. Something was wrong. Something had been wrong all week. I'd pushed it to the back of my mind and tried to act normally. Now, approaching Seaview Cottages, I felt it rearing up again. Every thought that came into my head was a bad one. I parked the bike against the wall of Mrs Rushton's cottage and knocked at the door.

'What's wrong? You look terrible!' Jeremy sounded concerned. I walked into the cottage and he closed the door behind me.

'You sure you're OK? What are those wrinkles for, eh?'

Jeremy touched my forehead. 'Is it a headache?' He walked through to the kitchen and began filling the kettle.

'No.' I followed him and stood in the doorway. Suddenly I was weeping. When Jeremy came back and held my shoulders, my body started shaking and my knees buckled. I put my arms around my friend, who held me tightly while I cried. The ugly strain began to give way to waves of release. Jeremy rubbed my back gently. After the worst of the sobbing, he spoke softly. 'What is it, love? Where's my bright little boy gone, eh? What's hurting you like this?' And after a moment, 'Has somebody hurt you?'

I shook my head. 'I don't know. Nothing's right.' I pushed myself back into Jeremy's body in a silent request to be held again.

Jeremy poured the tea and we went upstairs. My eyes were red and my voice was thick. I didn't speak any more about how I felt, but now that I was safe I could think more clearly. It was suddenly clear to me. Being ten had been great. Up till then I'd led an enchanted life. Nothing had ever gone wrong. It would have been good if I could have stopped wetting the bed, and by now I wished more than all the people who nagged me about it, that I could stop biting my nails, which were always painful and looked disgusting. But I'd been happy. That had all been lost. A cloud had gathered around my life and I knew that I'd never be happy again, that I didn't deserve it, that I was bad and deserved to be miserable. I wasn't sure that I wanted to live any more. Life had become, in the previous few months, more and more of a burden, and I didn't know if I could manage going through a whole lifetime carrying the weight that had settled in my stomach. I thought about all the odd things that had come into my mind when I was trying to go to sleep: about dying, and trying to work out whether anyone would notice, or whether they'd be relieved, or whether they'd feel guilty, or cry.

Jeremy distracted me, suggesting that we take the wheelbarrow down to the pier and collect some seaweed. 'Nothing like a bit of hard work to blow away the blues,' he said kindly.

We got two loads and forked them around the rose bushes at the edge of the allotment, then went back to the house for some coffee. Sitting holding my cup, I started crying again. Jeremy took the cup out of my hand. I curled up in his lap and wept and wept.

Thank goodness I had Jeremy.

*

Jeremy didn't work through the autumn and winter of 1970. He concentrated on various projects of his own and stayed in Shorefleet. He proposed a challenge: that we go swimming in the sea every afternoon through the winter, whatever the weather. So after school we'd meet down by the central steps on Whiting Bay, chaining our bikes to the railings. The changing rooms below had been sealed off by a fence, but it wasn't difficult to pull one end away and squeeze through into the chilly but dry cover to change. Each day we'd touch one another before getting properly undressed. Then we'd dash across the freezing beach and immerse ourselves in the grey water. To qualify, we had to put our heads under and swim at least two strokes: after that we could get out. Later we'd go back to my house for a hot drink. We kept it up until Christmas morning. Everyone thought we were mad.

Around the same time, Alex Jeffreys and I were sitting on a bus, perhaps going home from school.

'Suppose you're busy at the weekend again?'

'What – oh, probably.'

'Doing what, I wonder?' There was something knowing in Alex's tone. 'The rest of us are playing football at the rec on Saturday morning. Why don't you join us?'

'Thanks, but not tomorrow.'

'You seeing Jeremy?'

'Jeremy?'

'Yeah, that guy you used to talk about. I've seen you out with him. My mum thinks it's weird.'

'Oh.' The bus was just turning down towards the seafront. I had another minute, at most two, before I'd be on my own. There was no more conversation. The bus stopped.

'Bye.'

That brief conversation spelt the end of our friendship. Alex Jeffreys had become dangerous. He knew too much, and he and his mother thought about what they knew.

~ 9 ~

When I was around 30 – some 15 years ago – I hit what I thought of as rock bottom. Then, it wasn't just a case of imploding: the wreckage spread, infecting and destroying everything around me. It's what I'm most ashamed about – not Jeremy, but that.

It wasn't long after I'd ended my counselling sessions with Caroline. That had changed so much, but it had been a mistake to think I'd been 'cured'. I'd emerged believing in myself in a new way. I felt on top of the world. Everything seemed clear. I had choices and didn't need to be paralysed by fear and self-hatred. I'd been with Jayne about nine years and I'd put her through so much, and it felt marvellous then to believe that I was going to give her everything she could wish for. I meant it when I proposed to her. We were on holiday in Sicily. And we talked of having kids, and for the first time that felt meaningful too. I could really imagine it. Later that year we found out that she was pregnant. Everyone was so pleased.

Over the following months it all gradually fell apart. I tried to ignore it, to remain the grown-up. But the other me insistently reasserted itself, and that me felt so much more real. More and more it was like I was playing a role. The fractures opened out and deepened as the prospect of parenthood loomed closer. I had always felt lacking in a straightforward toughness. I'd felt skinless. I assumed that everyone was born skinless and developed skins only gradually and in the face of great agony, the way a baby crab is born with a soft back and only slowly forms a hard shell. I'd begun to worry intensely about the baby now safely and unsuspectingly snug in Jayne's body, about the terror it would feel on its expulsion. I doubted our capacity to alleviate its misery. I was afraid that I wouldn't be able to stand being close to it. I was scared of being a father.

I asked friends and acquaintances with families how their offspring had survived early childhood. I don't think they really understood what I was asking them. They described it as a time of great joy. It didn't help.

While I had lived by deception, somehow I knew I wouldn't be able to deceive my own child. Boy or girl, the baby would seek out and find my hidden failings, and both of us would be harmed in the process. I was a threat to the child, the child was a threat to me. Increasingly the vision of two loving adults, supporting one another in raising a secure son or daughter, was draining away.

I knew that I was going to love this child more than anything I'd ever loved in my life, and that the child's well-being would from then on be my first priority. This would mean having to stay with Jayne for ever. I would no longer be able to manage the day-by-day strains of a life of pretence by telling myself that it couldn't go on and that I could end it if I wished. The fantasy of escape would be taken away.

The birth went so well, better than I could have imagined. One evening in January, the previous weeks having dragged by, suddenly it was time. We phoned the labour ward and were told to come into the hospital. Jayne was given a room on her own. We were there all night. I lay on the floor when things quietened down. And then it all happened. The waters didn't break until right near the end, which I imagined meant that the baby would have been fairly comfortable up to that point. The midwife had attached a monitor that allowed me to see the baby's heartbeat, and it was only for the briefest period that it slowed right down. And then he was there.

I couldn't try to explain what that meeting was like. He was immediately beautiful, and appeared calm, happy to sleep and, later, to feed. I watched with a sense of wonderment, monitoring his every movement to see what it might signify of the person inside. It took time to digest, the sheer fact that he was there at all, another being that *we* had created. There was such pride and disbelief, and fear and joy. We had a boy's name ready: this was Jack.

I knew that my role now was to support Jayne through the period of her engrossment with the moment-by-moment needs of our newborn. I tried. I tried to keep going, to hide the chaos, to counteract the voices that told me that I had to get out, because only then could I save the child the hurt of being left sometime later, when he was older and more attached to me, and dependent on my presence in his life. I kept it up as long as I could, but in the end it was too much. Several weeks after Jack's birth, one awful night, I told Jayne that I was leaving.

The scenes between us, so recently happy and optimistic, were horrible. Jayne was bewildered and enraged and frightened. I wanted to cease to exist. It had always been a relief when a painstakingly constructed façade was pulled down and people were able to see the disgusting animal I really was. But this time was different. This was a crime; I'd done something that to all decent-minded people was sickening, selfish and abhorrent. My family were rightly ashamed of me. I couldn't think of meeting Jayne's parents, who'd taken me in with such warmth and love. Nobody could understand, and I had no reason to think they would judge me any differently if they knew everything that flooded my mind. Their opinion and my own were closer together, probably, than at any other time.

Jayne was amazing. I don't talk about it with her now; I don't think I could face hearing what it had been like for her. But she didn't fall apart. We had many terrible evenings full of recrimination and guilt. I couldn't stand to see her so hurt, so sad. I just clung onto the belief that she'd survive. And she did. Rather than hate me, she took some responsibility for what had happened. She was the only one I felt comfortable with. Despite what was said in moments of desperation, she didn't put all the blame on me, or reject me. Her first priority was Jack. She was clear that what he needed was to have a real relationship with his father, and she did everything to make that possible, even when it made her life much more difficult. I'll always be grateful to her for that.

I rented a room about a mile away, but I stayed back at the flat, in the spare room, three nights a week. After three months Jayne returned to work part-time, and I used my paternity leave and regular holiday allowance to look after Jack while she was away. Jayne required certainty in practical matters and soon organised a formal separation, setting out our various obligations. While each conversation concerning our lives was painful, we were able to establish a basis for our future, shared involvement with our child's upbringing.

For months, years, I ached terribly at each separation from Jack. It became a routine, Jayne holding him up at the window of the third-floor flat as I left, looking back and waving and blowing kisses, all the while pushing myself against the waves of hurt threatening me from deep inside my body. I felt desperate about the way I had brought the very hurt to Jack that I had worried about so much before he was born. But regularity and predictability eased the pain, and continuous indications that Jack himself was as happy and healthy a child as one could wish for, alleviated my anxieties and, to an extent, my guilt.

Where Jayne had never been able to count on me as a lover or partner, I did show myself to be totally reliable as a father. We two adults developed a close friendship based on our love of this tender and affectionate creature, and on our shared memories of the tempestuous but powerful relationship of which he was a product. I would always have a place inside me that worried about the hurt I'd caused 'the Little One', but Jayne had a different view, or a more practical orientation. She was preoccupied with his future safety and protection, and there could be no greater proof of her confidence in my love for our child than her letting me take over as father whenever she wasn't there.

Jayne told me on one occasion that our separating had also brought her some feelings of relief. Once I was sure that she no longer looked on me as a husband, my feelings for her became much less confused. Hatred and resentment had built up, and now the hatred dropped away, like snow drifts slipping from the roofs of houses during a thaw. I cared so much for her, and always would, not in the way she would once have wanted but in a way that was now certain and uncomplicated. There was little doubt in my mind that it was Jayne's ability to put her hurt and rage against me to one side, for our son's sake, that saved me.

For me, fatherhood was a revelation, not of the kind I'd anticipated but far more profound and positive. Whenever I tried to explain what it was like, I'd sound hopelessly sentimental. Out of the chaos grew one relationship that – though in one respect deeply marred already by my madness – I was determined would be real, real in the terms I used to assess how meaningfully I was involved in the lives of those around me. The Little One opened up inside me a seam of feeling that was so exquisite as to hurt, the contemplation of which often brought tears. It was life and beauty and my son's trust against which I now felt defenceless, and against which I didn't wish to defend myself.

*

In the year after leaving Jayne, my ties to her and to Jack kept me alive. I'm sure of that. Otherwise, it was a period of the deepest despair. I lived in a rented room that I kept somewhere between untidy and squalid, trying to keep a job I didn't feel equal to. During the nights there I faced my darkest moments. Tortured by the knowledge of having hurt those closest to me, I doubted that I was qualified to live in the world amongst other people. I seemed to see creeping up on me the destitution I'd long feared would be my fate. It was a relief that I was no longer living a lie, but I longed for some release from the full glare of the truth. I thought often of those who had willed their own escape from an unacceptable existence. I wished I could collapse under the strain.

Ella was living nearby, though I didn't see her much. But one day I found my way to the third-floor corridor in County Hall, where she was employed as a social worker. I wasn't sure, when it came to it, why I was there or whether I should disturb her. Leaning against the wall opposite the frosted-glass door I sank, exhausted, unsure whether I shouldn't just leave.

The door opened and a middle-aged man appeared. 'What are you doing here?'

I understood that I looked like I was just dossing in the corridor and struggled to my feet.

'Is Ella around? Ella Lowe?'

The man leaned his head back into the office. 'Ella, someone for you, I think.' He stayed watching until Ella appeared and left only when it was clear that we knew one another.

'Matt? What's wrong? Are you OK?'

Words stuck in my throat. I wasn't OK, but part of not being OK was feeling in a muddle.

Ella gave up on an answer. 'Let's go down to the canteen, come on.' She took my arm and walked towards some double doors and through them to a wide staircase. 'Matt, you've got to tell me what's going on.'

I turned to her and threw my arms around her neck, there in the stairwell. She held me and we stood like that, still, until I felt ready to continue.

We found a table in a quiet corner and Ella brought cups of tea.

'I'm sorry, Ella. I just couldn't face today on my own. I couldn't think where else to go.'

'That's all right, I'm glad you came. Aren't you supposed to be at work today?'

'Yeah. They won't miss me, I don't think. Ella, I don't feel well. It's such an effort doing anything. I don't know why I can't cope when everyone else seems able to.'

'Are you eating properly?'

'Off and on.'

'What does that mean? Do you think you need to see a doctor?'

'What for?'

'You don't look well to me. You don't seem to be coping.'

It hurt to hear her concern, and warmed me at the same time.

'You've been seeing Jack?

'Yes, of course. But I'm not due back there till Thursday.' I was thinking about Jack, about holding him quietly while he had his last bottle of the day. The way his eyes would lock onto my own for long moments at a time, and then grow drowsy until at last his head would fall back away from the bottle. I'd put the bottle to one side and gently lay him in his cot. Jayne would watch from the doorway, smiling, sharing in the wonder of it all. I hadn't heard Ella speaking.

'Are you listening to me?'

'Sorry.'

'I was saying that you should take this key and go back to my place. I think you need to have a bath and wash your hair. There's stuff in the fridge – cheese, anyway – and there's bread, so have something to eat. And just stay there till I come back this evening. Joe's bringing a take-away – I'll phone him to bring enough for three.'

'Thanks. I'd like that.'

'Things will be all right, Matt. I know they will.'

'Yeah, of course. Nothing to worry about.'

Breakdown and madness appeared to me as a great release into a world where nothing would be expected of me, where all self-awareness would cease. It became such a preoccupation, I felt so close to the insane, that I contacted the volunteer co-ordinator at the Maudsley Hospital, a cheerful, eccentric woman called Maria, and offered my services. And there, in the dingy and ill-lit rooms of the hospital social centre in Windsor Walk, I met the men and women whose ranks I aspired to join. I valued the work and liked the people I met, but it was immediately apparent that madness was not the answer. I felt guilty at ever having imagined it might have been. It was clear that a frag-mented mind didn't lead to a carefree existence: quite the opposite. I was suitably grateful that, somehow, my mind had stayed more or less in one piece.

Jack made the greatest difference. His straightforward love of life, his pleasure and good humour, confronted and counteracted the pessimism I saw enveloping everything else. It helped to realise how strong and resilient he was, despite his vulnerability. When I found myself surprised that he liked apricot yoghurt – something I loathed – I realised how I might have been confusing the two of us in ways that couldn't be healthy or helpful. Caring for him was about being attentive, attuned, following as much as leading. My love for Jack was the most painful and the most valuable thing in my life, and it made it possible to imagine, despite everything, that I could start to make a more positive contribution in other areas too.

So I found myself wondering if my experiences could be turned to some purpose, perhaps even equip me to do something good. I contacted ChildLine, where I was interviewed and accepted for their training course. During the role plays and discussions I discovered that being so undefended could, in certain circumstances, be an advantage. I worked as a volunteer telephone counsellor, once or twice a week and usually in the evenings, for about two years. I found that I could provide a warm and engaged response to calls made by children who, I was amazed to find, knew about abuse and that it shouldn't happen, and who knew too how to seek help, to tell someone. The most difficult calls – the only ones that left me feeling wrecked inside – were from the boys who couldn't talk, who would call only to freeze, or who through their tears and frustration would utter a few phrases about what was happening to them but who then, ashamed and confused, put the phone down.

The next aid to recovery was beginning a new career. With my experience at the Maudsley and ChildLine I was offered a position running the Rosalyn Centre, a drop-in in Clapham. It was the initiative of a radical clergyman, Nick Sperling, who provided his church hall to be the base for a new voluntary organisation, working for local people with mental health difficulties. I stayed there for nine years and helped the place grow to be the core of a range of community services and, more to the point, a thriving community in its own right. We – primarily myself, my co-worker Christine and our administrator Margaret – ran the centre as a home from home for a large number of isolated and anxious people whose lives had been disrupted and limited by a full range of psychiatric conditions. I don't think anyone realised how much of a home it was for me at that time. I found it hard leaving work at the end of the day. Christine had a natural flair for the work, such that it took time before I could believe that she needed or valued whatever support I could give her. Margaret was like a mother to both of us, bringing us packed lunches and worrying over us when we were stressed or ill or, as was more often Christine's difficulty, hung over.

The clients at the Rosalyn Centre were my family for a long while. I got hugs from Beth and Trudy, talked philosophy and politics with Brian, played chess with Anthony, and listened with real interest to the life stories of everyone prepared to talk to me. I heard about past lives of crime and of privilege, about lives in service, and about present lives on the estates of Wandsworth and Lambeth. The centre was alive, a place of romances and breakups, of birthday celebrations and Christmas dinners and discos, day trips and concert outings. There was a harsh side to it: the past of being ostracised, bullied, prostituted and bereaved; the present for many who lived within walls constructed out of paranoia and delusional grandiosity; or suffocating under the weight of prescribed medication, limited by poverty and defined by loneliness. There were tragedies: the young Jamaican man who lost an arm under a tube train at Charing Cross, the young English woman who lost her life under the tube train at the Oval. The cancers, heart attacks, and frequent collapses into full-blown psychosis. There was always the awfulness of being with people who had accepted the constraints of life as a 'schizophrenic' or 'manic depressive', and the pain of being with people who couldn't yet accept those constraints.

I took Jack to the Rosalyn. He was cooed over by everyone when he was small, and as he grew up he helped out serving drinks at parties or sweeping up after discos. All in all, I felt a sense of belonging there that I couldn't remember experiencing before.

And then there was Carmen.

Carmen had been a frequent visitor to my office before I worked for the Rosalyn – she was good friends with two of my colleagues. She always took the trouble to pass the time of day with whomever was about.

On one particular morning, she came when the rest of the team were away on a training exercise. She took a seat to write an extended note to her friends. I offered her a coffee. We talked, easily, about my work and the changes that were going on in the organisation. Funding was always difficult and Carmen made some suggestions. The conversation ran on. I wondered if she would join me for lunch. Over soup and a sandwich we talked more about her work – establishing projects for refugees from Latin America – and about the politics of work in overseas development. At two, she had to leave. She gave me her telephone number at work. We agreed that we should meet again sometime soon. Later that afternoon I phoned her and asked if we could meet the following day.

After that, we had lunch most days. I found myself looking forward to my lunch break, watching the clock. Now, there was something meaningful happening on days when I wasn't seeing Jack. I started paying more attention to how I looked. Each meeting sped by with me doing most of the talking. Carmen struck me as accepting and easy, though by nature rather a private individual. I gathered that there had until quite recently been someone important in her life, but that she was now on her own. She was vague, and I respected her vagueness. In any case, I preferred talking about the things we could share – our interest in the world, in music, in particular – than the things we couldn't.

It became our habit to meet in Kennington Park, equidistant from our workplaces. When the weather was bad we'd retreat to the rather shabby Parma Café in Kennington Lane, but if it was warm enough we'd buy filled rolls, and then walk and sit and talk while we ate. Once I came with Jack, and the three of us played together in the shade. Carmen watched while I fed and changed my son. Then Jack slept his usual peaceful sleep, lain out on a blanket on the grass. I felt adult and competent and proud.

There were other times when I was unhappy, and times when talking made me upset or angry. Carmen encouraged me and I felt safe enough with her to tell her something of the past, including a rough outline of my relationship with Jeremy. She was interested in what had happened between myself and Jayne, and I told her about that too. The inevitable problems arose, like how to talk freely about myself and yet not drive Carmen away. I needed her to see me as I saw myself, but then worried that that was just how she would see me. How to confide in her the failure I had been as a partner and a father, without her seeing me as pathetic or bad? I had, I told her, an exterior that fooled people: a smooth, metallic finish covering a squirming animal-like thing inside.

After one lunchtime meeting when I had made my self-doubt, even my self-loathing, clearer than ever, Carmen sent a card she had made herself. Inside she had copied out two verses of poetry:

> *Out of the night that covers me,*
> *Black as the pit from pole to pole,*
> *I thank whatever gods may be*
> *For my unconquerable soul.*
>
> *It matters not how strait the gate*
> *How charged with punishments the scroll,*
> *I am the master of my fate:*
> *I am the captain of my soul.*

I read these lines over and over, and placed the card on the mantelpiece in my room beside my photographs of Jack. The card reminded me of a strange phrase that Caroline, my counsellor, had once used: 'It's difficult for you to love yourself.' I'd spluttered when I'd heard that: it was unimaginable that I could. But here, in Carmen's card, there was again the suggestion that there was nothing wrong with self-respect, at least, or with a sense of one's own power.

I told Carmen more than she told me, but I didn't really mind. She talked about her family and her childhood and adolescence, her early boyfriends, all back in South America. She talked about her life in Britain, her work and her colleagues. A shroud covered the time when the army had destroyed the country she had known and loved, her world, and a number of the people closest to her. I learned nothing of her life under the military regime, and of her decision to leave. I imagined that there might be a time when she would trust me enough to share that part as well.

I'd always felt there was something fraudulent about my political convictions – because I could find no way of acting on them, because I was so irredeemably middle class and outwardly conventional. It was a pleasure to discuss ideas with Carmen, a real activist, and never to hear a hint of condescension in her voice. She talked to me as an equal. During one of our conversations she made a link between public and private sources of hurt, and in doing so seemed to legitimise much about which I felt only shame: 'You know, when you talk about your childhood, it reminds me of the damage done to people who are imprisoned and tortured. It's not the same, of course, but an adult does have more resources than a child. I was reading Primo Levi the other day, and he says something similar: that what we could learn from the terror he found in Auschwitz is that we must never allow similar suffering to happen in our homes. I imagine he wrote that because he knew something about both.'

*

A couple of months after our first lunch together, we were sitting on a bench, in a shelter we'd come to regard as our own, in the middle of Kennington Park. We were debating the merits of different classical composers and teasing one another about our widely differing tastes.

'I can see the beauty in Mahler, but Bruckner and Wagner are too dark, too self-obsessed. What you don't seem to appreciate is music that is about the joy of being alive: Vivaldi and Bach, and Dvořak.'

'I don't see what you get out of a second-rate composer like Dvořak.'

'What do you mean, second-rate? I doubt if you know much Dvořak.'

'You're right, I've never heard anything by him that really made me sit up and listen. Superficial stuff. I'm not sure I listen to music to get to this "joy of being alive". I like music that takes me deep into something heavy and complicated, that it's impossible to experience or convey in any other way.'

'Sounds to me that you're missing out on a lot if you can't find room for anything other than your deep, dark side.'

'Sometimes we seem quite close, but, if we are, it must be the backs of our heads that are touching, because we don't see the same things in the world, do we?'

'Do you know the Prokofiev violin concertos?'

'No. I like some of his music, though, the first piano concerto especially. I used to play that all the time.'

'I'm going to buy you a cassette of the violin concertos and see if you can't see the beauty I see.' She was laughing at me in a gentle way, and I looked right into her eyes to watch. I believed that you saw into people's real being through their eyes, which is why I usually kept my own well hidden. It was great to see myself reflected back with such lightness. The look changed. I realised that Carmen was looking back at me with a new intensity. Our gazes locked. I touched her arm. A moment later we were on the grass, our bodies locked together, me wondering at the clear welcome in her so-soft lips. We hardly spoke. Then we pulled ourselves together, refastened buttons and pulled up zips. And agreed that we needed to find a proper place to meet.

*

Carmen and I became lovers. A few weeks later, we were back lying together on the grass at Kennington.

'You have to love my cock always. I don't just mean like it, I mean love it, hunger for it, feel you can't live without it.'

'I love *you*.'

'That's not what I mean. It's more important than that. I want you to need it, to have to have it in your mouth, your cunt, your arse. To be in a state where you can't bear to be without it. Always. Tomorrow. In twenty years' time.'

She looked at me with a wry smile. 'You're expecting a lot.'

We both laughed. She knew I was serious, and I knew all we could do was laugh about it.

A little later she said, 'Men think they are their penises, and their penises are themselves. Women aren't the same.'

For weeks after we first made love I felt overwhelming urges to bite Carmen. I restrained myself, at least to the point of not hurting her too much. Then I felt driven by the fantasy of merging with her through sex, and was frustrated that only such a small piece of myself could actually get inside her. It seemed natural that I should identify myself with my penis. I was relieved that she understood, and satisfied to be classed as typically male, however ludicrous that made me. And grateful that she could have that understanding and not use it to put me down.

There was a honeymoon period, a year maybe, and then maybe two years of madness when I tested Carmen to the limit, not sparing her at all. I inflicted everything on her – that was the difference, I think. With everyone before, I'd hidden and lied and pretended; I'm not sure why, but with Carmen I needed to find out if she'd put up with me as I really was. In truth, she wouldn't: she left me after months of trying to understand and reassure, when the despair finally got to her and she felt I was damaging her too much. But I loved her, and, finally, it seems I trusted her. I continued to share with her the bleak and twisted way I saw myself, but I stopped testing her. And she came back.

~ 10 ~

'What's the matter?' Mum asked, when I walked in through the back door the day I broke down at Jeremy's.

'Nothing,' I smiled. 'I've been peeling onions.'

There was no need to bother her with this silliness. If I had to share my misery with anyone, I could do it with Jeremy.

There were so many advantages to being Jeremy's friend. Thanks to him I had a watch, a good audio system, a supply of clothes, records and a bike with 10 gears. As well as my ordinary camera, I now had an 8mm movie camera too. I'd become used to being taken places – to restaurants, shows, foreign countries. And all this when Jeremy's career was yet to blossom. What would it be like if he became a famous film director? It was strange: he was so imaginative and I was so dull, but by being with him I picked up all kinds of information and ideas that made me more interesting.

I was often low, and without Jeremy I could only cry on my own. He was always concerned and encouraging. He said I was too fragile for this world and needed looking after. I couldn't articulate, even to him, the harrowing thoughts that plagued me. I knew the change had happened when I was 10, but why remained a complete mystery. Until then my worries had always had clear causes and obvious solutions. Now, the source of the trouble seemed to be somewhere within myself that was beyond

my understanding or control. I became withdrawn and intro-
verted. Sometimes, when I didn't think I'd meet anyone I knew,
I'd walk about with a pronounced limp, imagining people pity-
ing me and wanting to look after me.

I'd been beautiful and now I was growing ugly. Jeremy never
said this, but he made it clear that younger children had charm-
ing characters and attractive bodies, neither of which survived
puberty.

I knew that I'd been at my most beautiful when I was about
eight. Now there were signs of hair growing on my groin, which
Jeremy encountered with silent distaste. It hurt badly: I hated it
when he found fault with me in any way. Like when I was
prescribed spectacles. For some time I'd had trouble reading the
blackboard at school, and when Mum saw me squinting at the TV,
a sight test was arranged. It was great when I collected my new
glasses, realising just how much I had been missing. That evening
I walked down to the beach with Joanna, and saw a full moon and
a skyful of stars just as they were meant to be seen. At the weekend, however, Jeremy greeted the sight of me wearing my black,
plastic-rimmed glasses with dismay and anger, and more or less
insisted that I only wear them when it was absolutely necessary.

Touching myself was one sure way of relieving the anxiety,
and it had become a regular, frequent and necessary activity.
Gradually, however, this too became a source of apprehension.
'Wanker' was a term of abuse at school to denote a degraded
and sad individual. As the compulsion grew, so did my discomfort. The urge now seemed to control me. It came to feel as if
I was giving in to a part of myself that I ought to be controlling, if not conquering.

My first ejaculation occasioned proof of this. For a while I'd
been sensing that the visible changes in my body were going to

result in a change in the nature of masturbation itself. The cycle from arousal to satisfaction was familiar, but the feelings grew ever more intense. I was drained afterwards and worried that I was doing myself harm. One day I was masturbating during the afternoon in my bedroom, when I sensed I was going to produce something from inside. I stood up and pulled out the bottom drawer of my chest of drawers and looked down to see what would happen. It was particularly difficult to reach a climax, but when I finally got there a thick liquid oozed from my penis onto the contents of the drawer. I didn't like it. It smelt, and I was shocked to find that amongst the whiteness I expected, there were streaks of blood. I'd not expected that, and I worried that I was injuring my body and soul by giving in to my impulses. I decided not to do it any more, a resolution that lasted less than a day but which I then reconfirmed. Only to be ignored again with increasing guilt and a strengthened sense of failure. The blood stopped after the second ejaculation and my fears in that regard were allayed, but the whole thing now seemed distasteful, confirming that growing up was both regrettable and shameful.

*

Our cat had been missing for some days: nobody could quite remember when she'd last been seen. This was not unusual: Fifi periodically took a brief holiday and always reappeared eventually. We weren't anxious until we heard a harrowing, unearthly wheezing coming from the shed. There she lay, having dragged herself along by her front paws, a gaping wound in her side and no movement at all in the back part of her body.

Mum found an old towel and brought the cat in. We stood quietly as she bathed Fifi's wound. Fifi was very thirsty but otherwise seemed distracted, disinterested, absent. When Dad came home I went with him to the vet. I carried the cat; there was no need for a box. Heavy and unmistakable hints were dropped that this was likely to be Fifi's last journey. I prayed that it wouldn't be.

We were called straight from the waiting room into a small surgery. Dad and I stood back while the vet, all smiles and freckles, unwrapped his docile patient. He made an inspection, listened to her heartbeat, pulled back her eyelids, felt – too roughly, I was sure – along her back. Fifi shuddered. Then he wiped at the wound. 'I think she's been in a car accident. Probably several days ago.' He paused. 'You're going to have to leave her here with me, I'm afraid.'

My heart sank and I moved closer to Dad.

'I can't be sure, but I'm hopeful that a course of antibiotics will deal with the infection. Her back's not broken, but I want to have her here under my eye, so I can get a clearer view of just how serious her internal injuries are.'

Fifi survived. She was never able to get her mouth to parts of her coat after that, and we had to brush it out for her. But otherwise she made a full recovery. I'd had vague ambitions before – Jeremy talked to me about becoming an archaeologist. But now I knew with a passion that I was going to be a veterinary surgeon. I went to my school careers library and found a booklet that told me what I'd have to do to realise my dream. My dad was pleased when he heard of my plan.

'I know what I want to be when I grow up,' I told Jeremy, anticipating a similarly positive endorsement.

'Oh good,' he replied with real interest. 'Aren't you going to tell me, then?'

'I'm going to be a vet. I'll have to be good at sciences and study biology, and go to university.'

'You mean looking after people's cats and dogs? Come off it, Matt. That's hardly a suitable ambition.'

'Why isn't it? This man we took Fifi to, he ...' I paused, not sure how to justify my excitement.

'All right, I can see your heart's in the right place. But neutering kittens and delousing dogs isn't a proper future for someone like you. I hope you're not going to set your sights below your true potential. I know you think that everyone is just as good as everybody else, but would I be doing all I do for you if I thought it was your destiny to end up as a vet?'

*

The previous year the family had had a holiday on a farm in Cornwall. The highpoints had been milking cows and spending hours diving into the Atlantic rollers. One day we'd gone on a long country walk and been caught in a heavy shower. The rain-water had drenched us, but it was warm and smelt sweet.

There had been an awful moment early one evening, as we all sat in the farmhouse lounge grouped around the TV. Joanna and I were sitting on the floor. Someone on the television used the word 'homosexual'. Joanna turned round and said, 'What's a homosexual, Mummy?' Mum replied, 'It's a man who loves other men rather than women.' Perhaps she said more, because she could always talk in a matter-of-fact way about such things. I was divided between the effort required to hide my burning cheeks and a furious processing of her words as they might relate to me and Jeremy.

It wasn't that I hadn't known what a homosexual was, but I'd never thought of the concept as having anything to do with me or my life. Mum hadn't implied that there was anything wrong in being homosexual, but I knew it was a bad thing. The range of insults used by my classmates was wide, but a high proportion of them, and the ones everyone was most uncomfortable about, were those that implied you were 'queer'. Now the questions rushed in. Was Jeremy a homosexual? I thought about him and Tony and wondered if they were in love. Then there was Jeremy's attachment to me. I had to conclude that he was homosexual. But did that make me one? Here my thinking became muddled. I couldn't follow through to a positive or a negative conclusion: the evidence of my inner preoccupations and my actual behaviour contradicted one another.

A week later I was with Jeremy in London.

'I want to ask you something.'

'Fire away: as a graduate in the University of Life, I can range over most subjects with a fair degree of brilliance.'

'No, something about you. Are you a homosexual?'

'Ha! Of course not! What gave you that idea? I find the idea of men's bodies absolutely disgusting. All that hair and muscle and sweaty smell. All adults are repulsive.' Then he went on. 'I can't be defined, Matt. They' – I knew that 'they' referred to some notion of normal people and the adult world upon which Jeremy looked with scorn – 'they always want to label you. You have to avoid that if you want to be yourself. I'm a lover of beauty and the mind, and I love you because you're beautiful and you have a beautiful mind. Because from the moment I met you I could see that you hadn't been spoilt, hadn't had your natural sweetness drummed out of you. I'm not attracted to adults of either sex. How can all that body hair be beautiful?'

Jeremy seemed to occupy some genuinely intermediate position outside the categories with which others were labelled, as if he really had created himself in defiance of all the pressures to which lesser mortals succumbed. I, on the other hand, would soon be getting hairier – Andrew Cousins, my class's chief bully, was already hirsute. I too would fall into the category of the smelly and disgusting. I'd been introduced to some beautiful pieces of writing that made it clear that the decline was going to be spiritual as well as physical. Jeremy had told me about the ancient Greeks, and I had struggled through a couple of novels by Mary Renault, so I began to see more clearly what he meant when he said that while the two of us formed an odd couple in Shorefleet in 1972, this was only because sight had been lost of the most respected relationship in the highest civilisation the world had ever known. This provided a category of a kind, a place in which 'Jeremy and Matt' made sense. And I was introduced to Jeremy's favourite poem by Wordsworth. 'Shades of the prison house' was an expression frequently on his lips, and now I understood what he meant by it. I was especially moved when I read *Ode: Intimations of Immortality from Recollections of Early Childhood* because it seemed so precisely to describe my own experience of a fall from grace:

> … *Not in entire forgetfulness*
> *And not in utter nakedness,*
> *But trailing clouds of glory do we come*
> *From God, who is our home:*
> *Heaven lies about us in our infancy!*
> *Shades of the prison house begin to close*
> *Upon the growing Boy,*
> *But He beholds the light, and whence it flows,*
> *He sees it in his joy;*
> *The Youth, who daily farther from the east*
> *Must travel, still is Nature's Priest,*
> *And by the vision splendid*
> *Is on his way attended;*
> *At length, the Man perceives it die away,*
> *And fade into the light of common day …*

This was exactly right: whatever had happened to me when I was 10 had happened to Wordsworth too. I barely read the more hopeful lines that followed.

Jeremy's position embodied an optimism of a kind: that with insight and will we could buck the trend and stay in touch and be alive. We could resist the relentless drive towards conformism and compromise, and remain honest and spontaneous. Jeremy thought of himself still as Nature's Priest, and he extended the same hope to me. But I knew I couldn't share that lofty ideal. I could feel the prison walls already closing in. The qualities that Jeremy loved in me were the ones that I wanted most to lose – my weakness and inability to effectively disguise my feelings. I both yearned to be left alone to become one of the teenagers standing around Giovanni's, and dreaded that such a fate should befall me.

*

At school I continued to study hard. My mind was becoming a sharp tool, and in particular subjects I could use it to tease out gaps or contradictions in the arguments of my betters. I enjoyed arguing and was good at it, and I twigged that adults liked working with a pupil who took things seriously enough to engage in these intellectual duels. On one of my reports a teacher wrote, 'Matthew is a boy who listens at just those moments when you hope he isn't.' I'd cemented an alliance with the brightest boy in the class, Terry Price, who brought sandwiches which he shared with me at break each day. Alex Jeffreys was in the same year, but he and I no longer acknowledged one another.

Academic prowess didn't bring popularity, but it provoked a response from the more aggressive members of the class, Andrew Cousins and Kevin Roseburgh, in particular. Kevin was angular and wiry whereas Andrew was built like a tank. Andrew was the quieter of the two, and the more terrifying, but it would have offended his self-respect to bother me directly. He limited his contribution to egging Kevin on.

'Lowe's a wanker. Hey, everyone, who's the wanker? Matt Lowe! Who did you suck off on the way to school this morning, Lowe? Are you playing with yourself now, Lowe? Hey, Lowe's wanking under the desk! You disgusting wanker, Lowe. Lowe's a queer! Lowe's a poof!'

Ours was not one of those schools where boys talked openly about their private selves. No one would ever have confessed to masturbating, for example. I was left unsure if I was the only one who defiled himself in this way. In any case, I lacked the front necessary to identify somebody else as the class deviant.

Once the fun had started, there was little knowing the direction it would take. Kevin might abandon his usual seat at the rear and sit directly behind me, making signs behind my head which the rest of the class would laugh at but which I couldn't see. Waiting until the teacher was facing the board, he would do something to create a stir, careful not to draw the teacher's attention. From time to time he'd thump me in the back. The punch carried with it an unspoken challenge to react or complain, to be weak and appeal for help, or to be weak and do nothing.

'You got a girlfriend, Lowe? What's she like? She got nice tits? Have you ever felt a girl up, Lowe? You've never been near one, have you, you wanker. Hey, I think Lowe's a girl. Should we find out for sure?'

'Stop being so stupid.' This was my usual arrogant response. It would have been far better if I could have strung together a few choice swear words, but I couldn't.

'Fucking wogs. Yeah, we should kill those fucking coons. What do you think, Lowe?'

'You are really ignorant.' It was like a red rag to a bull.

'We'll see you at lunch-time, Lowe. We'll meet you then, OK, by the pavilion.'

I didn't know what to do: go to the pavilion as a sheep to slaughter, or hide and excite their blood-lust further. On this occasion I allowed myself to be found. The punching started, not too painful but unpredictable, causing me to wince and dodge.

'Stupid, are we? Huh? Who looks stupid now? Huh? Answer me. Who looks stupid now? Well, what is it, Lowe, what's the answer?'

'Me.'

One of their acolytes crouched behind me so that when Kevin pushed I fell backwards. Kevin jumped on top, pinning my upper arms with his knees, leaving his own arms free to flick at my face. He put all his weight on his knees, on my forceps. The minion was out of sight, tying the laces of my shoes in a tight knot.

Eventually they got bored and wandered away. I got up and Terry, who'd been watching from a safe distance, joined me.

'Those bastards.'

'They're stupid. Bloody fools. Totally idiotic.'

'Let's go this way: they seem to be hanging around the labs.'

Avoiding Kevin Roseburgh was a priority. At ten to four each day I made sure I was sitting closest to the door and as soon as permission was given I was out of my place and running as fast as I could for the bicycle sheds. The aim was to unlock my bike and be out through the archway and off up the street before I could be cut off.

The only person who could see that something was wrong that year, as I mooned around the house, was Ella, who approached me as I sat looking out the front-room window one Sunday evening.

'Matt, I can see that something's up. Are you in love? Is that it? You can tell me, you know.'

'No, of course I'm not. Nothing's wrong.' I blushed. Love was an even trickier subject than being bullied. 'Just leave me alone. I'm all right.'

*

'I had a horrible dream last night. I was cycling down Steadman Road really fast, and it was really exciting and then I couldn't stop, and I whizzed past the Savoy Hotel and right to the end – there didn't seem to be any railings to crash into, and so I went on and out over the rocks and the sea, and I was falling and falling and falling, and then I woke up. I hate those kind of dreams.'

Jeremy and I were on the train talking as we watched the countryside passing by.

'In ancient times they thought that dreams were omens of the future. I wonder what that dream might be warning you about.'

'Making sure my brakes work properly, I suppose.'

Jeremy laughed. 'There was this guy called Freud who thought that dreams told us things about ourselves that we didn't want to know about. He thought that human beings were controlled by a part of themselves they were unaware of; he called it "the unconscious". And he thought that it was all about sex, everything in life, from the very beginning – even for a baby like Jenny.'

This sounded weird. I said nothing.

'It's something about the Jewish mind,' Jeremy continued. 'They have big ideas and think they have discovered the secret to everything with this one idea. For Freud it was sex. Then there was Marx who thought it was money. They both thought that we don't make decisions for ourselves, that decisions are made for us either by our sexual impulses or by our greed. It's nonsense, of course. We have the choice to be whatever we want to be, Matt. We can either be like sheep, or we can refuse to be like sheep. You can't use their theories to explain anything properly; you couldn't understand our special friendship like that, could you?'

I wasn't sure I'd followed his argument, but I agreed that these theories seemed very silly. It was a puzzle to think that there were adults who believed in ideas which Jeremy could so easily show to be shallow and worthless.

*

Jeremy sneered at team sports of any kind, and I adopted his arrogant disdain for my peers' enthusiasm for football. Cycling was his passion: to be on the open road, battling against the elements. Self-reliant, free and experiencing the rush that few other activities could offer.

When I was 12 Jeremy took me on a cycling holiday to Cornwall. We travelled by B roads through the countryside each day and stayed in youth hostels each night. I enjoyed that, mixing with groups of boys from Birmingham or men down from London, with family groups and students. People were friendly. We stayed at the mediaeval mill in Winchester, and in a cottage right on top of the highest cliff I'd ever seen at Tintagel. We enjoyed swimming in the rollers at sunset in Treyarnon Bay, and saw some gnarled apple trees in the rectory at St Ives that Jeremy's mother had helped plant when she was a little girl. We went go-cart racing in Penzance, and sang 'Uncle Tom Cobbleigh and All' as we walked up the hill out of Widdecombe-in-the-Moor. The cycling was hard, and the distances from one hostel to the next were sometimes unrealistic. Jeremy helped me up the hills, leaning down and placing a hand in the middle of my back. We usually arrived late at night, long after the evening meal had been served. The last hours of cycling were always difficult, and I dreamed – almost to the point of delusion – that youth hostels had buses they sent out to pick up straggling travellers. Jeremy often lied to me about how many hills lay between us and our bunk beds.

I had images of Dartmoor in my mind from the time when Jeremy had read *The Hound of the Baskervilles* to me. The road up onto the moor was long and steep, and I had to walk much of the way. The journey had again taken longer than planned, and by the time we reached the plateau the sun was low in the sky. Jeremy had arranged to phone his mother that evening and we were miles from the nearest village. He stopped at a crossroads and took out the map. 'We're here,' he explained, indicating with a fingertip where we stood, 'and we're going there. You just keep going on along this road for eight miles and wait for me where these two roads meet. You take the map. I'm going to turn off here and find a phone in that village, and then I'll come back up this road to meet you. We'll only have another five miles to go to the hostel.'

I cycled on through the barren landscape. The sun grew weaker and the sky became a screen of different colours, a vivid pink, an inky black, a deep and unusual blue. The tors and moorland took on a magical glow, bringing out the reds, browns and yellows that had been invisible a little while before. I'd seen something like this in the cinema but never in real life. The air cooled my face. There was something eerie but at the same time calming about the scene. It was like a dream. I felt completely at one with the place, a tiny speck lost in the ageless landscape stretching out away from me in all directions. I wished the scene could remain fixed, that the night wouldn't come, that I'd never reach the crossroads, that I could remain forever transfixed by the harsh beauty bearing down on me. I imagined describing the scene to Jeremy, who was perhaps having a similar experience. I wouldn't know how to. Words were hopeless, at least in my mouth. Jeremy would turn it into a story, a poem, a picture if he chose. But I was left simply opening my mind and letting it in, raw and unmediated, and I'd never be able to share it with anyone. I watched the way the setting sun was held amongst trailing strips of black cloud, found the first few stars that were visible directly above, and knew that after a few minutes it would be another ordinary night. What I was now part of was otherworldly but so transient, so fleeting. I wondered how I would ever get here again. I'd escaped the world of petty worries, the world of people with its endless complications. The tiredness had left my legs. I was no longer Matt, as I coasted along the deserted road feeling the chill breeze against my cheeks and the line of sweat on my brow.

~ 11 ~

We left Bayview Road when I was 13. The moving process took so long that any initial excitement gave way to indifference and scepticism, but eventually the purchase was agreed of a large detached house for sale in Park Road. At £22,000, I found out, it was the same price that Queen Victoria had paid for Osborne House on the Isle of Wight. Number 216 was not so palatial, but it was an impressive size. Seven bedrooms, two bathrooms, huge sitting room, separate dining room and a large garden with double garage and fishpond.

It was sad, still, to be leaving the only home any of us children had known or could remember. I'd lose my view down towards Whiting Bay; we'd no longer hear the mournful grinding of the foghorn. It seemed a shame to move so far from the sea. I was won over, though, when I went to see the new house for myself. It had two staircases, the main one by the front door and a back one that went up into one of the smaller bedrooms. I declared that this was going to be my room and nobody objected. Having a room of my own was a palpable step towards adulthood. I could leave behind a bedroom that had become a shrine to my and Jeremy's activities, its walls covered in memorabilia from the films he'd worked on or extracts from his scripts, and the corner that housed our Roman museum. The move struck me as a watershed, an opportunity for change all round –

a move from a soiled, compromised childhood to a purer, cleaner, more substantial future. Central to this project would be a change in the nature of my relationship with Jeremy.

'We could go round the new house if you want. We've got keys now. I can show you where my bedroom's going to be.' So we cycled up away from the coast to Park Road. My heart was thudding. I was trying to work out how to approach the subject, how to put my argument. At least we'd be on our own so I'd be able to speak freely. Once Jeremy knew how I felt, I was sure that we could come to some agreement. 'It' – there was no need to find an accurate word to describe what we did together – couldn't be that important.

I turned the key in the lock and we entered the kitchen. It was cold. Jeremy was unlikely to be impressed by something as boring as an empty house, but I was still hurt by his muted response. It suggested his criticisms of my parents again. Built in mock Tudor style, the place embodied everything that he despised.

He was talking about a possible new twist to the plot of *Matt's Film*. It had occurred to him that the story could be set on a Greek island: much more exotic than a farm in rural England, and with the prospect of finding a cave packed with real treasure; statues and gold in place of broken pottery. 'So maybe we'll go to Cyprus next summer. I've brought some books down which I'll show you later. And we'll need to learn Greek, of course. I'm probably going to spend a few weeks there with Tony in the next month or so and see what we can set up.'

My mind was on something else. My heart thumped, as if warning me not to speak. Yet as we moved from room to room I feared that I was going to lose the opportunity to get Jeremy to understand how I felt. It was so often like that for me: I'd be terrified of doing something, but once I'd done it and everything had turned out well, I'd realise how silly I'd been to worry.

We were climbing the stairs to the top floor.

'This is going to be Peter's room, and that one is going to be Joanna's. And look here, behind these doors is a great big attic.'

Jeremy put his hand on my shoulder. I moved away. 'There's no light in the attic and there's no torch.'

Jeremy's arms came around me. I moved away again. 'This is going to be a new place. I was thinking that perhaps we could love one another but without doing that. That that would be the best thing. I don't know what you think. But it doesn't seem all that important, and perhaps we could see how it was without doing that for a while.'

'Are you worried about somebody coming? We're here all alone.'

'No, it's not that at all. I'm glad we're alone because I thought we could talk about it properly. I don't want to any more.' I found it hard to think clearly. I could tell from Jeremy's expression that there would have to be a fight, and that I was going to lose. Jeremy took the initiative. 'So you don't love me any more?'

'I do, of course I do. But that's not the only way to show it, is it?'

'You're saying you love me like you love your cat, or your sisters. That's all.'

I objected to my feelings for my sisters being brought into the conversation but didn't say so. It wasn't my place to challenge Jeremy in that way. 'That's not right; of course I don't feel the same for you as for them.'

'You don't want to hold me any more, not to feel me close to you? That's not possible for me, Matt. The love I have for you is deeper than that. You're the most important thing in my life. You have been ever since the time when I first came into the Lowe family, and you were so sweet and we were all having dinner together, and you came and put your hands up, asking me to pick you up onto my lap, and then you announced to everyone there, "I'm going to marry Jeremy." That's when you won me over, Matt. It goes back that far.'

I had no recollection of this. I was dismayed.

'You came to me, Matt. I didn't come to you. You wanted me and I was drawn in and I've been yours and only yours ever since.'

I was hearing that I was responsible, that I'd actively sought Jeremy out. His attachment to me had been my doing, and I couldn't just walk away as if I had no responsibility for the consequences.

'I don't remember that.'

'Of course you don't, but that's what happened. I've given ten years of my life to you. And I thought you had to me, but perhaps you've been deceiving me.'

'No, I haven't. I've never deceived you. I love you and you've been the most important part of my life too. But I sometimes think that we'd be even happier if we didn't do that. Sometimes it makes me feel bad.'

'But you enjoy it, you know you do. There's nothing wrong with it. Everybody does it with the person they love, don't they? It's other people who make you feel bad. If you were strong, you could ignore them. It's awful to base your life on always taking the easy way out. I've been telling you that for years and you still do it. I've put so much into you, hoping that you weren't going to turn out to be someone who just goes with the flow, always finding the lazy way. You aren't going to disappoint me, are you, Matt?'

My new house was about to be contaminated and there was nothing I could do about it. I stood with lowered head while Jeremy unbuttoned my shirt.

*

The weekends in London became increasingly frequent. More independent because I was older, I could tell my parents where I would be rather than ask their permission to go. I liked being in London where there was no chance of being recognised, no need to scan the streets for fear of seeing someone from school. In London I walked differently, with my head held high.

Tony and Jeremy were once again sharing a flat, this time in Hampstead. I looked forward to seeing Tony, but he was out when we arrived. Jeremy prepared some pasta. After dinner we were going out to the cinema. Tony arrived with four or five friends while we were eating. After the plates had been cleared, Tony and Jeremy became involved in a long conversation about work. I took out a book, and the strangers talked amongst themselves. Occasionally, one or other of them would come over and chat to me. The conversations didn't last long, as I only made monosyllabic replies to their enquiries. After some time Jeremy and I left, and when we got home the flat was empty again.

A while later, back in Shorefleet, I was called to the telephone.

'Hi there, Matt. This is Simon – you may not remember me, but I'm a friend of Jeremy and Tony. We met in London a few weeks ago. I'm staying not far from you, down on business, and I thought I'd look you up and see how you were getting on.'

'I'm fine, thank you.'

'Good. How's Jeremy?'

'He's away at the moment. He's coming back next week.'

'Oh, that's a shame. Look, Matt, I wonder if you'd like to go swimming? I could pick you up and you could show me the best pool.'

'The best pool is in Lymbridge.'

'OK, Lymbridge, then. Would you like that?'

'I'm having my breakfast now.'

'Well, I could be there in about an hour's time. How about we say ten o'clock? You're at 216 Park Road, aren't you?'

'Yes.'

'Right then, come outside and find me at ten. I'll be parked a few doors down the road.'

'Goodbye.'

'Goodbye, Matt.'

I climbed into Simon's car. I recognised him vaguely – a tall, balding man with red, shiny cheeks. He was wearing a suit and tie. We drove to Lymbridge, and I directed him to the swimming pool, past the ticket barrier and through to the changing rooms. We spent a long time in the pool. While we were resting at the side, Simon pinched my waist.

'You're going to have to get rid of a bit of this if you want the girls running after you. Being fit makes such a difference to how good you are at sex. Did you know that?'

It had never occurred to me.

'Have you got a girlfriend, Matt?'

'No', I said quickly.

We ate lunch in the cafeteria and then returned to the car for the journey home. About halfway back Simon drove the car into a lay-by. 'I've just come back from a holiday in France, Matt. I've got a small place down on the Riviera, beautiful spot. I've got some pictures that might interest you.' He reached to the back seat for a folder that he placed on my lap. I opened it. Inside was a pile of enlarged colour photographs. I recognised the type of scenery: rocky cliffs, narrow inlets like small fjords, blue water. In each photograph there were a number of boys who seemed to be around my age, some younger, some older perhaps, all naked. I politely but quickly looked through the pile. I wasn't stupid. I knew this was a test, and I knew what the man was about now. I closed the file and handed it back to Simon.

'Nice, eh? Did you like them?'

'Not really.'

'You prefer young girls, do you?'

I didn't answer.

'I need to get home.' Simon started the engine, and I was relieved that he kept the car pointing towards Shorefleet. On the way back we talked about my school life.

When I told Jeremy on the phone about going swimming with Simon, he was upset and angry.

'How could you do that?'

'We just went swimming. It was all right.' Jeremy and I were always going to the local swimming pools, especially if he was in Shorefleet on schooldays. I'd meet him near the school and we'd cycle together to the pool. It provided an opportunity for us to be alone in a cubicle afterwards.

'Have you arranged to see him again?'

'No.'

'He's a dreadful man. He's dangerous. He's ... You have to keep away from people like that.'

'He seemed OK. He's a friend of yours and Tony's. He said so.'

'He's *not* a friend of mine. And Tony doesn't really know him. They just met at this party, that's all ... ' His voice trailed away. 'Just don't do anything like that again.'

*

On a shelf of old scripts in Jeremy's London flat I found one called *Medieval Tales*, a parody of Chaucer's *Canterbury Tales* that included the same kind of bawdy sex as the original.

Actually, it was a cross between Chaucer and *The Monk*, a gothic novel that Jeremy had also lent me to read. In one scene in his script a villager, dressed as the archangel Gabriel, presented himself at a young girl's window in an attempt to seduce her. Reading the script on the sofa at Jeremy's flat, I became erect and shifted so as to grind my groin into the cushions as I read. Jeremy came in while I was reading, and I quickly moved to my side and put the script down. He had seen and, I knew, noticed my blushing face.

Another time he saw me furtively looking through his *Stern* and *Paris Match* magazines, searching for pictures of attractive women. I'd assumed that he would feel betrayed and angry if he knew that I did this, but if that was his response he didn't show it. On the contrary, the following Saturday as we lay on his bed in his mother's cottage, he reached down and brought up a new issue of *Stern* which he placed on the pillow. I sat up and watched while he looked for a particular section. There was a girl posing in an empty room. I took over, turning the page to find a picture of the same girl with an older woman. The girl's breasts were bare.

'That's her mother,' whispered Jeremy.

I turned the page again. When Jeremy's hand reached into my trousers, he found an urgent erection straining against my underpants. I moved to allow him access and then gasped as he gripped me. Over the following weeks I arrived in high expectations of a repeat. I was disappointed if there was no magazine to look at, and I was thrilled when instead of *Stern* he arrived with copies of *Penthouse* and *Mayfair*. Still in complete silence, he steered my hand to touch the pictures. At the same time he tucked his genitals between his closed legs. I understood: I was to use him as if he were a woman.

There were other changes. My occasional rebellions meant we had to talk about what we were doing and why, about things which Jeremy had never talked openly about before. He became more confident in describing our relationship, and with me no longer so obviously a child, he was clearly beginning to wonder whether there might not be some common ground between his love for me and the wider world of homosexuality. This suggested to him that we might be missing out, that our love-making might be too restricted and that we should experiment more. Now that he had a ready means of making me more actively involved in the sex, he was bolder. One evening he surprised me by taking my penis into his mouth. Quite detached, and on this occasion physically unresponsive, I watched him, aware only of how oddly uncomfortable this felt. I always found Jeremy's attempts at oral sex strange and unsatisfactory.

Through his work at a London television studio Jeremy had developed a friendship with a casting director called Bert Tisdall, a diminutive man with a slightly hunched back, white hair and a closely cropped white beard, and small, penetrating eyes. Bert was outrageously camp, extrovertly and self-consciously 'queer'. His conversation would always revert to 'bums' and 'sand-wiches', and who was 'bonking' who, and which famous people were gay, and the size of their 'dongs'. Bert walked like Larry Grayson, even talked about Larry Grayson like he was a friend.

Bert, certainly, made no distinction between his own sexu-ality and that of his new friend, except, perhaps, to think that Jeremy's taste was a little quaint. As he came to know Jeremy better, he realised as well that Jeremy was inexperienced and uptight about sex. He was astonished to find out that no pene-tration was taking place. As far as he was concerned, sex without penetration was not proper sex at all. Jeremy relayed these opinions back to me in a half-humorous way. He also began to take a greater interest in my bottom. On one occasion, handing me a new magazine, he reached for a tube of cream. I jolted at the application of this cold lubricant. I allowed myself to be arranged, never taking my gaze off the pictures in front of me. I knew it wouldn't go in. I yelled at the awful pain. Jeremy apologised and withdrew, and then repositioned me. He tried again. It hurt horribly. Then I was elsewhere, lost in some story, focusing on the smiling, inviting girl looking back at me from the page, offering herself to me. After a while Jeremy stopped. I assumed he had given up, tired and bored of attempting the impossible.

A week later we met as usual. I didn't say anything until we were walking by the sea in the dark.

'Jeremy, you know what happened last week? My bottom still hurts.'

Jeremy never tried to get inside me again.

At different times I would respond to the sexual side of our relationship in different ways. Sometimes I'd be almost absent, an onlooker rather than a participant. At others, I'd get pleasure from the physical part of the experience but feel relieved when we could get back to the things I really enjoyed, like card games or cycle rides. Then there were times when I would get so caught up in what was happening that I felt myself to be a much more active partner. I would lose my inhibitions, forget my doubts, even believe that what we were doing – now that girls were acknowledged as the source of my excitement – really proved that I was 'normal'.

*

Around this time I became interested in politics, largely due to my father's influence. My parents had both been members of the

Communist Party – they'd met at a Party social. As children we'd played with the stack of CND banners and placards stored up in the loft. Our grandmother had stood as a Communist candidate in a local election in London during the war. At school and watching TV, I was subjected to continual propaganda insisting that Communists were degraded and inhumane beings whose minds had been perverted by hatred, whose slavish devotion to Moscow proved their treason and stupidity. I only had to look at Dad to know this was nonsense. I was proud, if sometimes also anxious, when he spoke out against racism, or refused to stand for the national anthem at school events, or got involved in a passionate argument with a guest at the dinner table. There were many questions I didn't understand, and I was curious to try to work them out for myself.

When I was 14 and leaving to visit Aunt Rose in Canada, Dad gave me copies of *The Communist Manifesto* and Lenin's *The State and Revolution*. The books took on an additional aura of danger when she told me to leave them behind, when we went on a day trip across the border into the United States. In the year that followed, I began to read about Third World liberation movements and revolutionary leaders. I ploughed through biographies of Castro and Ho Chi Minh, Stalin and Lenin, and later read Isaac Deutscher's trilogy about Trotsky. I read Edgar Snow's version of Mao's Long March in *Red Star Over China*. I read about Palestine and South Africa. I read Marx's historical essays, and both the political and the fantasy works of William Morris.

I think Dad was pleased that I was taking an interest in politics. My view of the world was different from his, however. Some years before I'd watched a TV programme with my parents about Hitler and the persecution of the Jews. I had a storybook about the Blitz and had always listened attentively to my parents' stories of life in wartime Britain. I'd been interested to hear how in Dad's home the enemy was Fascism and Fascists – of any and all nationalities – while for Mum's family the enemy was Germany and the Germans. While we were on holiday in France, Mum had explained about the Maquis. I knew that the Germans under Hitler had been a danger to peace and had been brutal and murderous. But this hadn't prepared me for what I saw that night on TV. I could hardly manage the hurt and rage. I thought I knew how the programme would end, with the victory of good over bad, a return to a world of safety and love. But it ended with Hitler killing himself. That wasn't good enough.

I wanted to go back and rewrite history, to make sure that everyone got their just deserts. And I couldn't, I wasn't big enough or strong enough.

When I awoke the next morning it was to a world that was forever changed. I could see no basis for Dad's attitude that, despite the horrors of the past and present, one day, right would triumph over wrong. That suffering would one day end. I came to share many of his attitudes, to be on the same 'side', with the same heroes and villains. But my philosophy was different. For Dad, optimism about the future was a matter of faith as well as conviction. Negativity and pessimism were signs of capitulation to the forces of oppression. I wished I could understand where this certainty came from, because my reading told me differently. Good did *not* triumph. The people Dad saw as the forerunners of a future in which ideas of equality and peace would triumph across the world, I saw as brave but doomed, heroes and hero-ines in a struggle for a world that would inevitably be swamped by barbarism, spoiled by people with money and power. The bombings in Vietnam, the forced expulsions in Palestine, the coup in Chile. The bastards always won, and there was no justice in the world. The weak were weak, and always would be, and I was inevitably allied with them.

Although I envied people who had no interest in the way the world worked, I thought it important to be intellectually rigorous. My mind was not of the quicksilver type that Jeremy had. I needed to work hard to think things through. And in this I believed I was like Dad who, in a somewhat embarrassed and indirect aside, had once warned me not to take Jeremy's political views too seriously. But he needn't have worried. I'd begun my own critique of the thoughts of Jeremy Rushton, and I found them inconsistent, liable to sudden and unexplained reversals, and guilty of ignorance or of wilful disregard of the evidence. I was establishing a degree of intellectual autonomy from my erstwhile mentor.

Jeremy had always been scornful of any serious engagement with politics, but in response to my interest he began to paint himself not just as a rebel, more as part of the struggle of the world's poor against oppression. Not surprisingly, he was attracted to some historical figures more than others. Che entered his world alongside Byron. However, he would have loved Che more if, like Byron, it had been rumoured that he'd slept with his sister.

To my mind Jeremy's arguments lacked coherence and substance. He seemed worried by my application of logic to a degree that would justify violence. For my part, I couldn't see any government or system that didn't operate according to this principle, and felt it was irrelevant and hypocritical only to hold left-wing views to such an unrealistic test.

Despite his romantic flirtation with rebels and revolt, Jeremy was nostalgically attached to the aristocratic ideal. In this, Byron was his hero. He was disgusted by the idea of 'the people' in anything but the most abstract sense. He felt that civilisation, literature and the arts – beauty itself – were dependent on an elite (though he would be scathingly condescending about any particular member of the aristocracy who chanced across his path). Against this, I'd developed a loathing of inequality, particularly the inequality of power.

I had a loathing too of the idea of the supernatural. I couldn't understand how anyone could contemplate life while also considering the existence of an omnipotent, omniscient God. To me, Satan was absolutely right to have rebelled: what a disgusting place in which to have found oneself, servile to some perfect potentate! The idea of a God brought on a physical sensation akin to suffocation. I felt oppressed in my very being and enraged at anyone who seemed willing to concede so much of their humanity to some ludicrous product of their own imagination. The very notion of existing in a state of such extreme inequality gave me the sense of being intruded upon. I ranted against religion at school, much to the delight of the religious education teacher, Mr Oldham, who was also the school counsellor. We became friends. Still, I was irritated by his evasive arguments when it came to the meaning of the word 'soul'. It was always the same: there was always a point in a confrontation with a believer when logical argument was openly dismissed in favour of some notion of faith, as if credulity were a point in their favour.

None of this scepticism and curiosity was applied to thinking about myself. I didn't reflect on my own life. The states of mind that I struggled with were real enough, but I didn't try to categorise them, to name them. The positive ones were easier to describe: exciting, exhilarating, mind-blowing, fascinating. These words were forever on my lips. But the cold mists that enveloped me remained nameless, formless, a mere backdrop, meaningless except as an indication of my own lack of worth.

I had words only for behaviour. Like bed-wetting, something that still occurred from time to time, to my horrible shame. And nail-biting. I knew that I'd also developed other strange habits. I went through a long period when I said 'What?' in response to everything that was said to me, forcing the other person to repeat what they'd said. The second time round I would 'hear'. Everyone had a go at me about this: Dad eventually lost his temper and shouted at me, and Jeremy accused me of doing it on purpose as a way of keeping myself hidden. Obsessively, and involuntarily, I played word games in my head and counting games on my fingers.

While I began to assert my own opinions when interpreting the world I could study or read about, in anything that implied questions of taste I had no confidence at all. I could trust my intellect but not my emotions. So I relied on Jeremy to understand how I should respond to films or books, because his views were always vivid and convincing while mine were shallow and contradictory. He was as single-minded as I was muddled. It seemed unwise to commit myself to anything until I had heard Jeremy's reaction. And having heard it, there wasn't much point in considering any tentative ideas that had occurred to me. It seemed obvious that he experienced everything more profoundly, with more originality and clarity, than anyone else I had ever met.

*

My aunty Rose and her husband Will had emigrated to Canada when we were small children. Peter and Ella had each spent a summer over in Toronto, and now it was my turn. Jeremy was against me going, arguing that there was nothing of cultural value in North America and worrying how six weeks there would change me. In any case he needed me to star in his film, which was due to be made in Cyprus that year. In the event, the invasion by Turkey delayed my departure, and although I went there for a month, I had to be replaced in the lead role. Jeremy had rented a house in Paphos. He 'discovered' Mikis, the strikingly beautiful eight-year-old who took over, playing football in the street outside. Mikis's father had died; he lived with his mother and grandmother just across the road.

So I was 14 when I finally flew to Toronto. I stepped out of the plane into a wall of humidity. Uncle Will met me, and we drove along a multi-track highway back into the city, then out to the suburbs where he and Rose lived. I had four cousins, the oldest five years younger than me. Rose had made the decision that I was best treated as one of the adults. This irritated her older sons, but it gave me an opportunity to find out just how mature I could be, managing on my own in a new and unfamiliar environment. Canada, for me, meant a world untouched by Jeremy. I looked forward to this more than any other aspect of the holiday. For five weeks his name wasn't mentioned.

The children took me along with them to play with their neighbours' families. Up the street there was a boy called Trevor who had a 14-year-old sister called Heather. She was taller than I was, with straight blonde hair and a strong North American drawl. For a few days we all went around together, but then Heather suggested that she and I go out for a walk alone. She took me along the banks of a river through a local park, and then we returned to her house to swim in the pool in the garden. This became our routine. We didn't touch one another, even to hold hands, and we never kissed, but I'd feel a warm glow as we stood close. I looked over the smooth skin of her back as she sunbathed. And I talked to her. It was bliss.

I was taken on holiday to a lake, a hundred miles north of Ottawa. We drove with a family friend, Julie, who took her own car. I drove some of the way with her, trying not to look too obviously at her breasts as they pushed, bra-less, against her T-shirt. She was very sexy. But when she offered to take me back with her on a longer visit to Ottawa, I chose to stay at the cottage by the lake. Its remote beauty outweighed even the prospect of enjoying more of her company. So I rowed and fished, and cooked over a campfire with Rose and Will and the rest of the family, until it was time to return to Toronto, and Heather.

Towards the end of the holiday, Rose asked about the arrangements for getting home from Gatwick. 'Will you be picked up at the airport?'

'Yeah, all that's arranged. A friend is meeting me.'

'Jeremy, I suppose?'

I tried not to blush. 'Yeah.'

I was dismayed that she knew about Jeremy. Although of course she would, as she and my mother continued a correspondence so voluminous and detailed that no one else in either family had the stamina to get through the letters that crossed the Atlantic each month. There was nothing in Rose's voice to convey suspicion or ridicule, nothing suggesting that she'd know what the very mention of his name did to me. I hadn't heard it for so long, and it was awful to contemplate returning to that unchanged world. Except, I was sure, I wouldn't let it be the same. I'd been treated as an adult in Canada: my opinion had been asked, my preferences taken into account. I'd managed well, had found new friends, had even talked to a girl. I didn't need Jeremy any more.

*

The plane touched down at Gatwick. I looked across at the terminal, knowing that behind the glass, amongst the crowds, he'd be there. I wished he wasn't. I wished he didn't exist. When he came forward, smiling with arms open, I let myself be hugged, more aware than ever of the unpalatable smell of his body and breath. He'd had to get up really early to be there on time.

'It's great to see you again! Did you sleep on the plane? Do you feel like some breakfast? Let's go and find a café and you can tell me all about your adventures.'

As we sat drinking tea I realised that I had very little to say that would interest Jeremy. No mention was made of Heather or Julie. Just something about those aspects consistent with the me that he wanted to contemplate: the campfires, the swimming, the books I'd read.

I felt tired. 'What time is the train downtown?'

'Downtown? Do you mean back to London? You've picked up that horrible Canadian accent, you know. In just a few weeks. It's very pronounced. I hope you'll get that out of your system soon.'

The train back to Shorefleet felt stuffy. The atmosphere was tense. I was trying to keep hold of the person I'd found within myself while in Canada, and Jeremy was becoming increasingly critical, picking up on any signs of change and complaining about them. Soon after leaving Norwich, two girls had walked down the corridor laughing and talking loudly. They'd caught my attention, and I was pleased when they turned round and opened the door to our compartment.

'There's room in here,' one called to the other.

'No, actually, there isn't,' Jeremy said. I hated him. Here was a chance simply to be in the same space as girls, and he was determined to prevent it.

'Yes, there is. Plenty of room,' one girl said.

'We don't want you in here. We're talking. Isn't there room somewhere else?'

I wanted to contradict him. It was awful that the girl should think I supported Jeremy in this.

'You're a rude bastard, you are. It's not your bloody train.'

'Yes, I am, and yes, it is. Just go away, will you.' Jeremy was really cross. The girls left.

He then tried to kiss me. I turned my head away.

'I thought this is what would happen. You're not yourself, you know that, don't you? You've become like some hard North American youth. It's so ugly. Where is that sensitive and open boy who left six weeks ago?'

'I don't like being like him. I prefer being like this.'

'Well, you can be like that if you wish. I'll wave to you as I pass you outside Giovanni's, along with the rest of your exciting new friends, and you can pretend not to know me, but inside you'll know you've made the wrong decision, won't you? That isn't the real you, is it, Matt? We both know that. So we'll have to go through this boring period while you lock yourself up in some kind of hard skin, before you feel it's OK to be yourself again. That's it, isn't it?'

'Just stop trying to touch me. I don't want that any more. I'm not like that.'

'Oh really?'

'Do you think I fancy you? I mean, do you?' This rocked Jeremy, who wasn't sure how to answer.

'Matt, that's not the point. Of course the nature of the feelings we have for one another is going to be different. I love you differently from the way you love me. Our feelings are all that's important. Things will change one day' – I took careful note of that – 'but it's not time yet.'

'I want it to change now. Why do we have to wait?'

'Because nothing changes overnight. Remember how good things were between us before you went to Canada. Look, I know it's hard, not being the same as other people, but we can't deny our true selves just to fit in. That's a kind of murder or suicide, not to be yourself.'

'I'm happier like this, being myself. It's been great all summer and I don't want to start it again. Please, just don't ask me.'

This time the rebellion lasted a fortnight and was only broken after a succession of painful rows and floods of tears.

~ 12 ~

While working at the Rosalyn Centre I continued to try different ways of sorting myself out. One momentous decision was to join a therapy group. It met for 90 minutes each Tuesday evening in north London. Brian, the group facilitator, was a thick-set, shaven-headed man dressed in a track suit – I thought he looked like a rugby player. He sat through the meetings largely in silence, a fixed and serious expression on his face, generally avoiding eye contact with any of the group's members. At times he said things that seemed cruel, that certainly upset and disturbed some of the more vocal participants – particularly those who continuously picked on him and his manner as the reason for the group's lack of progress. I said little for the first couple of months. There was a lady whose teenage son had been killed in a road accident: it hurt to look at her, to think of Jack and how she was going through, literally, my worst nightmare. Another woman had lost a baby. There was a man who said he wasn't there because he needed help, just because he wondered what it would be like, which seemed to rub everyone up the wrong way. There was a priest called Derek, notable for his full, prematurely white beard. Like me, some of the others were silent. I noticed how difficult it was for the group to stay with the awful feelings that emerged when people revealed their losses.

It surprised me to find that the group generated such powerful feelings. I was ashamed to realise that in the beginning I had

regarded the members with contempt, as slow, shallow and selfish. I knew that the facilitator expected the participants to
re-encounter some of the feelings that had arisen in their early
lives. This seemed absurd to me – I couldn't imagine becoming
attached to this rather sorry group of individuals. Gradually,
however, I learned to challenge my assumptions; I realised this
with a shock during a holiday break. I hadn't expected to miss
our weekly gatherings, but found I could think of little else. By
the time we reconvened, I had many times over rehearsed making
my first personal disclosure to the group.

Heart pounding, I waited for a moment when no one else
seemed to want to say anything. 'There's something I've got to
talk about. I've thought about the way I've been here, and I
think I've made sense of something. Talking about it seems
important, because telling you will, in itself, be changing something. I know that's confusing.' I paused, worried that my
thoughts would become jumbled or my mind go blank. 'I didn't
think much of the group to begin with. To be honest, I felt rather
superior.' I hesitated, not sure if the other members would
understand the link I was going to make. 'A lot of the time I
didn't really feel a part of my family when I was a child. There
were secrets. A lot of shame. A lot of things that kept me separate from my brother and sisters, and my parents. It's really
strange, but I've been keeping secrets from the group here, and
it's because I'm ashamed. Things to do with my son. Since we've
been meeting I've applied for a few jobs and been rejected, and
I was ashamed about that too. But when I got a job I really
wanted badly, I couldn't tell you because I was afraid you'd be
envious and spoil it.'

'So you've decided we're not so bad after all?' asked the
woman whose son had died.

I grinned with embarrassment.

'I understand that,' added one of the men. 'I'm glad you've said that, because I don't really trust the group at all, and I'm not sure why. Of course, things don't always go as well as they might, but we're only human.'

Another member spoke. 'It's awful the way secrets isolate you. I once had a drinking problem. I don't have it now, and it's not something I'm ashamed of the group knowing about, but at the time it was a terrible secret. Horrible. I couldn't look anyone in the eye. It made me feel awful about myself: I think it drove me to drink all the more.'

I left that evening feeling elated. The facilitator and the group as a whole seemed to understand that I'd been struggling with something significant. Testing their acceptance was only paving the way to a further revelation, however.

Two weeks later, shaking with a sense of terrible danger, I told them my 'big secret'.

'What I think lies behind my rejection of the group is a fear that, if you know me, you'd want to get rid of me. And the thing that seems to cut me off from you has been going round and round in my head all week.'

The group was focused and attentive.

'There was a man. I always used to describe him as a family friend. And he would take us out, me and my brother and sisters. And then I was somehow singled out, and I went around with him on my own.' I stopped. And then forced myself forward. 'It was ... he ... the relationship was an abusive one. He touched me.' I felt I was failing. It seemed impossible to be clear, explicit, direct. The shame bore down on me.

There followed a long pause. To me, staring at the floor, it seemed to go on for ever. Then: 'I'm so sorry.'

I looked up and found a saddened but open face looking back at me. Glancing round I took in faces showing concern, shock and outrage. Concern for me, outrage at what had happened to me. Several other group members spoke, all of them with a mixture of warmth and awkwardness. I didn't mind the awkwardness at all; I didn't even mind it when two members of the group started offering me advice. I just felt enormously relieved. I was going to be all right.

Then Derek, the priest, spoke. He had made it clear in previous meetings that he was gay. He had talked of his mixed feelings about women, which the group had found something of a struggle. There was something intimidating about him: the muscles in his face were set in a frown, and his voice was too loud for the room. 'I imagine, then, that you must hate me.' The comment was directed at me, but I found it hard to understand what had been said.

'What? Hate you?' Then it clicked. 'Because you're gay? You think I don't know the difference?'

'Your experience must make you feel emasculated in front of these women.'

It took moments again before I made any sense of what was happening, and this time I couldn't think of a reply. Other members of the group seemed embarrassed too.

'There seems to be some confusion here about whose pain the group can attend to.' This was the facilitator speaking. Everyone turned to look at him, but he didn't say anything else.

But Derek had more to say. 'I think it's a pity that one hears only one side of the story when it comes to this topic.'

A woman reacted quickly. 'Which side would you like to hear more about, then?'

'What I mean is that we hear these sob stories and everyone

reacts in the same way, as if we all know what there is to know about the subject. And I suspect it's a great deal more complicated than we think.'

'Go on. I think we've got to hear what you mean,' said the man who'd had the drinking problem.

'I'm not saying I know much about it. But last year I went to a conference on paedophilia. One of the speakers came from the Paedophile Information Exchange. He presented a different view, that sexual relationships with children may not always be coercive, or harmful. That some of the children involved initiate the relationships and appreciate the pleasure they gain from them.'

There he stopped. I was listening intently, churned up but unable to put a name – much less a voice – to what I was thinking. The man who'd spoken before wanted to know more. 'What did this guy say? Sounds like he convinced you.'

Afraid that somehow the group might stall in this now very muddy water, I found myself angrily asking, 'What do you mean? Tell me what you mean!'

'I don't have to say more than I have. I don't think this group is showing itself to be tolerant of unconventional opinions, and I'm not going to stick my neck out to have it chopped off.'

Time was moving fast. Others in the room expressed their dismay at the turn the meeting had taken, but, right on time, the facilitator ended the discussion.

It was only when I left the building and stepped out into the warm evening air that I realised how my body was struggling to manage the bewildering currents surging through it. I woke at three in the morning with a terrible stomach cramp that took an age to ease, with the help of a hot drink and Carmen's insistence that I go over and over what had happened in the group.

Over the following week I imagined subjecting Derek to a devastating attack. When we faced one another again, I was restrained, but I was now able to describe very clearly my feelings about the previous meeting, and about his intervention. It was soon clear that other members of the group had endured almost as disturbed a week as I had. They supported me, not in attacking Derek but in trying to get him to think about the timing of his contribution, the impact it might have had coming so soon after I'd struggled to disclose my own abuse.

Quickly, my anger turned to contempt. I couldn't remember ever being able to express such powerfully negative emotions towards anybody. I felt guilty, sure that I ought to be reprimanded and controlled, and I worried about Derek's capacity to retaliate. But the group's support remained solid. I realised that I was very lucky to have Derek there. Here was somebody who was determined to stand in as substitute abuser (for reasons he showed no interest in understanding). He remained stubbornly embattled, portrayed himself as the group's scapegoat, and provoked further and increasingly enraged reactions. He eventually apologised for the timing of his comments, which he conceded might have been insensitive, but insisted that they had been 'necessary'. He spoke of himself as being abused by me, of being a dissident and a martyr persecuted by a vicious and sadistic group. In the last session before the Christmas break, he announced that if I was going to be allowed to abuse him any more he was going to leave. Another group member called this blackmail, and Derek picked up his coat and walked out.

As far as I was concerned, the meaning of what had occurred was entirely the other way around. It was as if I'd told the group while the abuse was going on, and they had protected me, even driven the abuser from their ranks.

~ 13 ~

As a teenager I was in no condition to face life without Jeremy's love and encouragement. At the same time, being part of his world meant facing all the changes involved on my own, without the support that comes from being part of a group. I was alone, and had to work hard to remain alone, while feeling deeply envious of and inferior to those who moved more easily amongst their peers. I'd walk through Shorefleet enveloped in shame, hunched over, staring at the pavement, my girlish hair shaken down to obscure my face. So I was lucky to be able to escape for frequent weekends in London. There I didn't stammer and blush, as I did when I climbed onto the school bus under the scornful gaze of a score or so local schoolgirls. In London I not only walked with my spine straight, but, now anonymous, I revelled in attracting attention, dressing up in Jeremy's expensive clothes, delighting in a sense of freedom and allure. I was taken into a larger intermediate world: we went to see Lindsay Kemp's ballets at the Roundhouse in Camden Town, and *The Rocky Horror Show* at a theatre in the King's Road. Jeremy would talk to me about famous people who had lived like we did – composers, Russian novelists, pop stars. Bert took us to a gay club, which felt wild to me. I danced with abandon, knowing that there were dozens of eyes on me. I caught them looking, and they might smile or wink, or they'd share a knowing glance with Jeremy as if to congratulate him on his luck. This – and Bert's drooling over me whenever we met – was an antidote to the knowledge that, in Jeremy's eyes, I was becoming less and less beautiful all the time. I came to take in both positions: that I was increasingly disgusting to look at but also unbelievably gorgeous, to men at least. If I felt bad back home, my London experience suggested that it wasn't because there was something wrong with me but a result of the burdens imposed by convention and bourgeois morality.

Jeremy read me Shakespeare's sonnets. He encouraged me to read Gide's *The Immoralist*, Nabokov's *Lolita*, Plato's *Symposium* and Thomas Mann's *Death in Venice*, amongst others dealing with similar themes. All this sharpened my appreciation of what the relationship between an older man and a younger boy was supposed to be about. The older man – the Lover – was a bene-factor, a person who undertook the betterment of his charge. He had everything to offer in the way of learning, culture and virtue. He was the means by which the boy – the Beloved, or Friend – might himself achieve status and nobility.

The Beloved had at this point little to recommend him beyond his Beauty, though this was a fading asset. This was indeed the theme of the first dozen or so of Shakespeare's sonnets, where the Friend's two choices were to give birth to more beauty as muse to the poet or, as an inferior option, as father to children beautiful like himself. This held out a rather desperate view of my own future prospects, but in the present it fuelled my vanity no end. The Beloved had a choice: to benefit from the attentions of the Lover and be educated in the ways of the Elect, or to reject this opportunity in preference for the vulgar pleasures of the common herd. The latter would include spending time with his classmates or succumbing to the seductions of women. Feminine beauty was deemed inferior, cloying and limiting rather than ennobling, used to beguile and spoil. It was a symptom of my lack of worthiness that I should be so persistently distracted by sexual desires of my own. Another curious feature of this literature was that only the Lover was at risk – from the cruelty and indifference of the Beloved – while there were no apparent danger to the Beloved at all.

I noted too that these books seldom talked about what the Lover would do with the bodies of the beautiful boys they educated. I knew this through personal experience, of course. Works of literary art, often written by aesthetes, evaded the point, substituting a tragic lack of fulfilment for pornographic indulgence. It would hardly do to read of Aschenbach pressing his tobacco-reeking breath and prickly moustached face onto the soft mouth of Tadzio. While profoundly grateful for all the help I was receiving, I challenged Jeremy on the obvious weakness of these models. Why should the investment of the adult be paid for by the sexual services of the child? Jeremy evaded the issue too. It was simply the way things were, the basis of a particular kind of exchange which was never described as such.

So while Jeremy tried to present this other world as perfectly acceptable, actually more advanced than that occupied by ordinary people, the role assigned to me within it did nothing for my self-esteem. Rather it confirmed me in the role of inspiration and audience to the real genius. I was his pretty plaything. Acting the sexual rebel provided only limited scope for celebrating myself, and it was never sufficient to stop me aching to reconnect with the world that Jeremy despised. All of this resulted in regular confrontations during which I'd demand that we should stop touching one another, even stop spending so much time together. Although the outcome of my mutinies was always the same, defeat didn't prevent seditious thoughts from finding a permanent home in my mind.

While I needed to think about how to categorise our relationship, Jeremy was happy with the notion that it was unique. He was a romantic. When he described parallels in ancient Greece, he wasn't justifying himself but placing our relationship in a suitably glorious setting.

'I'm going to write about us, Matt.'

'Write what?'

'The whole story. A book about our love for one another. About the family I met on the beach in Shorefleet. About your mother, the most attractive woman in the town, about how I was accepted into the family and about how we found one another. I'm going to write it as it was, to show that this has been the most special experience imaginable, something that will make them all envious. I'm going to bring out all the tenderness and wonder of you as the little boy who chose me as your love. You'll see.'

His sincerity at such moments boosted my ego. So I developed two parallel but mutually incompatible outlooks, elaborations of the two worlds I inhabited.

*

I was flattered when Jeremy, one time we were down in London together, wanted to take erotic photographs of me. It was early evening, and we had finished a bottle of wine between us. Jeremy wouldn't be photographed: he was the artist who would dress, undress and pose his model. He arranged the furniture in his large bedroom and set up foil-covered boards to reflect the light properly. He'd bought himself a Polaroid camera. He draped my body in various ways, arranged my limbs and adjusted the position of my head. I lolled and flopped in voluptuous poses, pouting and lowering my eyes. I was told to touch myself. I revelled in the sensuousness of the lighting and the attention to my body. I gloried in the role of the girls in the magazines that I liked to look at. I enjoyed being so wantonly sexual.

Looking at the pictures later that evening, Jeremy declared that they were all ugly and vulgar. It was true that the reds were too red, the skin colours too pale. They were horribly crude. He seemed quite put out by the whole episode and I felt thoroughly deflated. I felt like saying, 'You should have taken them years ago, when I was still attractive.' But the words stuck in my throat.

Further anxieties arose about my looks when a light covering of brown hairs appeared on my upper lip. I had been obsessively monitoring facial blemishes for a while. A single spot would, I was sure, be the first thing any passer-by would notice about me. There were boys at school with severe acne, a state that the rest both laughed about and dreaded. I shook lots of pepper onto my food in the belief, which I kept to myself, that it must dry out the skin from the inside, and so lessen the chances of a serious affliction.

Now I needed to shave. But I couldn't walk into a shop and buy a razor: that would mean revealing pretensions of masculinity to a shop assistant. So instead I went to the beach and found some flints to smash together. I selected the fragments with the sharpest edges and took them home, only to find that while they were sharp enough to cut a finger they were ineffectual for the purpose of shaving. I found an old safety razor of my mother's in the bathroom and used that instead. Later on, when I asked Jeremy what to do, he bought me a wet razor and shaving foam.

*

Immediately after returning from the filming trip we took to Cyprus, Jeremy and Tony fell out. Tony had, apparently, accused Jeremy of brainwashing him, of suffocating his creativity, dominating his life, destroying his individuality. From the way Jeremy described it to me, he made it sound as if Tony had gone off the rails.

I was very sorry that this rift had occurred. I liked Tony. The atmosphere when the three of us were together was so much lighter. After many months during which the two men didn't speak, contact was made through mutual friends, and it was arranged that Jeremy and I would go to eat at Tony's new flat in Haringey.

I pressed the doorbell enthusiastically. Jeremy was uncharacteristically tense. It took a long time before the door was opened.

'Hello.' Tony spoke in a strangely detached voice, but he had often pretended to be unfriendly and I took it as a joke. We were led through the hall and into a large, open sitting room, at the top of which was a table laid for dinner.

'I'm still preparing the food. Help yourselves to some drink. I'll be back.' Tony disappeared.

'He's drunk', Jeremy whispered after he'd left.

'No, I don't think so.'

'I'm telling you he's drunk.' Jeremy poured two glasses of red wine and passed one to me.

I set about to explore the room, leafing through some large books of photographs. The walls were decorated with stunning photographs. There were landscapes – Moroccan deserts and castles, Sri Lankan jungles and beaches – and character studies of people from these and other Third World countries.

Tony called us to the table and asked how I was getting on at school.

To me this sounded fake. Tony was not one for small talk. I answered but realised that I'd guessed right and that he wasn't really interested. It seemed as if Jeremy and Tony had changed completely, from people who once knew one another's thoughts before they were spoken to strangers, or even enemies, who now couldn't discuss anything for fear of stirring up hurt and recrimination.

'When are you next jetting off to taste the pleasures of the Indian Ocean?' asked Jeremy. I'd heard that Tony was support-ing a school in a Sri Lankan village.

'Oh, never, probably. It's all gone sour there. Not safe now.' After a pause: 'And you, are you going to make the long-prom-ised visit to Morocco?'

'Maybe. I wanna do the Lawrence of Arabia bit, strutting round the sand dunes in my white robes!'

'Mmm.' There was an extended pause.

'Harry sends his love.' Harry was a film editor they'd both worked with frequently over the years. He was often the butt of their jokes.

'What's the old queen up to now? Last I heard he'd bought a wig, and a leather jacket to put over his paunch.'

'Yeah, something like that. He's discovered the scene in middle age and is finally letting his hair down. His poor old mum must be having kittens.'

'I'm sure he reverts to boring, balding Harry before he gets home.'

'You seen Bert at all?' I knew who they were talking about now, the camp man Jeremy and I sometimes met for lunch at the TV studio.

'I glimpsed him the other day, mincing across Waterloo Bridge with that young friend of his.'

'He's still seeing Simon, is he? Surprised that's lasted this long.'

I stayed silent and continued to drink my wine. The forced conversation simply emphasised the absence of the old spirit of trust and comradeship. They stopped talking too, concentrating on their food and drink.

'So it's true, then,' Tony had turned abruptly and was addressing me, 'that you have no personality at all?'

I hadn't been pushed or punched, but I might as well have been. Given the choice, I would have preferred a physical attack. I scrambled to find a way to understand what was happening, something that would enable me to carry on as if nothing in particular had taken place. The agony was not that Tony had such a low opinion of me; it was that anyone should speak the truth so frankly. For, of course, Tony was quite right. I'd never pretended to have a personality, so no one could accuse me of showing off. It was because I was a nobody that I felt so grateful to Jeremy and Tony for taking an interest in me. It was brutal, to speak the truth so undisguised, but perhaps it suggested a kind of intimacy as well? Jeremy didn't seem to think that Tony had said anything out of the ordinary, as the two had moved on to comparing notes about some film they'd both seen. I just sat there and listened. And wished there was some reason why Tony should like me.

*

Keeping Jeremy secret was becoming increasingly difficult, and the fear of exposure had become a constant companion. There were words that I couldn't hear without blushing. If I was in a car, for example, passing a row of cypress trees, I'd think of Cyprus, which meant Jeremy and me being away on our own, and I would assume that other people's minds would be making the same connections. So my heart rate would go up and I'd search to divert the conversation in some safe direction. The same was true of gypsies, or acting, or Latin, or Rome, or the theatre, or cycling, or a whole list of books and films, or sex or girls or love, or an endless number of other areas and anything that suggested them.

Avoidance became an art. It required a studied vagueness, a skill in changing the subject of a conversation or wilfully misunderstanding what was being said. It might require remaining in my bedroom for an hour to make sure that a visitor had left before I showed myself. It included the ability to disguise the truth, to allow an adult or a peer to remain with a completely false impression, but one that was safer than a true one would have been. I came to hate surprises. School holidays were a terrible nuisance, birthdays horrible. As far as possible I needed to run my life on a schedule that kept every part of it contained and in its place. Clashes of timetable and, worst of all, conflicting expectations could not occur.

I worked hard to control my world. It disturbed me to find my body insisting on having a life of its own. From time to time my stomach muscles would go into spasm, causing excruciating pain that lasted just an hour or two. The doctor suggested that I was overeating. Which was undeniable. During the first year sixth, my face, head and back periodically flared up with a fiery rash. The first time was during an English lesson. I yelled out, leapt over my desk and rushed out the door and down two flights of stairs to the toilets, where I dunked my head in cold water. The pain soon passed. It was unclear what had prompted this episode, but soon a pattern established itself. The rashes came on whenever I became embarrassed. It happened one time when a girl unexpectedly walked into the classroom during break, and another time when Mum and Joanna were in my room talking about Bayview Road, and Joanna started reminiscing about my Roman museum. This time the doctor described the mechanism – blood vessels that dilated but then got stuck and wouldn't return to their normal state – but he had no suggestions as to their cause. He imagined that it was connected with adolescence and hormonal changes, and would soon cease.

My own impulses and desires I kept hidden. Most evenings I'd slip out of the house and head down towards the coast, preferring it when it was dark. On winter nights I'd brace myself against the wind and spray, and make my way along under the cliffs, envying any couples I saw there and fantasising that every female I spied might initiate a conversation. We could go for a coffee together. But in fact it was easier if there was no one, just the sea, the sky and the cliffs.

*

Jeremy's work commitments changed in a most fortuitous way. He became sound editor on, of all things, a religious programme that went out on Sunday at midday. As a freelance he earned a lot of money, but the job meant working on Thursday, Friday and from Saturday all night until transmission time. He would arrive back in Shorefleet, mid-afternoon on Sunday, and would then need several hours of sleep. So we'd meet on Sunday evenings, and after school on Monday, Tuesday and Wednesday. This left me a lonesome teenager on the nights that mattered, Friday and Saturday, when I could press myself with particular effect against the sharp edge of my isolation.

Friends at school had begun going out, heading for the two nightclubs in the next town that specialised in under-age drinkers. Around the time of my 16th birthday I extended my coastal walks to spend some time with them, usually at the Quayside Inn. Steeling my nerves, I'd walk in through the masses of excited and chattering teenagers until I located my school friends Terry Price and Stephen Andrews.

'Hello, Matt! You finally got here.'

'Umm.'

'Can I get you a drink?'

'I'll have a tonic water.'

'Don't be a prat. Do you think I'm going to the bar to order a tonic water? He'll think I'm a complete wanker. What do you really want?'

'I want a tonic water. I don't like that other stuff.' I was referring with a condescending sneer to beer in all its forms.

'Well, you can go and get your own. No way am I going to buy a bloody tonic water.'

So I'd go up to the bar. It would take some time before I could get served, and then I'd rejoin Terry and Stephen while I eeked out my glass, watching the people around us and wondering how you came to be one of them. In particular, how did you come to be one of those boys with an arm around a girl, looking relaxed, chatting as if it was nothing out of the ordinary? I stared when, from time to time, such couples would seal themselves off from what was going on around them, entwine their bodies and kiss. Once I'd had my drink I'd announce that I was going to leave. It helped to remain unpredictable and eccentric, even in this. Terry would try to persuade me to stay – he himself was always clearly having a great time – but I'd leave, and walk around the coast back to Shorefleet.

I remained painfully shy. So how to meet a girl? Could a girl like me? These were the important questions, and, incarcerated in my invisible dungeon, it was difficult to see how they would ever be answered. Until, one day, Terry showed me the way. He helped draw me out, despite the fact that for years I had in my quiet but determined way discouraged any extension of our relationship beyond the school gates.

It was a Wednesday lunchtime, and Terry and I were sitting

on our desks, leaning out the classroom window. Being on the top floor, it overlooked Sidney Street and offered the opportunity to watch any girls from the local girls' school, and older women too, who happened to be passing by.

'There's a party on Friday night. Do you want to come?'

I was worried. How could I get out of this? Yet I was also intrigued. 'No, I don't think so. I'm not really the party sort.'

'What do you mean, you've never been to a party. Come on. There's nothing to it. Stephanie and Jane will be there, and the Shipton sisters. And their cousin Melanie might go: God, you've gotta see Melanie. She's only fifteen, but she's incredible.'

I was not indifferent to the opportunity to meet girls, but I was anxious. 'Sounds great. But I wouldn't know what to wear. Where is it, anyway?'

'It's in the church hall at St James's. There's no need to worry about clothes; just put on something smart. Leave that coat behind, though, makes you look like a tramp.'

'Are you sure? I think I'll look a fool.'

'No, you won't. It's just because it's the first time. There's nothing to it. Come round to my place first, and we'll walk over from there.'

'OK, if you say so.'

'You'd better be there. I might not invite you again.'

Jeremy was away in Cyprus, and I was glad to have a couple of months entirely on my own before August, when we'd arranged to work together in London editing his latest film, and then go on holiday together. I spent the remaining days of that week wondering what I would wear, worrying about making a complete ass of myself and demanding reassurance from an increasingly irritated Terry. Terry was a different species of adolescent – cocky, constantly cracking jokes –

though if you listened carefully, you'd notice that he himself was the butt of most of them – and vain. He was short, but his height mattered less to other people than it did to him. He would constantly draw attention to it, and to his crisp, unruly hair, his other obsession. Terry was an only child of parents who barely talked to one another. They barked instead. His mother organised coffee mornings for Conservative ladies and smoked in secret. When she heard her husband arrive home from work, she'd rush about trying to get rid of the smell. She was called Gillian, and she was 'Gillian' to Terry too. But Terry had, I came to realise, exploited her social connections and was on dropping-in terms with a number of families with attractive teenage daughters.

The evening of the party arrived. I was terrified. We walked in, me hunched over as if trying to bring my shoulders together in front of my face, hands stuffed in my pockets, sweating. I'd been told to bring a bottle and I'd chosen some cans of lager, but unsure if they were the right sort I tried to hide them as we passed through the crowd. I copied Terry in pouring myself a drink, this time a lemonade.

'God, you're weird. Come with me.'

I followed Terry into a large, half-lit room. Everyone was talking loudly, and there were occasional peels of shared laughter. Now and then a couple or a group would join another group or go outside. Everyone else was comfortable. For me this was heaven and hell combined. I wouldn't have left for the world, but I would've paid dearly to be made invisible.

'You see that girl there, in the doorway? That's Christine Morgan. She's going out with Peter Gibson, lucky sod. She's bloody gorgeous.'

We had talked about Christine before. Terry had pointed her

out one day in Sidney Street, and soon after had shown me where she lived, about 200 yards from my house in Park Road. This was the first time I'd seen her out of school uniform, and I was suitably impressed. She was beautiful. What you noticed first was her hair – thick, straight, deeply blonde, cut short. And then her slender figure, and her face. She was laughing, holding one hand up to her mouth. Small, pert nose, thick lips around a small mouth. Smiling eyes above rosy, rounded cheeks. For the rest of the evening I watched out for her and glanced in her direction whenever she passed close by. She didn't notice me.

A girl placed herself directly in front of me and was looking at me even while talking to Terry.

'How you doing, Terry?'

'Fine. It's too hot in here, though, isn't it?'

'Aren't you going to introduce your friend?' She looked at me. 'I don't remember seeing you before.'

'So sorry.' Terry gave an exaggerated apology. 'Catherine, this is Matt.'

I remained silent. Terry nudged me when I didn't reply.

'Hello,' I managed.

'He's shy, isn't he? What's your name again?'

'Matt Lowe.'

'You're not Peter Lowe's brother, are you? Oh my God, you are, I can see it now. I like Peter, I've known him a long time. He never said he had such an attractive brother.'

My blushes deepened by a factor of ten.

'So, what do you get up to? I don't see you down the bookshop.'

'I help out occasionally. It's not really my scene, though.'

Then Terry chipped in. 'I've just seen Stephen. Excuse

me, will you?' Terry walked away, grinning from ear to ear; my panic rose.

Catherine came to the rescue. 'I live down in Bridge Street, opposite the park. My parents have got a bed-and-breakfast place.'

'Oh, right.' Then: 'Which school do you go to?'

'Rutherford House. What about you?'

'Greendale.'

'Do you? Do you know Gregory Brown? I went out with him for a couple of months last year. Not my type, though.'

'Yeah, yeah.' Then silence.

'I think I need another drink. And it looks as if you do too. Let's go and get one.'

There was relief from the pressure to talk while we pushed through to the drinks table. But it rose again once we returned to the main room. The music was louder now, and about a dozen people were dancing in the middle.

'Do you wanna dance?'

'No.'

'Why not? It's fun. You're too shy, I can see that. Come on.'

'No, really, I can't. Sorry. You dance.'

'No, it's OK. I'd rather talk to you. Is that all right?'

'Yeah. Of course.'

My heart rate was slowing a little. I'd been studying Catherine through my fringe. Her most striking feature was a shock of shiny straight black hair that fell all the way down her back. I thought her make-up was a bit too obvious, and her skin seemed powdery, soft in a way I didn't find very attractive. But what she lacked in beauty she made up for in gentleness. She knew that I was suffering and was doing all she could to make it easy for me. She could have humiliated me – I was such an easy target. But she wouldn't do that. Another boy came up and started talking to her, and she got rid of him quickly. She kept our conversation alive. At one point she touched my arm and said she was going to the loo but would be back. And she did come back.

'How long are you staying? I've got to leave soon. My dad's picking me up at half ten.'

'Oh, I don't know. Is it that late?'

'Almost. Look, Matt, I was wondering if you'd like to see me again.'

'I would. That would be great. Are you sure? Yeah, of course I would.'

'Why don't you call at my place tomorrow, at two o'clock?'

'Fine.'

'All right, then. It's been lovely talking to you. I've really enjoyed myself.' She leaned forward and kissed me on the cheek. And then she was gone.

Terry came back. 'You dark horse. Catherine, hey! You bastard! So what's she like?'

'She's lovely. I'm meeting her tomorrow.'

'Bloody hell! You lucky sod. I'm not bringing you to any more bloody parties.'

That night I lay in bed going over the evening again and again. I felt calm, satisfied. I was pleased with myself for not sullying the experience, not bringing Catherine down to the base level of a sexual fantasy. She was lovely; it wasn't like that. This was pure, clean and good.

The next day I rang the doorbell of 16 Bridge Street at exactly two o'clock. Catherine came to the door promptly, and invited me in and introduced me to her mum.

'He's not a great talker, is he, Catherine? You'll suit one another – Catherine can't keep her mouth shut, can you, love?'

'That's enough. Come on, Matt, let's go.'

'Remember, you're to be back by five today; we're going to your sister's.'

We walked by the war memorial, round the promenade, down to the pier and then out under the cliff towards Coastguards Peak. As we walked, Catherine put her arm through mine. I found it easier to talk, and I told her about school. And about my family. I told her about my interest in politics, an area she declared herself to know nothing about at all. She told me about her older sister and her sister's children. And about Rutherford House. And what it was like living in a hotel.

It seemed no time at all before we were back standing outside Catherine's house. This time I could say, 'When can we meet again?'

'I'm working tomorrow. But we can meet at seven.'

'Good. Here?'

'Yeah.'

'Bye, then.' I began to move off.

'Hey, don't I get a goodbye kiss?' She sounded aggrieved.

'Oh.'

Catherine took my face in her hands and kissed me lightly on the mouth. 'See you tomorrow.'

*

The evening was warm and this time we stopped by a largely deserted Highcliffe Bay, and sat down in the sand.

'You are shy, aren't you. Haven't you kissed a girl before?' This was said without any hint of condescension. I shook my head and looked at her, wondering what she was going to do next.

'I'd like to kiss you.'

'Yeah, I'd like that.' But I didn't move.

Catherine shifted and lay back, at the same time drawing my

face down towards hers. Her lips brushed mine, then lightly tugged at my bottom lip. I felt her tongue gently explore my lips. I let my tongue join hers. She opened her mouth and pushed up against mine. It was a long kiss. The first of many.

Several days later we went to the afternoon showing of a film in Lymbridge. We paid little attention to the film. I loved kissing. With one hand I stroked Catherine's cheek; my other arm was around her shoulder. My hand went to her neck. She continued kissing me. My hand smoothed over her breast. Instantly, I jerked it back. 'I'm sorry. I'm really sorry. I'll never do that again. I promise. Are you all right? I'm really sorry. Oh my God. Forgive me.'

'It's all right. It's not a problem. Hey, don't worry.'

My head was in my hands. I'd done something terrible. All my pride in keeping my feelings for Catherine pure was gone. I'd shown her what a disgusting beast I was. I wouldn't listen to her reassurances.

The film ended. We walked up the street. I kept apologising.

'Matt, stop it. It's all right. It can be nice, you know. I know you're not horrible, that you didn't mean anything horrible by it. I like to feel close to you, like that.'

'Are you sure?'

'Matt, I'm not going all the way – I never have. I'm not ready for that. But I like us being close. OK?'

*

Jeremy's return began to prey on my mind. What should I do? I wanted to be left alone, to enjoy my vulgar, predictable, adolescent self, to lie on the beach next to Catherine while 'Seasons in the Sun' played on her tiny transistor. The idea of losing her was terrible. But I was bound to Jeremy. Everything in my life revolved around him. What could I do?

A package arrived from Cyprus. It contained a script entitled

The Killer Complex and a compliments slip. I read the script straightaway. It was the first story that Jeremy had written that I didn't like; a slight thriller, predictable and shallow. I wrote him a letter in which I gave him my honest reaction. At the end I added a note: 'By the way, I've met a girl called Catherine and I'm spending most of my time with her at the moment. Best wishes, Matt.'

I'd wondered how to end the letter. Normally I would have written 'Love, Matt', but this time I couldn't. I was trying to send Jeremy a message that I was sure he would understand.

The days passed quickly, and the date when I was due to go away with Jeremy got ever closer. I didn't want to leave. I didn't know how I would explain my departure to Catherine. I decided that I needed to recruit Jeremy's help, to get him to understand my dilemma so that we would find a workable solution. I wrote again.

Dear Jeremy,

I have a problem I'm not sure how to solve. If you've received the letter I sent, you'll know I've been going out with a girl called Catherine. We're getting on really well together at the moment – and I don't want to have to say goodbye on 1st August or whenever. Since you and I have known each other, I have been able to get to know hardly anyone – when you're around we go out together, when you're not I stay in. This time I didn't stay in and now I know Catherine. She's about the only person I have ever been allowed to see for over five years, apart occasionally from a few school friends and I don't want to give her up.

I'm sorry if it sounds like a letter from the problem page of Princess Tina. I don't want any trouble like last time. I'm just not sure what to do. I remember a long time ago, you used to say if I ever wanted to go out with friends, just say so. I know we've arranged to do everything but I thought the best thing to do was to write frankly and tell you the situation.

My going out with her is not a permanent thing and I certainly don't want to say goodbye to you, but I certainly don't want to leave her yet either. I'm sorry about all the problems this causes. I'm feeling sick at the moment. I don't know if you've got any suggestions.

Love, Matt

My letter crossed in the post with one from Cyprus, which I opened with awful trepidation. I was right to have been worried. Jeremy began by expressing real hurt about my criticism of his screenplay. He accepted that it was cliché-ridden and cheap, but said this was because he was writing it for someone else, just to make money. He complained about the Cypriots, the heat, the family he was staying with, before getting around to my 'amatory conquest'. 'I suppose', he wrote, 'you are "in" to sex now and hope you are enjoying groping her breasts or whatever part of her anatomy you have managed to get your hands on.' His derision was followed by a torrent of self-pity and cynicism about the world. He accused me of having disillusioned him and let myself down, commenting, 'But even if your idealism drops off in proportion to the number of girls who'll drop their knickers for you, at least one does get a second chance when dying is no great sacrifice and all the animal satisfactions taste only of acid and salt.' Worst of all, Jeremy made it clear that, as far as he was concerned, Catherine's existence made no difference at all to the plans we'd made for the rest of the summer: 'If you are still keen to assist on the film, I start about 1st August. Also the cycle trip, which I'm looking forward to very much, if you still want to come and the pleasures of the flesh are not a greater counter-attraction to heads down against the wind, etc …'

Jeremy phoned while I was out and left a message to say he'd be back in Shorefleet on a particular day and would be up at Park Road after breakfast.

I didn't sleep well that night. I'd lulled myself with the idea that he'd understand the importance of this moment for me. I'd imagined the two of us talking it through calmly, making adjustments. The letter put paid to that idea. A stern, god-like figure was bearing down to show me the error of my ways, with his monopoly on mockery and moral authority. I was confused as to what I wanted too. I knew Catherine's shortcomings; I could see her through Jeremy's eyes. If he met her, he would accuse her of being fun-loving and superficial. To him that was vulgar. Above all she was a girl, and therefore part of the trap society sets to fog the mind, to waylay the spirit. The part of me that loved being with her was the very part that I'd been shown I must despise. Keeping Catherine meant surrendering to my baser side, to my mediocrity. How could I choose her over Jeremy? More to the point, could I manage without him? It was a nonsense, a non-starter. I was looking defeat in the face.

I did my feeble best. When at last, after passing the time of day with my mother over a cup of coffee, we were alone in my bedroom, I wondered aloud whether we couldn't reorganise the summer. But no, this couldn't happen. Jeremy explained how the cutting room was booked, and how we had to work hard to complete the editing work before he ran out of money. Of course, if I no longer wanted to be involved, if I wanted to renege on my commitments, he wouldn't make me do anything. But the way this was said, made it a test of my moral fibre rather than a genuine choice. I reassured him that I didn't intend to back out. The worst part was when he asked about Catherine. What was I to say? That she had decided to leave school and was thinking of going full-time at W.H. Smith while working out which tech course she might apply for? I said as little as I could, assuring Jeremy that I didn't really care about her, that there was nothing to it really, just harmless fun. I would end it with her.

I wrote Catherine a brief note. I apologised for not talking to her directly but said I'd been thinking that perhaps it would be best if we didn't see one another any more. I thanked her for being such a good friend and wished her luck with her exam results.

Jeremy and I went to London to work. There were a couple of Scottish art students renting rooms in his large Hampstead flat, and their presence did something to ease my longing for Catherine. One of them, Gwendolyn, was particularly sexy and extrovert, and flirted with me shamelessly. 'Oh I wish I were a sixteen-year-old in Shorefleet, I'd have eaten you up by now, I tell you. I bet the girls are all over you, aren't they, Matt? Goodness me, and he blushes too!'

When I'd arrived from Shorefleet she'd given me a warm hug. 'I'm all a-tremble, Matt. I hear you're going to lie on top of me tonight.' She was referring to the fact that I was going to sleep in the bedroom directly above hers.

I enjoyed her teasing, but I also found out that she was not just a tease. One afternoon, I came back to the flat alone. Walking downstairs to the kitchen I passed the bathroom, and there, through the heavily frosted glass, I could see her making vigorous love to some man I didn't know.

Preparing the roughly cut pilot of Jeremy's latest project was laborious. The work itself was mechanical, breaking up film into loops, and then measuring out the wider magnetic tape to run for the same length of time, looping that, and then marking up both and putting them in their own can. It was also an unusually hot summer, and the small editing room was stifling. After a week Jeremy proposed that we forget the work and go on holiday early. We returned to Shorefleet to collect my bike and then crossed the Channel. After two days travelling south from Calais, Jeremy suggested that we take the train to some more exotic landscape. He chose Mende, in the foothills of the Massif Central, from where we resumed our journey south by bicycle. As we didn't have enough money for hotels, we bought a plastic sheet and made a makeshift tent.

We cycled through some stunning countryside – the Tarn gorges, the watershed of the Cévennes, and then down the course of the Hérault, through Clermont and onwards to the sea. We crossed the Camargue and rested in Cassis. There were near-naked girls everywhere. After a day spent clambering around Cassis's rocky coastline, swimming and then moving on, I was unable to think of anything except gawping in wonder at the exposed flesh of these confident, wiry young women, many of whom seemed around my own age. Those were the ones I sought out with my eyes, and by late afternoon I was desperate for relief. The youth hostel where we put up was not the best place for sex, so I dragged Jeremy out onto the scrubby headland away from the path and demanded action.

At the end of August I returned to Shorefleet to find a card from Catherine, congratulating me on doing so well in my O levels. She added a note saying that she'd been sad to receive my note and wondering if we might still be friends. Perhaps I'd go and have a coffee with her one day.

I hid the letter, taking it out from time to time to reread it. I waited, unsure that I would be welcomed, but eventually plucked up the courage to phone. She sounded pleased to hear from me, not resentful at all, and invited me to visit. Back at the Bridge Street guest-house, we sat in the kitchen drinking coffee while Catherine's mother went to and fro. Her mum commented to the effect that intelligent people were always complicated, and that it was best to avoid emotional entanglements with them. I had the impression that she liked me but would have been anxious if her daughter had become too attached to such an unreliable type. That day we parted as friends. Later, we resumed our habit of going into the room between the kitchen and the lounge which, it seemed, was where Catherine was allowed some privacy in the house. It was here that I had become more prac-tised and less guilt-ridden at exploring her full breasts, while she would occasionally put her hand on the front of my trousers. While these explorations also resumed, I regulated my visits so that no one could mistake them to mean that we were a couple again. They ceased some time later when Catherine herself found a proper boyfriend.

The brief relationship with Catherine left me wondering when something like it would happen again, but quickly this turned to the question of whether it would *ever* happen again. There were invitations from Terry to more parties. Occasionally I'd end up snogging a girl – I hated the word 'snog' but relished the experience. 'Snogging', 'petting' and 'groping' were all, I thought, horrible names for the most heavenly of activities. These parties both relieved and accentuated my feelings of being a freak, an outsider, split between two incompatible selves.

Marion, a friend of my parents, was the next person to take on the role of catalyst in my life. From the age of about ten I had stayed with her, and her husband Ron and daughter Suzy, every couple of months on a Friday evening. I had regular tasks: to clean out the bird table, to go to the off-licence to buy ginger beer and to make my bed in the morning. From there, I'd walk down to Jeremy's on Saturday.

In the late spring of 1976 Marion invited Jeremy and me for a meal. Hers was the only house we visited where we were known to be very close. Ron, the taciturn net-maker and boatman, seemed to tolerate us: he would go to bed about eight o'clock, leaving the three of us to talk into the evening. That particular time, Marion had also invited a 21-year-old student they'd met, who was keen on sailing. Her name was Margaret. This made the evening special for me: I was sitting within an arm's length of a real young woman again. Margaret had a high voice and a rich Irish accent, and after the meal she brought out her guitar and sang us some Celtic ballads. She had wide-open eyes and a round face surrounded by blonde curls. Her tight figure reminded me of a discussion in an English lesson about a line by Keats. Mr Bentham had asked the class to name their associations with the word 'ample'. There was a profound silence, and an exasperated teacher finally answered his own question: 'Why, *bosoms,* of course!' Margaret was wearing a white blouse that left a distinct cleavage visible.

A couple of weeks later, Marion invited me again, this time on my own. She'd invited Margaret as well. Another evening passed pleasantly. I listened to the conversation between the two women and again formed part of the audience as Margaret played and sang. One aspect was strange and stayed in my mind. When we left the dining table to move into the small sitting room, I sat down on the sofa. When Margaret joined me, she sat in such a way that our legs touched from our hips to our knees. She said nothing to me.

Later, I described this to my friend Terry. He was appalled that I had so misread Margaret's communication and apparently passed up on what he regarded as an open invitation that might never be renewed. I wasn't so sure. However, the following Saturday morning Terry, Stephen and I were standing outside the Colliers' Barge, down on the pier, when Margaret walked by and called out to us. Both Terry and Stephen were more able at small talk than I was, and I didn't take part in the conversation at all, but I was aware that for much of the time it was me that Margaret's eyes were on. The other two boys were convinced that I was 'in', though both felt pretty hopeless about my prospects of realising the opportunity. When I protested that Margaret was 21, Terry brushed my objections aside as typical Lowe negativity.

The following day I was working in the bookshop, helping my father out, as I occasionally did. Margaret came in. She didn't want a book; she was simply there for a chat. I glanced at Mary, who was in charge of the shop that Sunday. Mary smiled and said encouragingly, 'Go on, I'm fine here. Be as long as you like.'

We stood in the street, leaning against the window of the toyshop next door, and talked. At least, Margaret talked and I tried to participate. In my mind I was asking her out, but the words wouldn't come. This distracted me from what she was actually saying, but she didn't seem to notice. There were awkward silences and I was sure she'd make her apologies and leave, but she didn't. I decided I had to end the conversation, and this provided me with the chance I needed. 'I think I'd better go back to work now. Would you like to meet up later?'

'OK. What do you suggest?'

'I don't know. We could go for a drink, I suppose.'

'OK.'

It was so easy when you tried!

'What time?'

It was agreed that we would meet exactly where we were at eight o'clock.

We chose the Ship. It was a horrible pub, but I'd been there a couple of times with Terry so I knew where the bar was. It was unlikely I'd bump into my brother, and I knew I'd get served. Our earlier conversational efforts were repeated as we drank. Our glasses were soon empty.

'What shall we do now?' Margaret asked.

'I don't know. Would you like any more to drink?'

'Not really. I'm not much of a drinker myself.'

'We could go for a walk along the cliff.'

'OK, but let's keep away from the pier; I know too many people down there.'

'OK.'

'After that, we could go up to my place for a coffee.'

'Yeah, that'd be great.'

We hadn't been walking for long when Margaret wondered if I felt ready for coffee.

The stairs up to her flat smelt damp; the walls were a dull yellow. Through the featureless, flat door and we were in a tiny hallway and then straight across into the sitting room. The furnishings looked tired and drab, but the double windows gave a wonderful view all the way up Clarion Street. I was looking down on a familiar part of the town but from a completely unexpected angle. It was dusk. Not dark, but the streetlights were on. The bookshop was still open, and there was a constant flow of holiday-makers slowly making their way back to their bed-and-breakfasts, as well as occasional groups of young people just beginning their evenings out.

'Here's the coffee.'

We sat side by side on the sofa, and this time I took the initiative. I placed my arm around Margaret's shoulders and leaned over to kiss her. We fell into one another.

'Phew! That was unexpected! But great.'

We fell together again. We wound ourselves up in one another, locking mouths and exploring and encouraging each other. Margaret shifted around so that she lay along the sofa with her shoulders on my knees, looking up into my face. I looked down at her, at her face, her cleavage, and then raised her face up again to meet my own.

'You're good at this. You've had a lot of practice, eh?' This jarred, but I ignored it.

We remained on the sofa for a long time. It grew dark. There were occasional noises of shouting or laughing from the street below.

Margaret heard the key in the door first and sat up straight. Someone entered.

'Is that you, Sue? You all right?'

'I'm a bit wrecked, to be honest. I'm making coffee – do you want some?'

'No thanks.'

Sue appeared with a mug. 'Oh hello – didn't realise you had company.'

'This is Matt. Peter Lowe's brother.'

'Really.' She introduced herself.

I thought it might be time for me to leave.

'God, it's late! You don't have to go yet, do you?'

'No, not at all, no.'

'Perhaps it would be better if we didn't crowd out the sitting room. We could go into my room, if you like.'

'OK, fine.'

Margaret's room was a small rectangular box with a single bed on one side. Beside it, filling the rest of the width of the room, was a small chest of drawers that also served as a bedside table. It held some bottles and a small transistor. Margaret turned it on to Radio Caroline. 'Not much space, I'm afraid.'

We sat on the bed and were soon lying entwined along its length. Margaret unbuttoned my shirt and ran her hand inside, along my tummy and up to my nipple. She didn't object when I copied her.

'I need to go to the loo.'

'It's on the left, first door.' I buttoned up my shirt and went out. I urinated and then washed my penis. I'd had a bath before coming out, but I was anxious not to repulse. I stood by the door while I took my shirt off, looking down at Margaret. Then Margaret got up and went to the loo herself.

This was the realisation of a dream, yet I felt surprisingly calm. I knew how to play this role. At the same time it was entirely new. I drank in the new sensations, the new odours. Margaret reappeared. A few moments later I was struggling with the clasp of her bra. Her breasts were large, but her nipples were almost flat and I struggled to grip them. I pushed my fingers into her jeans. She shuffled herself free of them, leaving her white lacy knickers behind. My hand traced between her legs. She had a gentle grip on my rigid penis. Her mouth left mine and travelled down my chest, and then further down. She moved so she could rest her head on my belly and look at what she was holding. She leaned forward and held me against her cheek, then pressed her lips against me. She moved back again and watched as she pulled down the skin and then let it up again. Then she brought her head back up the bed. There was no rush. I half sat up, my arm reaching round for her breast while she lay her head on my chest.

I wanted to investigate further. It took some minutes to gather the will to push her back and to move down her body. The strong smell of suntan lotion became mixed with another powerful scent. Here I was, Matt, with a real woman, mind-blown but comfortable. It was wonderful. But I wasn't sure I wanted to taste, to drink, as well as inhale.

'Come up here. I'm on the Pill. It's OK.'

She pulled me on top of her. I looked into her face while feeling her hands directing me. I felt her flesh give way.

I was conscious enough of the moment to glance up and take note of the time, a time I would surely never forget. It was 2:34 on the 5th of the 6th.

I left the flat soon after six the next morning. A perfect summer dawn. Out in the street I winced at the gyp from my strained stomach muscles. I walked, though, with head held high. I was immediately conscious of this involuntary change and revelled in its obvious significance. A huge weight had been lifted from my shoulders. The sun was already warming the air. An occasional seagull broke the silence. Two young men were unloading bundles of papers at the newsagent's halfway up the High Street.

At home the doors were all locked – Mum and Dad must have assumed I'd come back earlier. Lying down on the grass, I fell asleep.

~ 14 ~

For a couple of weeks I kept Margaret a secret from Jeremy, but this time my skills at dissimulation proved inadequate. It was obvious that everything was different. I was sullen and argumentative, distracted and impatient, but when he asked what was wrong I denied that anything in particular was the matter. Still, the hostility was distressing to both of us, and for me the tension grew unbearable. I steeled myself for another confrontation.

'There's something I need to talk to you about. I know I said there wasn't, but there is.'

'Wouldn't be another girl, by any chance?'

'Yeah.'

'Why didn't you just say? We've talked about this, haven't we? There's no need for this to cause more awfulness between us.'

'I was just sure there would be, and I couldn't stand any more of that.'

'Well, you can see now, can't you? I'm not angry. I'm not trying to stop everything that you want in life. You shouldn't see me like that any more. I'm happy for you – I can enjoy your triumphs vicariously, if only you'll let me. All I ask is that you keep a place for me as well. Is that too much to ask, after all we've been through? There's no reason why we should love so possessively. I know that's unrealistic. So, what's she like? Have you slept with her yet?' He was trying to be light-hearted. The last question was asked with a laugh, as if we were two lads sharing tales of our conquests. The whole scene was unreal.

'You know her, actually.'

'Do I?' Jeremy had turned serious. 'I can't think who it could be.'

'Do you remember, ages ago, we went to Marion's and—'

'You don't mean that Irish girl – she was awful. You can't possibly have got involved with her!' He was angry now, pacing round the room. 'I could feel all right about it being a girl your own age, someone nice, but how could you think of spending yourself on a woman like that?'

There was much more in this vein. I didn't try to defend myself. Jeremy left.

The following day I was upstairs and so didn't hear the phone ring. Mum answered it, then called up the stairs.

'It's me. I'm on the pier.' Margaret sounded petrified. 'I've just had a conversation with Jeremy.'

'It's all right. I'm coming. I can explain. I'll be at the flat in ten minutes.'

I jumped on my bike and sped off.

'I didn't realise. It's sick, isn't it? I mean, what's going on? He said that you were his lover, that you're sleeping with both of us. He was laughing at me. It was horrible. He's twisted. What did he think he was doing? Well, if he thought I'd ditch you, he's got another thing coming. But do you love him?'

'No, of course not. We had a relationship, that's true. But we're not together any more. I found it difficult to stop it when I wanted to, but it's all over now.' I wasn't sure where the truth ended and the lying began. The no-man's-land between the two was a place I'd made my own. Still, I believed that something had changed from the moment I'd received Margaret's phone call.

Jeremy had threatened my 'normal' life, the life that connected school friends and Friday and Saturday nights, and the odd party and the space where I might just be ordinary. All my instincts of self-preservation had been mobilised, and from one moment to the next everything had gone from being impossible, paralysed, stuck, to being clear as day.

Margaret and I talked and then went to bed. I left at one in the morning – without telling her I'd picked up a kitchen knife and put it in my trouser pocket. Before going downstairs I'd spent minutes at the large window overlooking Clarion Street, watching for any movement, any sign that I was being shadowed. I decided not to walk home by the obvious route but to go down Market Street and then turn right along the promenade before cutting inland. It was a beautiful summer's evening, the dark night lit by the coloured bulbs that snaked along the clifftop.

As I passed an alleyway leading up into the town, I was surprised to see two policemen walking quickly towards me. I was also shocked to see a police car with a flashing light coming along the promenade ahead of me. And behind me a police motorbike that would have cut off all plans to escape, had I had any.

'What's your name?'

'Matt Lowe.'

'And what are you doing out here at this time of night?'

Jeremy had been stopped by the police while carrying a large bag full of washing home from our house once, and had refused to let them see inside it on the grounds that they had no reason to be suspicious. I was not as brave. 'I'm going home.'

'And where's that?'

'216 Park Road.'

'Where have you been this evening?'

'I've been at my girlfriend's.'

'All evening?'

'Since about lunchtime.'

'The reason we've stopped you is that you meet the description of a young man who's been observed damaging boats in the harbour. Do you know anything about that?'

'I haven't been near the harbour. I wouldn't do that.'

'What's that sticking out of your pocket? Why are you carrying a knife?'

I was flustered. 'I don't know. I wasn't aware it was there. I must have just picked it up by mistake.'

'Picked it up by mistake? Does that sound convincing to you? Where did you get it?'

'Must have been from my girlfriend's.'

'Where does this girlfriend live?'

'Just over there, bottom of Clarion Street.'

One of the other policemen was speaking into his radio. The police car had stopped, but the engine was still running. The policeman who'd been speaking to me, then walked over and bent down to talk to the driver. When he stood up, the car reversed back along the promenade and disappeared. The motorcyclist also drove away.

'We're going to have to go and talk to this girlfriend. Clarion Street, you said?'

We climbed the dingy stairs in silence. Margaret looked worried when she opened the door, searching my face for an explanation, but within minutes she had confirmed that the knife was hers and had corroborated my alibi.

On leaving, the policeman said 'We're going to give you a lift home. You shouldn't be out this late, should you, lad? Perhaps we should come in and have a word with your parents.'

I was relieved that this idea had been forgotten by the time we drew up outside Number 216. The car waited until I had walked round the house to the back door. I walked in and was surprised to hear that there were people still up in the front room. Pushing open the door I was confronted with the sight of Jeremy sitting beside my mother on the sofa, Dad standing in the bay window. Something broke, or broke free, inside.

'What are you doing here? Get out! How dare you come here!' It must have been the first time I'd shouted in real anger in front of my parents, but I was oblivious to their presence. 'Come on, get out! Now! Just leave, OK?'

Jeremy stood up, looked bewildered, but showed no sign of moving. I strode forward, grabbed him by the shoulders and dragged him out of the room, up the steps towards the front door. I slammed the door behind him and locked it. It was all over in seconds.

I became aware of my heavy breathing in the sudden silence. My parents were waiting, perhaps expecting an explanation. I turned and went upstairs to avoid seeing them. I was lying on my bed, trying to think about what had happened, when Dad knocked and came into the room. 'Are you all right, Matthew? Quite a business, eh? I don't want to interfere. Your life is your own, I know that. But we're quite worried, you know. Your mother has been quite upset.'

'What about?'

'Jeremy thinks that you're being taken advantage of. He thinks that – is it Margaret? – that she has plans to marry you.'

'He's mad. Dad, that's just bloody nonsense.'

'Well, I hope so, Matthew.' There was a long pause, and then he spoke again. 'Jeremy has given you an awful lot over the years, you know. You shouldn't be too hard on him. He's very hurt. Perhaps you should go down after a few days and see how he is.'

*

There was, from the outset, an end date set for my involvement with Margaret. She had to return to Ireland in early August, after completing a catering course at the local tech. Nor did we share much, or do much, except sex. We never visited friends or went to the cinema. The two halves of shandy we'd shared on our first date were the only drinks we ever had in public. We once went for a walk along the coast, but we couldn't stop touching one another and there were people about, so we cut the walk short.

I would cycle to school in the morning and lock my bike on a lamppost around the corner from the Lower School entrance. After being marked as present, I'd walk out and cycle back to Clarion Street. In the middle of the afternoon I'd get dressed and cycle back to school in time to show my face at final registration. Then I'd cycle back to Margaret.

While hugely grateful to her, I was aware of how little we had in common. I tried to tell her about the history essays I was writing and the novels I was studying, but though she showed interest, these attempts merely accentuated the gulf between us. My special fantasy was to have a girlfriend that I could talk to. I dreaded Margaret's departure, but I knew that the relationship wouldn't have lasted, whatever the circumstances. In the meantime we enjoyed ourselves.

From the start, I found sex easy and fun. I wondered when I'd lost my virginity. In Margaret's flat, was one obvious answer. This was real sex. And I had much to learn. I was eager, and from time to time she would adjust the pressure I applied, or when the rhythm didn't suit her she'd whisper, 'Slow down, slow down.'

Yet, for all my excruciating shyness with girls, in bed with Margaret I felt like an old hand. It seemed that this was what I'd been trained to do. I had few hang-ups and liked taking risks. It was easier than sitting in a pub or meeting her flatmates, much easier than talking.

Outside Margaret's flat I couldn't tell what my world was like. It seemed as if a bomb had exploded at the centre of my life, a volcanic eruption that had broken everything apart and sent the bits miles up into the stratosphere. It wasn't clear what the landscape was going to look like when they all fell back down to earth. I feared that nothing would have changed. Part of me, a part I was deeply ashamed of, was afraid of what change would mean.

I'd lost all interest in schoolwork. When I did settle down with my books, I couldn't concentrate. I failed to hand in several essays on time. The efforts I'd made were uncharacteristic: scrappy and thin. It was not simply the sex that distracted me but a persistent fear – a kind of paranoia – about Jeremy coming after me. I made an arrangement to see Mr Oldham, the school counsellor. Mr Oldham was different from the other staff, adopting a slightly satirical attitude towards the macho, sport-obsessed culture of the school.

'Come on in, Matt. I was wondering about you the other day – saw you looking down in the dumps. What's going on?'

'It's difficult to explain, really. I'm not sure why, but I'm finding I can't work at the moment. I've got essays to do and I don't think I'm going to be able to do them. When I'm not here, they seem so pointless.'

'Perhaps there are other things that seem more important.'

'Yeah, there are. I've got a girlfriend …'

'Aha.' It seemed that this was what he'd expected, and explained everything.

'No, it's not only that. It's more complicated. I've had this other relationship, with a man. And I'm confused. Actually I'm frightened.'

'Frightened? Look, Matt, it's very normal to be confused at your age. There's really nothing to worry about. Most boys go through periods when they're unsure whether they're straight or gay. You know, I did wonder about you, because during one of our ethics classes last year we were talking about relationships, and you were very careful, I thought, never to talk about relationships with girls but always to refer to relationships with "people". I've learnt that that's a bit of a giveaway. The point, though, is to keep a clear head. You mustn't let this sidetrack you completely. Things will sort themselves out, but it might take some time. In the meantime, all play and no work makes Jack a dull boy, eh?'

My mind had wandered. I wasn't sure what I'd expected, why I'd thought it might help seeing Mr Oldham. Faced with his down-to-earth response, my anxieties simply seemed groundless.

'I'll talk to your form teacher and let them know you're in a spot of bother. I won't say any more than that. This is, as I've explained before, confidential. But if you want me to, I can make sure they don't go overboard if your work over the next week or so isn't what it should be.'

'Yes, please, that would help.'

'We'll meet again, shall we, just to see how things are going. You come and find me next week and we'll make a time.'

Then a letter arrived from Jeremy.

It was an intriguing missive, written, it seemed, in a state of elation. 'We' were over, but whatever feelings he might have had about that, he seemed enormously satisfied that 'the last chapter' had ended with 'a stunning climax'. It had freed him to begin work on the book about our relationship, and he was pleased I'd provided him with a fitting finale. He described in detail his confrontation with Margaret on the pier. 'You know,' he wrote, 'the most horrifying thing about the way I had behaved is that, faced with a sort of Hardyesque series of dramatic scenes and coincidences, I couldn't resist playing the last scene.' The lines came pouring out. From Hardy and Noël Coward, the letter took on the tone of Humphrey Bogart talking over a Raymond Chandler script: 'You were being destroyed anyway, and I was, I couldn't stand the predictability. I was the one who had to do something, so I shuffled the pack because the game had come to a standstill.'

What was clear was that Jeremy felt liberated, in more ways than one. He described breaking down at Marion's and telling her everything about the two of us. After that he'd told his sister, his work colleagues and his closest friends. It was, he said, like breathing air on top of a mountain: 'You've no idea how sympathetic everybody is; I don't know why we bothered to be so paranoid about it.' On the advice of his sister, he had played down the sexual details when confiding in his mother. He wrote that he hadn't been too explicit when talking to my parents either: he'd always assumed they must have known but my father had been extremely odd that night (I assumed he meant the night I threw him out), '... going on about interfering with your natural development. I thought it was a bit funny,' he continued, 'as I could hardly be accused of turning you into a screaming poofter, and even if I had, it's a bit late now.'

Gwendolyn, his flatmate, had also been taken into his confidence. He'd cried with her: 'She's been incredibly sympathetic, saying it was so unusual to meet a man who felt such things.' And they'd made love. They were now, it seemed, an item, and Jeremy described himself as 'bisexual'. He was hoping I would go and spend some time with them. 'The one thing everybody takes as unquestioned, you see, is that I love you.'

I now had what I had craved: freedom. And it terrified me. I had, it transpired, left the safety of the family at some unmarked point in a long-forgotten past, but I had not – as I now saw friends like Terry and Stephen had – begun to take steps of my own away from the nursery. I'd always had a loving adult at my side, a wise, supportive, all-knowing Friend to lend me confidence or relieve an impossible burden of self-doubt. Now that Friend was telling me that I didn't need him. I'd been replaced overnight, and – despite everything that Jeremy had ever said about himself – with a woman. I was envious. I would have liked to be with Gwendolyn, if I'd been given the choice.

It was not as if I could imagine a woman taking Jeremy's place with me. I knew something of the depth of my need – its true dimensions, which I glimpsed more clearly as I felt him recede into the distance. What I saw, I knew no girl would ever help me with. Any girl would want to find a man who was as true on the inside – even truer – as on the outside. And my insides were putrid. The only chance of getting close to a girl was to hide all that from her, and to do that I needed Jeremy. I couldn't imagine that either of the two girls who had, briefly but miraculously, let me get close, could have had any notion of what would've hit them if I'd burdened them with that part of myself that Jeremy helped me live with. They wouldn't have been strong enough, they couldn't possibly have understood. They were both from the Shorefleet I'd said goodbye to years before, the life of *Crackerjack* and taking jam sandwiches to friends' birthday parties, and being a son and brother and friend. I could feel either contempt or envy for that life, but I couldn't rejoin it. I was an alien, a product of Jeremy's but without his stamina or self-belief.

So his letter confused me. What was I doing to this man who loved me, who had made me, whom I had loved back? When he said he was relieved that everyone had heard about our relationship with acceptance rather than condemnation, I shared in his relief. Perhaps I could be honest with people about the past and still look them in the eye after all, still be invited to eat at their tables!

The anger I felt was at his betrayal of me. He'd provided me with so much – why wasn't he helping me now? Why hadn't he provided me with a woman? Why hadn't he arranged for me to sleep with Gwendolyn? I was sure it could have been done. Why didn't he start making sex films for me to star in? Why was I left with this monstrous need that was driving me into the wilderness where I couldn't cope? I raged against myself. Why did I need women at all? Why couldn't I crush this appetite that threatened everything that kept me safe? Why did I always take the easy way out? Why couldn't I be homosexual and be satisfied to love the man who loved me?

I believed that I'd cut myself loose from Jeremy the moment I threw him out of my parents' house, the night after he'd confronted Margaret on the pier. This is how I pictured it to myself later, and I wasn't lying. But I was mistaken. I repressed and forgot about the months after that extraordinary day, a period of vacillation and shame, and betrayal and misery. Not the strange sexual fumblings of my early childhood but the compromises I made in my late teens.

A few days after receiving his letter, I met Jeremy at the top of the central steps on Whiting Bay. He was with Gwendolyn; I was on my way to find Margaret. Bizarre, both men with their women. There was a conversation of a kind unimaginable only days before. Jeremy was friendly in a way that betrayed no hint of recrimination or possessiveness; quite the contrary. I responded with my adult part, withdrawn and unemotional, and there was no sense that this stirred his resentment. He seemed rather to be proud of the young adolescent before him, showing me off to Gwendolyn as one of his, but not as belonging to him.

When he contacted me again to invite me to see a play in London, I said yes. I felt at home amongst the crowds of people from the sexual fringes that the show attracted. Afterwards, I kissed him goodbye outside Chalk Farm tube station with an ardour that was as much about identifying with our collective rebellion against established sexual mores, as it was an affirmation of my love and gratitude.

Then it was time for Margaret to leave. On her last day in Shorefleet I stayed up all night with her, but I could tell she had already sealed herself off. Amidst the sadness and regret, we didn't make love at all. At home in the bath the next morning, I cried for her, and for myself. We'd half-heartedly agreed that we'd meet again, that I'd visit her family in Ireland, but I knew I'd never go. I didn't love her. She took no part of me away with her. We didn't phone one another either. I soon wrote to cancel my planned visit. The first copy of my letter was smudged with tears, and I had to copy it again before I could post it. But these were the last tears I cried for Margaret.

So my peculiar dual existence limped on. I resumed my visits when Jeremy was in town. Even our sex life resumed. He had tired of Gwendolyn within days and came to dread their coupling, even before he found himself incapable of it. I went through the motions, sometimes for relief, sometimes for a quiet life. Sometimes I refused and we fought. For now there was no point in hiding anything from one another, for either of us. Jeremy accused me of ruining his professional life, insisting that for 15 years I had drained him of all the energy and resources he'd needed to succeed as a film director. He said I was ungrateful and owed it to him not to change. He grumbled that I was awful to be with and awful to be without, and that anyway I was a man he didn't find attractive any more, who wore glasses and thought about women all the time.

I gave as good as I got, flinging at Jeremy all the loathing I had for myself. I knew how more than anything he hated seeing me weak, passive, pathetic. We behaved like an old married couple who'd grown used to hating one another, living constantly in the shadow of divorce yet hanging back from facing the consequences of separation. We rowed and fought, and made up and fought again.

It was an unedifying spectacle. Jeremy said he loved in me the aspect which I most loathed in myself – my defencelessness. I walked about like a crab without a shell, desperate to find some armour that fitted, to arm myself with weapons to repel all intruders. But every time I seemed to find some protection, Jeremy rejected me, and I was out in the world alone until I brought back to him the needy infant he'd first fallen for. We discussed it pretty much in these terms. It nearly broke him, I think.

*

Not long after Margaret returned to Ireland, I was at another party: soft lights, a table with bottles of drink, slow music – at this one someone kept putting on a record of the Carpenters' greatest hits. This was to facilitate dancing which wasn't dancing much at all, more an opportunity for two bodies to sway against one another in slow time. The big deal was that Christine Morgan was there – on her own.

I'd continued to admire her from afar. She would occasionally walk past our house after school on her way home. Or I'd see her mother's green Ford and instantly glance towards the passenger seat to see if she was in the car. Terry and I had made friends with a new boy at school, Andy Mitchell, whose house was just across the street from Christine's. The three of us would sit up in Andy's bedroom listening to Led Zeppelin and Jimi Hendrix, Andy drawing our attention to the bass guitar lines, always with an eye out for movement across the road. If a door opened, we'd all leap up to see whether Christine would emerge.

Now she was just a few yards away, talking to another girl, sipping a drink, her short, thick blonde hair cut to expose the light in her eyes, and the hint of a smile on her small mouth. Her compact figure was clad in a classy-looking red velvet jacket. I hung back, rehearsed what I might say, something that would minimise the humiliation should she reject me. I had a glass of cheap red wine, and then another. I stood rooted to the spot, watching her. Terry and Andy appeared from time to time to jeer at me in a kindly way and egg me on.

And then suddenly I'd done it: I was talking to her. She hadn't sneered or fallen back in hysterical laughter. Her eyes hadn't said, 'Come off it, you ugly lump of shit.' I was there with her, awkward and inarticulate but there, and listening for the first time to the laughter in her voice, the cheeky edge that was none-the-less kind and accepting. Her eyes on me were steadier than mine were on her. My limited repertoire determined that within a brief few minutes I knew what she was studying, which subject she felt the most passionate about – French literature; her father's and mother's occupations – factory manager and teacher, respectively; what her favourite novel was. And I shared similar information with her. Then the inevitable question.

'Will you dance with me?'

'I don't dance.'

'Of course you do.' She guided me towards the area where a dozen or so couples were smooching to the Carpenters, and I put my arms around her and felt her form nestle itself into mine. My face lay against that wondrous hair – the hair that had helped me pick her out from a crowd of Rutherford House girls at a hundred yards or more – and I breathed in deeply. As the record ended, the party's host approached us – or rather Christine – and asked if she'd dance with him. She smiled, said yes – my stomach lurched – and then tapped me on the arm. 'I'm coming to find you in a few minutes, so don't run away.' And she did come back, and I quickly jumped the next hurdle for fear of further distractions, and she agreed that I could call on her the next day after lunch.

Christine was my first love. The pain was exquisite, almost too much – just bearable, wonderful. I mooned about when she was busy, got ready an hour before our agreed meeting times, and would restlessly hang about by the window of the spare bedroom – through which I could just see her garden gate – while waiting for her to call. We started walking to school together; I'd carry her bag for her. We'd kiss repeatedly and get a little more intimate as we went through Derwells Avenue, a pathway over some rough land covered with elder and neglected apple trees.

I wasn't thrown into an erotic frenzy when I questioned Christine about her past loves, as I had been with Margaret. I was tortured hearing that she'd slept with some before me – the image it left in my mind sickened me, and I couldn't go to school for two days.

Our sexual life was subject to various unwelcome constraints. Christine didn't have her own flat like Margaret, so for much of the time we had to make do with fumbling around in my bedroom, with the risk of Mum walking in unannounced. She did that once, carrying an armful of washing for the airing cupboard – I was sure she did it on purpose to embarrass me – and there we were lying on the bed, me with my shirt off. Christine was understandably reluctant to go beyond a certain point under such conditions. Then Nanny Langton came to convalesce at 216 Park Road after an operation. Mum suggested that perhaps we might not spend all our time alone in my bedroom while she was there. But Nan's presence meant that there was the option of using her empty flat, just a few minutes' walk away, if I could get hold of the keys. When Nan's flat was no longer available, I copied the key to a small backstreet store which Dad rented to house stock for the bookshop. It was sometimes cold in the store, and then we'd make love, fully clothed, on the floor among the piles of cardboard boxes.

The best times were when we were both off school during the week, our parents away at work. Such opportunities became more frequent as first the mock A levels and then the real exams approached. On one such day Christine's father came home from work unexpectedly, trapping me upstairs while she dressed hurriedly and went down to discover how long he'd be stopping. Somehow, Mr Morgan picked up that something was going on and asked outright if I was there. She couldn't lie, and I was called downstairs. We were told off. Though he ended by saying that it would have been a different matter if it had been anyone but me, and that he wasn't thinking of telling Christine's mother. At the end of this awkward encounter, Mr Morgan clipped me on the head and muttered something about my being a dark horse.

It was a Saturday night and I was dancing with Christine at a disco in the church hall off Blenheim Square. She undid all my shirt buttons and ran her hands over my smooth skin. I knew we made a striking couple, and I was thrilled at her exhibitionism.

Afterwards, we walked to the shelter overlooking the sea and I unbuttoned her blouse and pushed up her bra. The next evening I was at Jeremy's house, looking down as my trouser zip was opened and he reached in to find my penis. I wondered that it always responded, even when I had no sense of erotic excitement.

'Do you think I fancy you?' was a question I began to ask Jeremy more and more often.

'No, of course not' would be the reply.

'So what are we doing, then? Doesn't it matter to you that I don't want this from you?'

I'd help Jeremy to orgasm all the same. But it wasn't easy. The strain grew. I was aware that I was betraying Christine, that I was lying to her, and it bothered me. I carried on, though; it was, for me, quite normal.

When he'd learned about Christine, Jeremy had assured me that he was pleased. 'I'm glad you've picked up another girl-friend. I don't feel a bit jealous. I told you that's all over with. You're a young man now, I suppose. What I'd like more than anything is for you to feel strong enough to want to spend some time with me. Whatever you want, darling. I'll be all in for what-ever you want because I know you love me, even though you don't say so any more. So, you decide what you'd like to do. Don't feel that anything you do with me is giving in or anything; that's all part of the past, like me being possessive and jealous. OK? I still love you as much as ever, you know that.'

I would grasp at the promise of this new era of friendship and acceptance. But somehow it would always fall apart. It was difficult to understand why. To me, Jeremy was unpredictable and unreliable. He'd arrive back from working through the night exhausted, short-tempered and demanding. And I would give in, and then the hatred would seethe in both of us. I wasn't accomplished at verbalising my resentments, but I expressed them powerfully in other ways. I became quite paranoid about Jeremy's power, and although I chose to remain within its orbit I attacked it as malevolent and destructive. He then became bewildered and despairing.

'I still don't know what it is we're having such an awful row about this time. All our phone calls this week were filled with hate. Why is everything so serious? Is there something the matter I don't know about?'

'No. It's you who started on me this time. I don't know what you expect of me.'

'It's your tone of voice. Just listen to yourself. It was the same last weekend. I hoped it might have changed back by now, but there it is again. You really seem to hate me, as if I'd done something awful to you.'

'I know you haven't done anything awful. There's nothing to worry about. Everything will be all right again. I just don't know why you must criticise me all the time. I'm doing the best I can.'

'Why can't we just talk any more? It all seems inappropriately heavy.'

More rows, more kissing and making up. Several times we agreed that everything had to change, that we could now begin a new phase of warm friendship. The warmth couldn't be sustained.

'I'm glad that one of us had the courage to put a stop to the sex, but why all the bitterness? We weren't going to be able to sleep together for a month from today, anyway – I'm going away, you know that.'

'It felt great for a week, but I can't deal with it any more.'

'Look, I was ecstatic all week, singing in the street. It's all been a bit of a strain, and it's nice to feel really free. I've got so much coming up – with the new film and everything. It's been difficult for me having to adjust to less and less of you, and still I try to persuade myself that you're the centre of my existence.'

'I don't want you to do that; it just makes me feel so responsible. It's too heavy. We're not married.'

'Of course not.'

'But it feels like that sometimes.'

'I'm just hurt by your total curtailment of all communication, and your bitterness even before I started making all sorts of black threats. I'm out of my depth. It's so disillusioning to think that I'm regarded as somebody who's been a bad part of your life and that you don't want to see me again. Or that you've been hating me for months and not showing it.'

'You don't understand the strain. If you ever find yourself in this situation again, you should think twice about it. I'm not saying you're bad, or that you've been a bad part of my life. But you don't know what the strain of it has been like.'

'You never say "thank you". I don't know if you're as bitter as you sound. Look, I have to thank *you* for coming back to me when I was very hurt, and for making yourself unhappy because you were lying to Christine. Surely you have to thank *me* for gradually adjusting to what you wanted, without too much bitterness. Even though I've said bitter things, I haven't actually done anything to affect your life. And I want to thank *you* for letting us go on being lovers, which has been very nice. You can't dislike me so much suddenly as to never want to see me again, unless you've disliked me for ages without showing it. I must still be your friend, aren't I? I find it difficult to envisage the future if I've failed to love you to your advantage. After all I've put into this relationship for so long, to have a hateful ending seems to make life all a bit bleak. Leave me something, unless you feel it's all been a waste of time.'

'Of course not. Of course not.'

'Just give me the chance to go on loving you without want-ing anything back. Otherwise, it's as if you really believe that I never loved you properly and only wanted the sex part, and just quoted Plato as a ploy. I can adjust to more or less not seeing you at all, out of love, if only I can feel that you thought well of me and were grateful for me keeping out of the way. I wanted to love you properly, without making you unhappy. I want to feel I'm doing something good. I want to be able to come round and see the family. I don't want the family to think I've hurt you, because I haven't, have I?'

'Of course not. Of course not.'

This corrosive bickering revealed Jeremy's deep pain and, to my confusion, his vulnerability. In the past I had always been the weak one, but now I sometimes found myself in the position of ministering to Jeremy's hurt.

On one occasion he pleaded with me to look after him. 'I want to ask you not to hurt me any more. I can always see my sensitive little boy in you, and it hurts so much when you hide him, and come to me as this cold adult. When I was eighteen, before I went abroad, I fell in love with a girl. She hurt me terribly – she left me for a fisherman. It must sound silly to you, but I became very disil-lusioned with everything, with everybody. It was after that that I worked on the beach, and met you, and it was so important to me that you smiled and were glad to see me. It was a real experience. You meant it. And since then, you've smiled at me like that many times. But these days you smile and you don't mean it. Now your eyes are cold, and the little boy has vanished.'

It was excruciating to hear his distress, to be confronted with my role in causing him such hurt. I softened and held him, and he wept.

'As long as you have any traces of that little boy inside you, please don't hide him from me. You were so positive then. "I'd like to learn Latin" – you said that. I can't kill that part of me which is still a child, and it is that part of me which is in this awful pain and makes me cry like a baby all the time. You helped me wipe away all the awful years of trying to be a grown-up. I was always afraid that you'd laugh at me, but you never did. You seemed golden and gifted, but you let me into your life and I tried to give you my ten-year-old self, the part of me I'd tried to preserve. We had this secret from everyone, that I was really a child in disguise.'

I, too, felt the nostalgia for a time when Jeremy had seemed to make life exciting and different, before all the problems arose.

'I'm still in love with that golden little boy. Please – please try to be positive. The most awful thing about the last few years is that you have let yourself become so self-doubting. "I don't know this, I can't do that ..." Perhaps it's my fault.'

He was no longer crying. His voice had grown quiet. 'You have to know that you can inflict terrible pain on me, because I have no shell. I crawled out of it when I gave my whole soul to you, and I can't get back inside. It's something I couldn't give you, a tough skin, and I know that you need to develop one. You don't need one with me, though; I don't want you to pretend to have the hide of a rhinoceros when you're with me. I miss you so much. Reading poetry. The cycle trips. Listening to music. Talking. I miss you hugging me and telling me you love me.'

He reached for a tissue and dabbed his face.

'In Cornwall we had a fight and I remember hurting you. You put your arms around me and said "Please don't hurt me." Now I'm saying to the sweet and special little boy in you, "Please don't hurt me." I know we can't go back but ... if only my beautiful little friend could come and comfort me, smiling his wonderful smile, put his hand on my arm and ask me to come out to play.'

Jeremy sobbed while I held him tightly, aware of how incapable I was of filling the gap in his life.

*

School encouraged me to delay going to university so I could take the Oxbridge entrance exams. I didn't want to stay in Shorefleet a day longer than I had to and refused. In an attempt to change my mind, Mr Webster, the history teacher, invited me to his flat after school one afternoon. He served tea and scones in an untidy sitting room, leather furniture scattered with open books and papers. I was unimpressed with his description of the virtues of Oxbridge life; he made it sound too much like boarding school. We moved on to politics – we often clashed during history lessons, and Mr Webster was clearly spoiling for another duel.

'It was Suez that politicised me, Lowe. I was at school then, and I remember sitting on the school bus, a frisson of pride rushing through me at the news of our lads going into action. And the lily-livered came out in force then, I can tell you. No stomach, no patriotism.'

I was happy to be provoked, and an argument ensued on the virtues and vices of colonialism and empire.

'The trouble with this country now is that it's soft, there's no spine, not like in Victorian days.'

'So you'd like to go back to the days of backstreet abortions, no rights for women, locking up homosexuals ...' I was waving a red flag in front of a bull, but I hadn't bargained quite for the bull's reaction.

'Whaaat, Lowe? I'd wondered about the muttering at school, and now it all falls into place. Now I realise why you're so hated, Lowe! So you believe in equality for queers, do you? Whatever next, I'd like to know.' Mr Webster had got up from the table and was striding about the room, gesticulating wildly. He wasn't exactly foaming at the mouth, but his eyes were rolling uncontrollably in their sockets. 'I used to love the music of Tchaikovsky, Lowe. I had all his symphonies, the piano concertos, the ballet scores, and I played them all the time. And then I found out he was a pervert! I smashed every one of them! That's what I think about homosexuals!'

Eventually he calmed down, and I stayed for another half an hour in the rather strained atmosphere that now pervaded the room.

I applied to two London colleges. I didn't know if I was hoping to live in London because Jeremy lived there or because Christine had applied to UCL. Jeremy helped me prepare for my interviews. The one at King's was intimidating, but at Bedford the two academics had arranged a more homely setting and they did their utmost to relax me. When I couldn't speak, they waited calmly, and one of them, a Dr Bishop, told me to take my time and answer the question when I felt ready. Then he stood up and spent several minutes failing to make the Venetian blinds work, looking like the archetypal scatty academic. They offered me a place, on condition that I attained two E grades at A level.

Long before it was time to go to London, a final parting took place. The complications and the tension had become unbearable. The change came in a deepening of my commitment to Christine. My feelings for her were simply taking over the areas that Jeremy had once occupied. They were more compelling, more all-consuming. When I was lonely, she was the one I craved; it was her presence and not his that seemed to make the world a slightly more tolerable place. Christine was not only beautiful, she was mature and intelligent.

Something totally unexpected happened one Saturday night. We were at a party in Lymbridge. Christine's father picked us up as arranged at eleven o'clock, but when we got into his car it was obvious that something was wrong. He was breathing heavily, didn't seem able to talk and drove recklessly. He occasionally took a pill out of his pocket and swallowed it. From the back seat I could see Christine's face – she was terrified. I put it down to a heart problem, as there had been talk of her father having had a mild heart attack sometime before. On any other night I would have gone in with Christine for a hot drink, but she told her father to drop me off first, and I was left baffled and worried as they sped away.

The next day Christine called to say that she wouldn't be able to see me. Her voice was croaky and thin. She said that her father had beaten her mother, and that it looked as if they were going to divorce. I could, however, visit the following day. I wasn't prepared for the bloated patchwork black and purple of Sue Morgan's face when she let me in. I blinked back tears and managed, I hope, to be sensitive and supportive, keeping myself together until I walked back in the door of my own home. Then I couldn't talk, but reached out to my bewildered father and held him tight, and sobbed and sobbed.

My role in the Morgan household shifted after that. Christine's father left. I helped her help her mother, picking up the younger sister from school, getting shopping, staying around the whole family more. I felt needed and responsible. So I simply announced that I wouldn't be going to Jeremy's place again. This time I meant it.

It was that easy.

~ 15 ~

It's taken me all this time to work out what happened next. I was aware of the facts, most of them, but they were all jumbled up. Events had been rearranged in my mind to preserve certain myths that I nurtured about myself.

Jeremy had gone. Without the scenes and the sordidness and the secrecy I could get a better perspective, or at least that's what I thought. As Dad had suggested a year before, there seemed so much to be grateful for. Without Jeremy, I told myself, I might never have properly appreciated classical music, or read so widely or, for that matter, started my own vegetable garden. Now I found myself playing this Jeremy role for Christine, taking her to concerts, plays and foreign films. I thought of myself as continuing his work and it made me feel good.

At the same time I was in a mess. I had no confidence. My attempts to make friends or to join in some activity – I tried various political groups – came to nothing. There seemed to be a Jeremy-shaped hole in my life. I missed his certainty, his guidance, the way he counteracted my lack of self-esteem. I had used him as a touchstone for so long that I found myself trying to imagine his response: 'What would Jeremy do about this?' And quite often: 'Jeremy would despise me for doing this' or 'wanting that' or 'not doing that'. It was hard living up to the expectations that this Jeremy-part demanded of me. I saw myself as superficial, lazy and weak. Without him I didn't really know what direction to take. I missed him.

I blamed Christine for not being able to help me in the way that Jeremy had. It seemed inconceivable that a woman could provide this inner bolstering. I felt the absence of the arms of someone bigger and stronger than I was, and came to resent the idea that I was expected to provide Christine with this, while she couldn't reciprocate. I wanted to collapse onto or into somebody, to be looked after, to rest, to give up from time to time in a place where I did not need to be strong or cheerful. I could only imagine enjoying this kind of comfort with a man. With Christine I assumed I had to hide the strangeness, the loneliness, that cut me off from her. I was angry with her and all women for expecting me to be grown up and reliable.

I had assumed that splitting from Jeremy would be like throwing off an unbearable weight, and that my life would regain the unity I imagined it would have had before it had become necessary to camouflage and deceive. But my days of leading a double life weren't over. To the outside world, to Christine herself, we were like all the other student couples finding out what it was like to be living together in the Big City. I both hid behind her and kept from her just how desperately out of place I felt. I stayed in touch with Bert and Tony, and on a fairly regular basis secretly enjoyed the role of being treated and flattered and paid for. Meanwhile, such independent steps as I tried to make, only confirmed how gullible and gutless I still was. In college halls I was allocated a born-again Christian as a room-mate, so I decided to move out. Through the Capital Radio flatshare list I found the perfect solution: 'Single room, Primrose Hill, £5 a week, gay or understanding'. It sounded too good to be true, so cheap and in a perfect position. I phoned the number and a visit was arranged.

I was let into a cramped flat – a tiny bathroom and kitchen, two medium-sized bedrooms – by Ross Gibbons. Ross was of medium height and barrel-chested, with thinning, greasy black hair and a dirty grin. He spoke loudly and barked at his own jokes. He showed me round and made me tea, helping himself to a tumbler of vodka and Coke. The interview ranged from 'Where are you from, Matt?' through to 'You saw on the advert it said "gay or understanding", what did you think about that?'

I answered honestly: I wasn't gay – I'd a girlfriend living nearby – but I thought of myself as understanding. I'd been friends with gay men. Ross seemed happy with that, and it was agreed I would move in the following Saturday. In the meantime Ross would clear his junk out of 'my' room.

Ross had told me he was a television cameraman. I had already arranged to meet Bert for lunch at the studio where he worked, later that week. Since my break-up with Jeremy, Bert had maintained a keen interest in my life and bought me lunch on a regular basis. I wasn't surprised that he knew Ross; he seemed to know everyone. But his eyes grew the size of an owl's at the mention of Ross's name.

'You can't live there.'

'Why not? It's perfect.'

'Ross Gibbons is an evil man. Just stay away from him.'

'Don't be ridiculous. What do you think he's going to do to me?'

'Just take my advice. You're better off where you are, whatever you think.'

When I moved into the flat that Saturday, 'my' room was still packed with Ross's belongings, and there was only space to deposit my suitcase and two boxes of books and cassettes. Ross walked back into his own bedroom. 'I'm sorry, Matt. I've been too busy, just couldn't find the time to get round to it. But no problem, hey. You can spend tonight in here, and I'll sort it out tomorrow.'

I looked at the double bed.

Ross appeared manically active, talking constantly, breaking for brief moments to take a drag on a cigarette or have another swig of vodka. I sat on a chair, sipping tea in the cramped kitchen, while he cooked a large bagful of fresh sweetcorn in batches to freeze. They were in season, he said, and extremely cheap.

I went to bed around one in the morning. Ross said he usually stayed up till three; he didn't need much sleep. I drifted off to the sound of clanging saucepans, then woke as the mattress sank with the weight of another body. I felt large, strong hands on my shoulders. Protectively, I shifted so that I was lying on my stomach. Ross ran his hands down my back and then under my pyjama top. Then he sat up and pulled back the duvet. A moment later my pyjamas were being pulled down, and Ross was strad-dling me. Hands gripped my bottom; I clenched my muscles. But Ross was not intent on penetration. I felt him lower his body and manoeuvre his penis into the cleft between my buttocks. He pressed his body down to increase the friction. His breath reeked of tobacco and alcohol and garlic. I knew it would be over at some point; I just had to remain still. After a time – a minute, five minutes? – he fell to the side. And then threw a cloth at my head. I cleaned my back as best I could and went back to sleep.

I lived at Ross Gibbons's for about four months. Even after I reclaimed the room I was renting, he refused to allow me any privacy. There were no further attempts at physical intimacy, but he wouldn't let me put a lock on the room and insisted on his right to enter at any time of the night, even if Christine was stay-ing. Thoroughly intimidated, I secretly packed my belongings and called a minicab while he was sleeping off a hangover one afternoon. I spent the rest of the year in a damp but safe and private, basement room in Tufnell Park. For the second year, Christine and I set up house together in a small flat in Willesden.

*

I still felt horribly inadequate. Growing up had never seemed a more unpleasant prospect. I was frightened about the future, about failing, about letting everyone down. At times I tried to talk about it. Like the time Christine went back to Shorefleet for her mother's birthday. I phoned Tony who, as I'd hoped, invited me over for the Saturday afternoon and to stay for a meal. Tony and I ate alone. It felt easy. There was some conversation about Jeremy but not much. The food, as always, was delicious. We had a few glasses of wine. The more I relaxed, the more I struggled with the idea of leaving. As Tony was a man, I could at least try to share my worries with him.

'Tony ... I can't explain properly, but I'm finding it all very difficult. It's all such a strain.'

'You mean college work? Or something else?'

'It's not that. I'm enjoying the work at the moment. It's ... There are times when I just don't think I'm going to cope with it all, with the whole thing.' Tears had begun to run down my cheeks, and then I was shaking and sobbing into Tony's jersey. 'Why am I different from everyone else? Why can't I grow up?'

'You're OK here. You're safe.'

'I don't want to go home. I can't stand being on my own.'

'Don't worry, you can stay. I'd like that.' Then Tony added sympathetically, 'We all thought you'd come through it unscathed. But perhaps we were wrong.'

I heard what he said and knew what he was referring to. But it didn't mean very much to me. I knew the relationship with

Jeremy had caused some difficult moments, but it didn't explain why I felt so weak, so defeated.

We went to bed, sharing Tony's futon. I was calm now. We talked. I lay back when he moved his head down my body and took my penis in his mouth.

Another time, Dad and one of his colleagues, John, visited London for a book fair. The three of us ate together in a hotel restaurant and then moved on to the bar. I felt close to Dad, who was clearly enjoying his visit and entertaining John and me with a succession of amusing anecdotes about the book industry. He was interested too in how I was getting on, wanted to find out what being at university was like. I tried not to sound too negative. I knew that he was intensely proud of the fact that his son was studying; he simply assumed I'd do well. And while I squirmed every time this pride revealed itself, I didn't want to spoil it for him. But I needed to try to connect on another level.

'Dad, you know, I'm not finding it easy here.'

'Not easy? How do you mean?'

'The work isn't too hard – I mean it's a hell of a lot harder than school. We have to work on our own, so it's difficult knowing if I'm making progress or not. Each time I get an essay marked and discuss it with the seminar leaders, I feel back on track and it seems they're OK with how I'm getting on. But a few days later, the doubts come back again. But that's not really what I mean. I feel, suppose I've always felt in a way, that there's something lacking in me. Difficult to put my finger on it, but I find everything so difficult. I'm too anxious, and I'm too shy. It's difficult to feel good all the time.'

'Look, Matthew, I think I know what you're saying. It's in your blood. I've always felt anxious, and I think that my dad did too. He covered it up, as we all have to. But there's no getting away from it. We inherit these things, and we just have to live with them and make the best of them, and not allow our inner doubts to get in the way. Best not to dwell on it. Think about what you've achieved – you've got so much more confidence than I had, I could never have done what you have. Don't let it hold you back.'

I didn't answer. It upset me to think of Dad as beset by anxiety, and I could see he was uncomfortable by my revealing my own sense of inadequacy. When we parted he gripped my shoulders as if he was trying to inject an extra dose of love and self-confidence.

*

Soon after this a letter from Jeremy arrived, redirected from Park Road.

Jeremy began by saying that, having disappeared for two years, he thought he should be allowed to write and find out how I was getting on. He said he'd heard all sorts of gossip about me (from Bert), and advised that if I had heard any about him, I should ignore it. His silence had followed from the realisation 'that if one claims to really love somebody as I was always claiming, then one ought to know when one's absence is actually in the better interest of the beloved object than one's presence'. He apologised for not having realised this soon enough.

The bulk of the letter was an update on developments in his life. He'd finally directed a television series, called *Son of Midas*, with the familiar theme of a boy who discovered a treasure trove. He'd sold it too, on the basis of a rough cut, and now had a deadline to complete the final version. The star was Mikis, the boy who'd taken my place as his lead actor several years before. 'I managed my estrangement from you,' Jeremy wrote, 'by deliberately, almost forcing myself to fall head over heels for my model ...' They'd had 'a bit of physical on the way', but there was no basis for a relationship once the filming had been completed. He listed what he'd bought Mikis, and what Mikis had given him. 'The ease of cataloguing everything is an index of its superficiality; I don't think I could say what I gave you, and what you gave me, or what we took away from each other.' Since then he'd been visiting Morocco, where he'd befriended someone called Rashid. He concluded by expressing the hope that I'd phone to arrange a meeting.

The letter had a peculiar effect on me. I felt instantly in his orbit again. He was so immediately familiar. I walked up the road to the nearest phone box, a stone's throw from the rooms Christine and I were renting in Willesden. I rang the number Jeremy had given me and asked to speak to him.

'Shall I say who's calling?'

'It's just a friend. Matt.'

After a brief pause a more familiar and friendlier voice came on the line. 'Matt, how are you? You received my letter, then? I'm so glad you called.'

'I was going to write, but I found it difficult knowing what to say.'

'I'm glad you didn't. You were never very good at expressing yourself on paper. You always come through as yourself when you speak directly. So how's life as a student? What you expected?'

'More or less. I like the history. I don't have to spend much time in college, so I'm reading and writing essays most of the time. Last year was harder – I almost dropped out, but in the end I decided to give the second year a chance, and I'm glad I have. It's easier now.'

'And how's the lovely Christine? Are you still together?'

'Yeah, we're living together now, in Willesden. She's great.'

'So what do you think about meeting up, sharing our news? I hope I made it clear in the letter that I'm really proud of what you've become. I'd just like to think that we could still be part of one another's lives. In a civilised, grown-up way. Not as a threat to you, not making any demands.'

'Yeah, you were clear about that. Your letter was a relief in a way. It's seemed a bit weird not seeing you but knowing you were around.'

'Good. It's felt like that to me too. Cycling round Regent's Park or seeing groups of students walking about, and wondering if you might be one of them. Why don't you come down to the studio? All the old faces are here. I could buy you lunch at the Verde Vallee.'

'Not today. But I could tomorrow.'

'Great. Around half twelve, then?'

I'd visited the dubbing studios many times before. I pushed through the heavy glass door, walked up to the first floor and rang the bell. Jeremy's voice came through the intercom, and when the buzzer sounded I let myself in. I found him in a cramped cutting room: some years before I'd secretly searched through the rows of small aluminium cans that filled the shelves, opened the ones with the most suggestive-sounding titles and watched short movies depicting schoolgirls being spanked on the tiny screens of the editing equipment. Jeremy theatrically threw his cigar into an ashtray and leapt up. 'Hey, hello! Welcome to the real world of hard graft and Havana cigars!' He came towards me, held my shoulders. I put out a hand to prevent him coming any closer.

'Don't worry! Just wanted to give my old friend a hug! No more of that, eh? How about a coffee? I live on the stuff – that and these fat Havanas. But first take a look at this.'

I looked into the screen: 'Episode 4, *Son of Midas*'.

'Written, produced, directed, designed, cast, wardrobe and all post-production by yours truly!'

A group of villagers appeared on the screen, following a man pulling a reluctant goat past some cottages. The scene cut to a bird's-eye view of the crowd, and then to a close-up of Mikis watching it from a nearby hilltop.

'The dream came true, eh? Eight episodes. It's all going to happen now. The Italians have already bought it – for peanuts, as it happens, but enough to pay for the finishing touches. And then I can sell it to everyone else.' Jeremy gave me a rundown on developments, filling me in on what I'd missed. We went for lunch and over pasta he quizzed me about my studies and caught up on news from Shorefleet. He relayed the saga of his relationship with Mikis. We clicked like old friends.

Before parting, Jeremy made me an exciting offer. 'You know, I could do with some help with the dubbing of *Midas*. I wondered if you might be interested. It's no problem if you're too busy – perhaps you think working for me would be too compromising – but the offer's there. I'm here working my balls off Monday to Wednesday and then I'm back at the television studio. Depending on which days you were available, we'd be working together or you'd be here working on your own. It's all stuff you know already. You'll remember it all pretty quickly once I show you again. I'd pay you the proper rate: seventy-five pounds a day. Think about it.'

I thought about it and agreed. Here was Jeremy, at last in a position to make me relatively wealthy. Seventy-five pounds a day was unheard of as a rate for casual work amongst students. The work was moving out of Dean Street and into Jeremy's studio flat in Waterloo. It turned out that he had no kitchen and cooked lunches on an electric ring. The place stank of cigars. But for £75 a day I'd have put up with much worse. We listened to Radio 3 or played Jeremy's cassettes. Pink Floyd had just issued *The Wall*, and I played it over and over. Jeremy himself was on a roll: full of energy and back to his most optimistic about his own career prospects. There was a tight schedule for completing the dubbing of *Son of Midas*, as he'd entered it in a number of film festivals as well as selling it to the Italian company.

It was while I was working for Jeremy that he arranged for Mikis, the film's star, to visit England for a short holiday. I wish I could say that I was troubled when Jeremy referred to this boy – he was probably 11 or 12 – as 'my lover'. If I'm honest, such discomfort as I felt was jealousy. It wasn't easy to listen to Jeremy say he was going out to buy Mikis an expensive turntable and a camera, or asking me to help to rearrange the tiny studio so there was room for an extra camp bed. I remembered Mikis as an arrogant and contemptuous little boy, and when we met this time I decided I'd been right. I found his attitude to Jeremy difficult to tolerate. He seemed to harangue Jeremy, who was doing everything he could to appease and satisfy the demands of his now adolescent star. The whole scene felt distasteful, and I found myself taking sides, resenting the bullying to which Jeremy was being subjected. When he phoned a couple of days later to say that the visit had been a disaster, that Mikis had been impossible and that he'd sent him packing earlier than planned, I was quietly pleased.

So Jeremy remained there in the background. I continued to work on the episodes until they were completed. Jeremy then embarked on a campaign to promote and sell the programmes, which took him abroad a great deal. He left the studio in Waterloo and, whenever he visited Britain, lodged with my sister

Ella and her partner Joe in south London. He and I occasionally met for a meal. He wrote regularly.

*

By the time I started the last year of my degree course I was no longer with Christine. Her departure for a year in Paris, as part of her degree, came at a point when we were both, I think, ready to move on. A few weeks into the new academic term I was introduced to Jayne. She was spontaneous and fearless. And strong. And striking: as dark as Christine had been blonde. I set out to persuade her that we were made for each other. As we seemed to be, on the basis of an attraction of opposites. Now I was with an 18-year-old who had more of a grasp on life than I had at 20, and who had little interest in the kind of sterile introversion at which I excelled.

What I loved about Jayne, and what made it so hard to be with her, was her insistence that she could deal with the truth in whatever form it came, but that she would not tolerate lies and deception. 'What I need,' Jayne would say, 'is to feel that we are like a rock, that we create a place which is really safe and good, so that we can go and face the awfulness of life outside.' It was Jayne's strength that liberated me from the delusion that I needed a man, somebody physically larger than myself, to look after me. I found myself finally living without the yearning for male intimacy and care that had seemed to compromise my view of myself as 'straight'.

My degree result was good. I spent a year in London living with Jayne, considering what to do next. In the end I secured a grant to do research in Warwick. I moved there at the end of the summer of 1981. Working entirely on my own took some getting used to, after life as an undergraduate, but I applied myself, working hard in the university library every day. With an inner voice, whose origins even I recognised, warning me against wasting my time and taking the easy way out, I did not stint. In the second year Jayne, having completed her degree, joined me, and we were able to live together again.

We meant the world to one another, but it would be difficult to say that Jayne and I were happy. She loved life, and I loved her for that. Yet I couldn't really feel the optimism and joy that sustained her. I confused battling with my depression with an intermittent war with Jayne herself. It was as if I couldn't bear being too close to her, too dependent, but neither could I stand being too distant from her. A pattern emerged: I sabotaged our brief moments of real happiness to the extent where I reduced Jayne to the point of wanting to leave me; then I'd switch gears, and do everything in my power to convince her to stay, believing that my survival required her absolute devotion. It was a cycle that continued for the whole 10 years we were together.

*

For some while Jeremy had been spending most of his time overseas. I hadn't kept his existence a secret from Jayne; there was no need for that. I'd introduced him to her on a brief visit that he'd made to England about a year previously. Now, though, he announced that he had signed a six-month contract with the BBC in Birmingham and would therefore be living quite close to us. I thought that I should tell Jayne more about the background to my connection with him. It was all in the past now, and I'd made a pact with her that there were to be no secrets. I wanted to live by that as much as possible. Jayne was not narrow-minded at all; I wondered why I hadn't told her before.

We were at a restaurant behind my college. It was a cold night and they had a fire burning that, along with the red shades on the wall lamps, created a warm and comforting atmosphere. At other

tables there were more young couples and a few parents up visiting their student children. Jayne and I didn't often eat out, and
each time we did, we made it something of a celebration.

I waited until we were eating our main course. 'I told you
that Jeremy's coming to work in Birmingham. He's talking of
coming over to stay with us soon.'

'Oh, right. I'll see if I can be away that weekend.' Jayne was
joking but also saying that she hadn't particularly taken to the
idea of having Jeremy as a friend. I must have frowned, because
she added, 'Don't worry, I'll be there. Not sure he'd mind if I
wasn't, though.' She seemed to be hinting at something, and that
disconcerted me.

'I'm sure he would. I'd like it if you were friends. He's all
right, he can be a laugh. There is one thing I was going to tell
you about, should have explained ages ago, really, but never got
round to it.'

'What's that?'

'You know I said that he'd always been around, you know,
when I was a kid.'

'He was a family friend.'

'Yeah, that's right, he was. But he was also a lot more
than that. I mean that we had a relationship that was separate
from that.'

Jayne was paying proper attention now. 'What do you mean?'

'Well, a relationship.'

'A sexual thing?'

'Yeah.'

'You're sorted out now, though, are you?'

I smiled.

'Pretty weird, though, isn't it, having a thing with a family
friend. How old were you?' Jayne seemed to have heard me as

saying that Jeremy and I had got together during some confused adolescent phase. She seemed to be expecting me to confirm that. I could tell that she found this idea distasteful, but that it was something she would accept, adjust to. But I wanted her to know the truth.

'I don't know really. When I was small.'

'Small? What does that mean? You mean, when you were a child?' Jayne's voice had risen, and the expression on her face showed clearly that I had miscalculated.

'Yeah, I don't know, all through my childhood, really.'

'From when? Until when?' Jayne was almost shouting now, and her face was snarled up in an expression I couldn't quite translate. Was she going to hit me, or be sick?

'Oh, it finished when I was fifteen.' The truth had been abandoned, the priority now was damage limitation.

It didn't work. I glanced around, worried that we were attracting the attention of other diners, but before finding out whether we had or not, I had to turn back to face an onslaught from Jayne, who clearly hadn't understood what I'd been saying at all.

'It's foul. It's terrible. I can't believe that. Are you asking me to be friends with someone who interferes with children?'

I was stunned to see that she was crying hard. There was misery written on her face. I hated to see her suffering.

'That's not what happened. It's all right. It wasn't a problem. It was a bit different, but it was OK.'

'It? It? You called it a relationship a minute ago. How can you possibly mean that you had a sexual *relationship* as a little boy? Oh God, I can't deal with this. How can it be OK? What does it mean that you think it was OK? Does it mean you'd go and fuck a child and think it was OK?'

'No, of course not. I don't want to do anything like that. What a ridiculous thing to say.'

'Is it so ridiculous? If you're twisted enough to think that it's OK for him to do that to you, how am I supposed to know if you don't think it's OK for you to do it to somebody else? What did your parents think? Did they know?'

I answered honestly. 'I don't know. I've often wondered.'

'You didn't tell them? Why didn't you tell them about what that bastard was doing to you?'

'He wasn't doing anything *to* me. He's a bit eccentric, but he's not a monster.' I was getting lost in her questions and in the sheer force of her emotion. I didn't understand it and didn't know how to deal with it. Becoming angry myself, I resorted to an attempt to put the genie back in the bottle. 'Look, I wouldn't have mentioned it if I thought you'd have this reaction. I just wanted to tell you about something that happened a long time ago and doesn't matter to me any more. It doesn't matter any more, do you hear me? So let's talk about something else!' I was trying to equal Jayne's passion and certainty.

'How can we talk about something else? You're describing something barbaric. Terrible. Monstrous. I can't bear it.' She was crying hard again.

'Look, stop it!'

Suddenly Jayne was pushing her plate away, scraping her chair back and standing up. She whipped her coat off the back of her chair as she headed towards the door, still moaning through her tears. I looked around: this time heads were turned. I looked down at my meal, calculating how I was going to get out of the restaurant with the minimum of fuss.

When we met back at the house, Jayne's anger and grief had subsided. There were a few more tears as she put her arms around me and said she was so sorry this had happened to me. I could bear that, though it seemed an odd thing for her to say. I told her that I didn't ever want to talk about it again, and made her promise that she would never raise the subject. Then we went to bed.

Writing this, thinking about that scene now, my skin goes cold.

*

Jeremy arrived a few weeks later. That first time I was on edge, but his visit passed without incident. We showed him the cathedral and then took him to another local restaurant to eat. He got into an argument with some rowdy undergraduates and enjoyed himself immensely. I could tell that Jayne disliked him, probably disliked him intensely, but she made it all right, for my sake. I was grateful. I could tell that she was observing the way he and I were together, checking perhaps that there was no reason for her to feel threatened. Jeremy went out of his way to be amusing, helpful and generous. After that, he visited us in Warwick on a fairly regular basis.

One time he and I were eating alone in an Italian restaurant in Coventry. The feeling was good. We'd shared a bottle of wine, and this had fuelled conversation on a subject that I, at least, knew nothing whatsoever about: comparative linguistics. Having argued to a stalemate about the existence of a subjunctive tense in English, I said, 'Life is so complicated. I'm doing this research, and more and more I'm feeling that there's something empty about it, something about the complexity of life that I can't convey or take account of when I'm studying history.'

'I'm not sure what you mean.'

'I mean that my own mind is such a muddle. I've got a sense of how contradictory my own motivations are, for even simple things. And then I read somebody's diaries, for example, and I take them as a fairly simple representation of the facts, of the way the diarist was thinking and feeling. And then I use that as evidence. But I don't really believe it myself.'

'Perhaps this is just another version of your now famous self-deprecation, an "I may be studying for a PhD but really I'm a complete louse" line. I don't buy it. Just like I didn't buy it when it was "I'm going to fail my eleven-plus" or "I've messed up my A levels." It's really quite wearing, Matt.'

I laughed. He was revisiting a theme we'd played over dozens of times in the past. 'Maybe. But you don't really understand what lies behind it. You don't know how hard things are some-times.' I hesitated. 'Sometimes I don't think I can go on. I can't see the point in it all.'

'Well, we all have to cope with the great philosophical ques-tion: what is the meaning of life? In the end, what is it all about? We live and die, the earth falls into the sun, or the sun goes out.'

'I don't mean that. It's not about some intellectual quest. I mean that inside I feel dead already. It seems such an effort, just going through the motions.'

'Oh, I see. You don't think that's my fault, do you?'

'What do you mean?' I was irritated. It seemed so difficult to get anyone to understand. 'No, of course not. You've given me most of the things that do help – music and the rest. Forget it, it's not a real problem.'

*

I thought of myself as sick then. I was sick, but not just in the ways I knew about. When Jeremy's contract came to an end, he went abroad again, working in France and the United States, and holidaying in various exotic locations. He wrote frequently and at length. He could be frank about his activities with me in a way he could not be with anyone else, except perhaps Bert. Rereading these letters now I can't help but be ashamed at having been their recipient. In mock pornographic style, he described his sexual encounters with a succession of poverty-stricken children, mostly in the Philippines. 'I changed partners again, I'm such a slut. I've shacked up with my "ex", he of photos I sent you ... I had another go with a thirteen-year-old nymphette the other day. There wasn't much going for it. Think I'll have to admit I'm never going to make a dame happy.' In another letter he reviewed the year's achievements in true Byronic style, listing highs and lows, bottles of wine drunk, cigars smoked, number of times he'd had sex with however many different partners.

I was concerned about his lifestyle, but my worries were distinct from those that Jayne would have had, had she read the letters. I worried about the ethics of sex tourism, but I made few distinctions on the basis of age or gender. Jeremy assured me that he was very different from the French and German tourists who bought the children of Manila, describing instead something with which I was already familiar: how he became accepted by a local family – usually through a street encounter with the child – and how this developed into an accepted and open relationship in which the boy's mother and father seemed grateful for the extra help they received, and which could be viewed as rescuing their child from a life of straightforward street prostitution.

Jeremy, at any rate, felt that it was OK.

While I disapproved of buying sex from impoverished people in underdeveloped countries, I was more worried about the boys exploiting Jeremy than the other way around. I could not imagine them really caring for him, like I had done. I knew how head-over-heels he'd fall, how unrealistically exposed he'd be to hurt. He wrote again and again, insisting that he was having real romances with real people who loved him, but this only increased my protective feelings and my exasperation that he should insist on putting himself at such risk. I hated reading about the expensive presents, the setting up of bank accounts, the payment of school bills and accommodation for months ahead, sensing that nothing real or lasting would come of it all, except Jeremy's own continuing disillusionment and lack of any financial resources. I was relieved, though, when his letters showed that he was cheerful and productive rather than full of despair or ill, and thousands of miles from anyone he knew. I felt close to his suffering, and partly responsible that he suffered alone.

For the most part Jeremy adopted the persona of a travel writer, having extraordinary adventures in strange parts and getting into fixes as he encountered the bizarre ways of people living on the edge, where bare-faced poverty, corruption and exploitation held sway. Behind the humour, there was anger about the way the world had denied him opportunities to fulfil his professional ambitions, and the way it denied meaningful chances to the children he befriended along the way. But mainly, he upheld the comic aspect.

I never referred to our shared past, though Jeremy often did. He described it in the same terms that I would have done, as a relationship different from but akin to any other. I didn't question its legitimacy. I didn't shy away from its negative aspects: it was too much of a strain for a young boy to be asked to shoulder. I wouldn't approve of it happening to anyone else, as I was aware of how hard it was to maintain an ordinary life at the same time. It wasn't fair to have to lie all the time to one's family and friends. When looking back at my life, I'd sometimes feel that I'd always been married, always been committed, and I'd regret that, because being committed was difficult. It meant that I'd never had to manage on my own, and I was beginning to think it might be this that had left me so ineffectual and floppy. I *had* made decisions, some of them based on the selfish motives that I assumed inspired Jeremy's 'friends' in Manila. But I had also felt a need for Jeremy himself. It was true that he had been too possessive and controlling in the final years of our relationship, but I too could be possessive and controlling. Ending a marriage, I knew, was a heart-rending business, a savage experience in which everyone behaved badly. I could not find grounds for seeing my relationship with Jeremy as so different from my subsequent attachments, which I had also experienced as a strange mix of the magical and the malevolent.

So I kept something of a balance sheet of my life, and the part Jeremy had played in it, and it was from this perspective that I viewed all subsequent turns in his career. Even when most aware of the 'bad' aspects, I had, on the other side, the belief that I'd been 'the love of Jeremy's life'. This was something he always maintained and continued to allude to in his correspondence, and it meant a great deal to me. Giving a detailed account of spending time on a beach, snorkelling with a boy in the Philippines, he wrote, 'Of course, all this is really an echo, which is why I subject you to a description of it. Only you and I know that I am really looking for you, though I realise the search is hopeless.' Another letter ended with the comment, 'I'm aware that 1963–76 was "it" for me, and it won't happen again, so it's just lovely that I can still be such friends with all these kids.'

Such sentiments seemed to make all the sacrifices worthwhile. The drawback was that it was a precarious privilege: I was left vulnerable to feeling displaced. A letter from Jeremy had once fallen out of a book I'd picked off a shelf in Bert's flat, describing some boy he'd met in Morocco as the best thing that had happened to him. I'd been devastated.

Another setback came with the publication of Jeremy's two children's books, *Son of Midas* in 1981 and *Inca Adventures* in 1985. If I was the love of his life, then surely he would have dedicated one of these volumes to me. In fact, the dedications were to people I'd never heard of. I was hurt and confused, and only partially mollified by receiving personal copies in which Jeremy wrote long and effusive tributes to my part in launching him on his story-telling career. But these were short-lived shocks. It seemed obvious that none of the holiday 'romances' he enjoyed, however he painted them, could ever really push me from the central place in his heart.

*

In the midst of all this, Gracey died. When I visited her for the last time, she was staying at her daughter's flat in Islington, in London. I found her in bed, a fraction of her former self, shrunken by the cancer that was killing her. But she was still Gracey, still laughing, still looking me straight in the eye. She seemed pleased that I'd called, and we reminisced about life in Bayview Road. Gracey told me about the plans for her funeral.

Six weeks later she was buried in the beautiful church of St Gregory's in Shorefleet. It was where I first heard 'The Old Rugged Cross', and the music-hall lilt of this hymn spoke of Gracey's love of life, her ordinariness, her being rooted. At the reception afterwards, her husband George said, 'The vicar came round before she died, to get to know her, like, and they were talking over the old days so he could have an idea of what to say at the service. She told him about the morning she had to chase you up the road because you'd refused to have your face washed.

But she suggested he not mention that; she didn't want to make it too hard on you.'

I wished the vicar had used that story, had made it clear to everyone that Gracey had been someone special for me. It's hard now to picture how close I'd been to her as a small child. She and Jeremy represented different worlds, and I ended up in the flashy, perverse, vapid, contemptuous one. I regret that so much.

~ 16 ~

It was around the time that I married Jayne, just before the wedding while optimism still held sway, that I sent a letter to my parents. It was a difficult moment. Dad had been ill for some time: first a heart attack, then severe angina while he waited for the operation which, when it was carried out, left him with chronic pain. As a result, he had become severely discouraged and preoccupied.

The aim was to get close to them – to tear down an invisible wall that had made them strange to me and, although they were unaware of it, me strange to them. My attempt at demolishing this obstacle was only partially successful. For a start, though I was now motivated to try to undo the damage of the past, I could not name things for what they were.

As a way in, I told them about my counselling, wondering whether Dad wouldn't find something similar helpful for his depression. I was quite bold – for me – in talking of the difficulties I'd been through, the self-denigration and lack of confidence, and about my feeling an outsider in the family. I explained that the therapy had changed the way I thought about the past and that now I wanted to make an attempt at getting close to them again: 'I have never really wanted to tell you about this. Not because you weren't involved, but because the past is past, and because I didn't think it was fair to start getting het-up about that when you were both having very difficult, real problems to face in the present. This is still a very big consideration for me – I'm not trying to cause any distress.' I reassured them that I didn't think they had done anything wrong; it was more what hadn't been done that I didn't understand.' I went on, as bravely as I knew how:

> If there's one thing I would have had different in my life, and which I believe would have made a huge difference to me as a child and growing up, it's the influence of Jeremy that I would change. I would remove him completely. And what I don't understand is why you did not remove him for me. He doesn't have a well-balanced personality. He's obsessive and has any number of irrational traits of his own. He is also a very strong and possessive character who came to dominate me in an unhealthy way. Not only was that bad, but it totally confused me about your attitude towards me. Long before I even thought of trying to do anything about my problems, as a teenager and after, I wondered over and over what you had thought about it all, whether 'parental non-interference', in principle, was the reason, or just indifference. Or did you think it was all a good thing? I don't understand why it was me that it happened to – whether I turned to Jeremy because there was already something lacking for me before that, or not.

I said that I knew we weren't a very demonstrative family, but I had to find out if there was real love and affection, because I couldn't be sure any more.

Some days afterwards I had a reply from Dad. He explained that he and Mum had decided it would make more sense if they wrote to me individually, 'without showing our offerings to each other'. He said that he had been extremely upset reading my letter, and felt guilty too. Taking up my description of Jeremy's influence, he said that 'since we allowed the situation to arise, we must bear total responsibility for that relationship'. It was difficult, he continued, to remember exactly how it had all come about:

> We were both of us very busy indeed, working very long hours, and, with so many of you, also working very hard at home. Probably we did not pay enough attention to each of you as individuals, but, if so, it did not seem so at the time. We loved you all, enjoyed you all. As a child you were lovable, very lively and it always seemed to me very happy. Jeremy, in the early years, often took you all out, doing things in the open air which seemed harmless and exciting, which neither of us had the time or energy to cope with. As the years went by, Peter and Ella opted out and Jeremy centred on you. It did worry us, and Jeremy and I had several upsets about it when he tried to monopolise you. But it seemed that you were, yourself, enjoying the extra excursions and that he was helping you in your educational development. I also believed that Jeremy would find a job which would end the relationship, or at least curtail the frequency of the meetings. As time went on, I think I shied away from the idea of breaking up the relationship, for fear of the damage it would do you. In any case, you were even then not so inarticulate that you would not have made any unhappiness known to us. But, obviously, we were very wrong.

My dad assured me that, whatever doubts I had, I was totally wrong to think I might have been rejected or unloved, 'even to the extent that I might have had a sense of guilt that you were something of a favourite'.

While going a long way to address the issues I had raised, he did wonder when I had become so unhappy. The hypothesis he proposed to explain my anxieties was one I'd heard before: perhaps, he suggested, it was my 'inherited personality'. He urged me to look to my strengths rather than rely too much on any therapy I might be having. And then he added a paragraph which, I thought, explained why he'd wanted to write in confidence.

> I must make one confession. You may have no memory of it, you may have a shadowy spectre of it. Mum and I had a near bust-up when you were quite young. It was my fault – getting involved with someone and Mum getting back at me by doing likewise. We were apart for only a brief time, but it was very traumatic while it lasted. I remember calling a meeting of all of you and telling you about it in true democratic fashion, one Monday afternoon when Mum had gone! It took me a long time to get over and I bitterly regret it ever happened, but it did. I think we were so engrossed with all of you for so long that we lost contact with other people. We rediscovered the outside world with catastrophic consequences. It could be a source of insecurity. I very much hope it is not.

Mum's letter arrived a few days later. She too commented on my relationship with Jeremy, saying that with hindsight she accepted that Jeremy was not a good influence.

> Many's the time I've wondered whether we should have had more foresight, but whatever reasons let us foster the relationship, indifference and lack of love and care were certainly not amongst them. When we first met Jeremy, he was a lonely, intelligent teenager lacking a father and normal

family life. He's now a lonely, intelligent, middle-aged man, still lacking a home or any normal life.

At that time he was more friendly with Peter; you weren't more than a toddler. Time passed and he was accepted into the family, and gradually found you more interesting, sympathetic and intelligent than the rest of us. Try to put yourself in our position. We had four young children, Dad was working seven days a week – and seven evenings as well in the summer. We had very little money and few opportunities for outings and trips. Jeremy was a chance for you to escape from a back garden full of nappies and a dining room full of book-keeping. He took you cycling, he introduced you to archaeology, and may well have sparked off your interest in history – and in cooking. You climbed cliffs, sailed in dinghies, acted in films, visited gypsy camps and travelled abroad. At that time you were quite definitely happy with the situation, and by the time any anxiety arose in us, it would have been very difficult for us to put a stop to it without doing a very heavy-handed parental job, and probably locking you up!

On one occasion when you were in your early teens, I talked to him like a Dutch uncle and told him that you had friends of both sexes and plenty to do with your time, and that if all his spare time, money and affection was lavished on you, he was the one who was going to get hurt! I apparently underestimated, as the hurt seems to have been pretty widespread.

She then attempted to prove that – whatever the cause of my current 'resentment' – it couldn't be Jeremy. After all, I had never rejected him, even after going to university. I'd continued until recently to be his friend. It was clear, she thought, that I'd had a cataclysmic row with him, and had extrapolated backwards to find him, and by extension her and my father, responsible for all my problems in life. 'Strangely enough,' she concluded, 'although he must realise that we know about the quarrel, he still sends us cards from time to time. At present he seems to be doing quite well.'

The letters were confusing. We were, finally, talking about Jeremy, and Dad, in particular, seemed willing to examine whether his presence in the family had been beneficial or not. He'd sounded much warmer and less defensive than Mum. Her attempt to rebut my whole emerging outlook on my life left me crestfallen and determined to try once more to explain myself. So I wrote again, saying that I was sorry for whatever bad feelings I had stirred up and thanking them for having written so frankly. Still, I noted, there were a few things in their letters which were not right, and I wanted to explain more. I told them that, far from feeling worse than in the past, I was feeling less burdened and much stronger than I had for years. I assured them that I hadn't swallowed a line fed me by some analyst. I described how the work with Caroline had been about me constructing a way of understanding my own life, that at last made some sense. I told them again that I wasn't trying to apportion blame and acknowledged that I hadn't always been unhappy. At the same time, I wrote, it was now clear to me that there were many reasons why children found it difficult to articulate their feelings openly. But I had to challenge their assumption that getting on well in college and having a girlfriend must mean that one was OK.

Although I still could not spell out the nature of my relationship with Jeremy, I did try to convey more clearly my current feelings about him:

I think Jeremy is evil. And I say so because I feel that Mum sees nothing very wrong with him, and even feels sorry for him, and wouldn't mind continuing as before with him. I never had a row with Jeremy. He was out of the country when the total change in the way I think and feel about him took place. We haven't heard from him since then. I'm not totally surprised he still writes to you, because we were all something of an adopted family, but I find the whole thing totally sick.

This isn't just a phase. Until sometime last year, the future and even the present didn't seem all that real. Now I'm actually forward looking! And only when that happened was it possible to decide to get married.

Do you understand that I care for you both very much, but didn't think I'd be able to show it before getting these things out of my mind? I hope so.

After this exchange we didn't talk about Jeremy again. I talked briefly to Ella and Joanna, but I was as vague with them as I had been in my letters to Mum and Dad. They were initially shocked and angry on my behalf, but when they realised that I'd upset our parents, they made it clear that I should stop. For many years, the name 'Jeremy' wasn't uttered in my hearing by any member of the family.

~ 17 ~

During my thirties, things held together pretty well. Further therapy, including that important group experience, helped. With my love for Carmen and Jack, and with a new career, my life seemed to have a clearer and more secure foundation.

Jeremy – rather memories of Jeremy – came and went. Once, a dinner conversation unexpectedly turned in his direction. Carmen and I were eating with our close friends, Richard and Sylvia, and a compatriot and friend of Sylvia's called Tom. Tom, a Norwegian film-maker, was in London for a week's holiday. The food was good, the wine flowed and the talk was snappy. I warmed to Tom's dry humour, and the two of us spent most of the evening having our own conversation up one end of the dining table.

'Are you working on a film now?' I enquired.

'No, it's a while since I was directly involved in the film business. I have two occupations at the moment. I'm concentrating on doing nothing most of the time, and, occasionally, I work very hard at looking busy.'

'A tough life!' It wasn't that funny, but something in Tom's timing and accent made me laugh.

'What about you? You're in the same business as Richard, I heard.'

'Yeah, we met on a course ages ago. I work in a children's home, with adolescents.'

'It sounds fascinating. But I wonder what took you into that line of work?'

I wondered how to answer. It was a familiar dilemma. To break the taboo on discussing the past, or do the polite thing and find some innocuous explanation. It bothered me that friends could talk easily about their early lives, good or bad, and I felt I could not.

'I was brought up in a small seaside town called Shorefleet. Everyone there is either mad or looking after people who are.'

Tom laughed. 'Funnily enough, Shorefleet is about the only place in England that I know, apart from London. I was taken there for a lovely weekend, oh, must be ten years ago. I was assured that while there I ate the best ice cream in the world.'

'At Giovanni's, of course. How did that come about?'

'There was a film festival in Oslo, and a young English director presented a children's series there and won a prize. I met him and was very taken with him. We invited him to stay. He visited us a couple of times, and once I was able to see him in London. And that was when he took me down to his home-town by the sea.'

'His name was Jeremy Rushton.'

'You know him! I suppose you would, Shorefleet is not such a big place. Are you still in touch with him? We were close for a couple of years, but then he disappeared. I wrote once or twice, but nothing, not for many years now.'

'No, I haven't seen him for years either, longer than you.'

'Oh, he's a complicated character, I think. Crazy, but then, aren't we all? His films had a certain naïve charm, but I had the impression that he could have achieved so much more. You knew him well?'

'Umm. When I was younger I knew him pretty well. He was complicated, like you say.'

*

Sylvia and Richard were our only friends who knew about Jeremy. Sylvia could be direct to the point of bluntness, as well as being an extremely loving friend. On our first weekend away together, the conversation took a particular turn, and she too had asked why I'd wanted to work in the social care field. For the first time I'd chosen to tell the truth. Sylvia hadn't pressed for any details, but she had asked one supplementary question: 'Did you ever report the abuse?'

I told her that I hadn't. The idea had never occurred to me. For years I'd been haunted by visions of what would happen if I ever ran into Jeremy. Behind the wheel of a car I might see a cyclist up ahead that looked like him: should I run him down and then reverse over his legs? Or stop and suggest we go for a coffee? Or drive past and ignore him? I no longer felt afraid of meeting him. I was curious, above all, about whether I would demonstrate strength more by venting my rage or by not venting it. But the idea of involving the police had never come into my mind.

Now the question had been posed it couldn't be ignored. The purpose of reporting crimes was, for me, to prevent a criminal creating more victims. Although I'd been fully aware that Jeremy had continued abusing other children during my twenties, it was as if I hadn't integrated that knowledge, not wondered whether I had any moral responsibility to act. Sylvia's question awakened me to that possibility. What did it mean that I'd done nothing? Was I so self-obsessed that I didn't have room to care about anyone else? Was I protecting Jeremy? It was true that sometimes, when listening to Carmen talk about him, I felt she was too crude in her condemnation. She hadn't known him, didn't know the full picture. Didn't know, above all, how fragile he was. I realised that while at times I nursed a murderous rage against him, for the most part the image I had of him was of a basically pathetic and friendless individual. But this didn't resolve the issue, because having been made aware of the choice before me, how could I put Jeremy's needs above those of the children he might still be hurting?

I put it all to the back of my mind. But it kept forcing its way into my thoughts again. It was difficult because it meant, for the first time, really imagining him as someone who was still alive somewhere on the planet, older – but in essentials, still the person I'd known decades before in Shorefleet.

In March 2002 I ran an internet search on Jeremy's name. I came up with a number of films and television programmes that he'd played a part producing, usually as second director. Most were several years old. I chose the most recent and found the name of a production company based in France. Then I e-mailed Tom for the company's contact details – I guessed another film-maker would be able to find it more easily than I could. Tom came up with the goods, and I sent the company an e-mail.

A week later a reply arrived from Mexico: 'Any friend of Tom's is a friend of mine! Hope you are doing well. How can I help?'

I wrote back saying that I didn't need help in the sense of asking him to do anything for me, but that I wanted to start a dialogue with him about things that had been bothering me. Jeremy replied with a jaunty 'I'm prepared to help in any way I can.' He attached a photograph of himself, hardly changed at all, standing between two Mexican students. Confused as to why I was doing this and what I expected from it, I wrote my first proper message. Rather clumsily, I threatened that unless he engaged in this correspondence and attempted to be honest with me, I might report him to the police. I defined my purpose as succinctly as I could:

> For many years you purported to love me. I heard you explain and justify what happened in many different ways, but then I was a child. Even in the last years when I knew you, I was still very much the person you had created. I wasn't capable of speaking to you from an independent position. I want to know if you can engage in a conversation in which I speak to you as an adult, while we think about what happened and what it meant to me.

I heard nothing for what seemed an age, though in reality it was less than a week. Believing I knew what lay behind Jeremy's failure to respond, I lost patience and fired off another message of my own. Perhaps now, the underlying motives for beginning the correspondence surfaced, because I directed a tirade against him. I accused him of living behind a thin, brittle façade of lies. On the surface, a creative and sensitive soul, a victim of circumstance, a man in love with life.

> Imagine all these good things and the utter incapacity to have an honest relationship with another person, except one of your own kind. Another, whose whole approach to life is based on the greatest lie, the biggest self-deception, that what you do is OK, ordinary, constructive, as good as – no, better than – the lives that others lead. That what you do is love; that you have relationships; that you care for the children you exploit. I have always – since I could think about such things – pitied you in the extreme. I can't imagine what it must be like waking up to find that one's sexuality is as yours is. Finding it drives you to do the things you do, and

drives you to find some way of continually justifying it to yourself, twisting your mind and the minds of those who get entangled with you. Do you still warble on about Socrates and Plato? Do you still view yourself as the outlaw aristocrat, swanning over the ranks of ordinary mortals?

I suggested that he imagine the impact on my parents of telling them the simple truth.

I know, that if you would listen, I could show you what you did to me. Apart from the things you might like to think of, introducing me to music, reading me Dickens and the rest. I mean what kind of a sense of myself I had and how this was related to what I had been carrying for you, for so long. To be prostituted for as long as one can remember. To spend one's whole childhood under the emotional domination of someone like you. I would demonstrate that you contributed to years of depression and self-doubt, of self-destructiveness. And I'd want to know if you still thought that was all right. Whether, I suppose, you didn't care what the consequences of your way of life were. Because that's the bottom line, isn't it? If you don't care about the consequences of what you do, on those you claim to love, then what kind of a person are you?

If you're doing a piece of work, you do research on it. You find out all there is to know. But do you do the same about your way of life? Have you been looking to understand what the impact of sexually interfering with children is? If you have, what have you made of it? I think I already know: a lot of fuss dreamed up by interfering social workers and crackpot psychologists! I could have shown you differently, made it impossible for you to hide behind that kind of blindness. And then what would you have done? If you were to see why you hunted out the vulnerable, the immature; that you were not worshipping their immaturity, but feeding off it.

After trying to describe in detail the pain and distress Jeremy had caused, I concluded:

> I have written in anger and hatred, because that is what you inspire; it's what you will inspire in all the children you go near, though you will never stay around long enough to see it, for them to become strong enough to show you. You can't let yourself see what you are doing to them. That being the case, all your intelligence and sensitivity and generosity simply make you the more dangerous.
>
> I've often wondered what it would be like to bump into you. There's nothing worthwhile to say, no possibility of real communication. What you did was commit a destructive assault on me, lasting the years of my childhood, and I am left with a vast rage.

A week later, a message from Jeremy finally appeared. It was pained, and painful to read. He wondered whether I had any positive feelings left for him, and referred nostalgically to our meetings in London and Warwick, 'when you had this lovely sense of humour and made fun of me a lot. Nobody dominating anybody else and we were just friends. That was a good time, wasn't it? The worst thing in my life was when you cut me completely out of your life. Maybe you still think the worst thing in yours was meeting me in the first place'.

Ignoring Jeremy's complete evasion of everything I'd said – unable, it seems, to give up on this opportunity to rant and rage across the ocean at the man I held responsible for so much that had gone wrong in my life – I wrote again. I asked him straight out whether he thought that adults forming intense, emotional and sexual relationships with children were OK or not. I wrote to him as if he needed help, as someone who'd be there while he faced the truth about himself: 'I want to know how you respond to me trying to tell you what it did to me. The nature, the quality, the meaning of what happened between us. It's not edifying, the image of you wistfully missing the laughter and refusing to listen to anything else. Take your time, but I hope your next message will read like a reply.'

Jeremy's next e-mail was anything but that. It marked the end of our correspondence. He took it that I was asking for the opportunity to vent my rage, to confront him, as part of some therapeutic exercise. He could see the point in that, 'as we both have a considerable portion of our lives which we'd want to do over again and do differently'. He carried on, imagining how 'we could walk around the Aztec temples at Tenochtitlan and you could scream at me or whatever you liked, but we'd end up in some way friends again …' But he worried that perhaps all I wanted was revenge, and complained that my letters sounded malicious, saying that I misjudged him in thinking that he hadn't already confronted his past 'and been more or less destroyed by it':

> It was like having a major portion of my life surgically removed and I had to start seeing myself as somebody who didn't really deserve to live at all. You're correct only when you say I'm this sad and pathetic and lonely person underneath, but not exactly for the reason you said. It's not because I've gone on blithely not facing up to what an awful person I am or was, but because I have.

Far from having sinister motives towards the young people he was now teaching, Jeremy had found a goodness in himself. The students thought he was wonderful. In fact, he wrote, 'I've lived like a Buddhist monk for years and years.'

Jeremy's e-mail ended on rather a pathetic note. 'I still talk to you', he noted. 'I often find myself doing it. I use exactly the same tone of voice and intonation and everything, and then I feel awful because all that has gone.' He appealed to me to move on from the rage and hate; this would rescue him from a thought that had long plagued him: 'I've often thought that the moment before I die, I'll think of you, and then I'll think what an awful person I am, and that'll be it. It's almost inevitable, really. You don't have to forgive me or give me your blessing or anything, just say hello, I suppose. Wouldn't that be something for you too?'

Jeremy's claim to be living a celibate life let me off the necessity of reporting him. And then the whole issue receded again into insignificance. My mum had been suffering from breast cancer for many years, and around that time her condition took a turn for the worse. She spent many months in the local hospice, stoical as ever but now more demonstrative. She'd overcome her former reserve, and wanted to be held and kissed. Changes in both of us, it seemed, had done away with the awkwardness I'd experienced in the past. I felt very close to her at the end.

We never, of course, mentioned Jeremy.

~ 18 ~

Slip a copy of Mahler's Fifth Symphony into the CD machine, turn up the volume and turn out the lights, and let the first two movements do their stuff. I've little faith in my ability to convey what it's like, being depressed, but Mahler does a pretty good job, at least for me. No doubt everyone's experience of depression is different. Psychiatrists have a stream of words that dissect and distinguish depression's various common strands: low mood, disturbed sleep, diminished appetite, loss of libido, ideas of guilt or unworthiness, agitation, reduced concentration, lack of self-esteem, pessimism ... Yet these terms have the quality of something described from the outside. So much more difficult to convey the inner reality. It's easier to describe positive states of being, of happiness or even of sadness, than of ceasing to feel, of not feeling real, of not being oneself.

When you're there you can't do anything constructive, and when it's passed the memory is vague and imprecise. You can make a list of your distorted thoughts, but it's difficult to put across the manner in which they slice into you. Everything you come into contact with is besmirched: the home you've put so much into making just how you want it, has lost its charm; the people you know you love, whom you need so desperately, turn bad too.

When I'm depressed I think about death all the time. Fortunately, perhaps, I'm so miserably lifeless that I can't find the energy to *do* anything. 'Fellowship is life, lack of fellowship is death.' I agree with that. In the grip of it all, you know there's a way out and that the key lies with the people around you. But all you can think about is to get away from them, to hide, to pretend.

When a depression starts, I do try to keep in contact, not with the people around me but with words and music: Mahler, Leonard Cohen, the poets. Quite often it's enough; a few days of them and I pick up again. That's brilliant, to feel that you've stopped it in its tracks, hauled yourself back into the real world. You get up, dust yourself off, pick up your hat, turn and give it a sneering goodbye, and walk on.

But this doesn't always work. Sometimes the music and poetry themselves get chewed up, become meaningless. Then there's nothing outside the depression. Everything is defined in its terms. It's a state in which you can think anything. You can envy people in car crashes because at least they know what's destroyed their lives. You can wish you had a terminal illness because then you'd know the death you faced was real, and that soon it'd all be over. You can believe that your only son would be better off if you died, that he wouldn't be bothered because it's obvious that you've nothing to offer him. And the fact that you wouldn't see him grow up, a thought that would be like a torment in ordinary times, doesn't bother you either. You feel empty, but at the same time you're overflowing with negation and violence.

Even after all this time and all the work I've done on myself, I don't understand quite where this hate comes from, what makes it so virulent. And it doesn't matter who tries to reach me then. There's no way I can respond, open myself up, share, find comfort. I'm on my own. I'm supposed to desire my partner, but the urge has gone. I have to shop, but the supermarket has become a place of particular terror. I have to cook, but I have no appetite. Every part of my day is made up of obligations I don't want to meet. Other people need me. When Jack is with me I make the best effort I possibly can, pushing myself to be ordinary, and after he's gone I collapse with exhaustion.

Eventually something breaks. And what had seemed hermetically sealed and perfect gives way. As Cohen wrote, 'There is a crack in everything, that's how the light gets in.' And you thank the gods you don't believe in. It might take days or weeks or months, but it happens eventually. You never know how you got out, so you don't learn how to stop yourself falling the next time, but so what? At the time you're just too happy to live in a world of colour and light, with a past and a future, a family, a life. Reconnecting is clearly part of it. Talking obviously helps. As you talk, you wonder why just hours before you despaired of being able to connect again. And then the tears are not just tears of frustration; they work as they should, sluicing out all kinds of poisons and hates and dreads. And you begin to sense a goodness that you couldn't have found if you'd looked the day before.

For weeks you worry that each bad thought might signal a return to solitary. You wake up in the morning and feel about for reassurance; you give your body a careful scan to check for the kind of twisted-up feeling that's a sign the depression's coming back; you smile to yourself when the report comes back 'All clear'. You avoid heavy music now, for fear of tipping the scales, and seek out the happy stuff, family films, thrillers and the like. It's wonderful to find that you can love and make love again.

When my latest depression struck, establishing itself gradually until it surfaced around the time that Martin broke into the staff office at the children's home, all I could think about was Jeremy.

*

'I was only buggered once.'

'*Only* once?' the therapist answered softly.

'Well, I told you last time that I'd been abused. I didn't want you to get the impression it was worse than it was.'

'You say "only once", as if you think I might not believe that what *did* happen to you was all that significant.'

I lay on her couch, my arm over my face and my fist clenched as if warding her off. I *was* warding her off. I wanted her to know everything, but I didn't want to be with her when she found out. While I hesitated, she continued, 'You imagine that I've formed quite lurid pictures of the abuse in my mind, and that when you come to tell me what actually happened, it might not seem as bad, and I'll think you've been making a fuss out of nothing.'

'Something like that. "Sexual abuse" covers a multitude of sins, doesn't it? And I'm not clear even if the abuse was the worst thing about it. And why is that the first thing I tell you about? It happened ages ago. I'm here because of what's going on in my life now.'

'It's a struggle, perhaps, to know just how and where to start: with what's most shocking, to find out how I'll take it? But I think you want me to know you as a person too, not simply as a victim. I suppose it'll take time to get to the point where the abuse fits into the wider picture.'

'There's a lot of bad stuff. But there are loads of good memories too.'

It was my second session with my new psychotherapist. After resigning from my position at the children's home, I had waited to check that rest wouldn't grant me a spontaneous remission and then telephoned a leading psychotherapy organisation. I'd asked to be put me in touch with a therapist living reasonably close by. The following week I had my first appointment. The clinician had turned out to be a woman about my age – mid-forties – who saw me in the basement room of a tall Victorian house, in a quiet street in north London. She struck me as quite stern, and I worried about her disapproval and disgust. But at that point I was desperate enough that nothing would have held me back. I sat – or rather lay – on the armchair. I was crying before I started talking, and I cried throughout the meeting. At the end of that first 50 minutes I had to pull myself up the steps because my legs had turned to jelly.

Going back to see a therapist seemed like an admission of failure. But I was scared. I'd come close to the edge – the 'edge' suggesting some vague notion of giving up completely, of signing off. It was a euphemism for some kind of death, though I didn't believe I'd ever be able to kill myself. This obsessing about death was quite familiar – it was also a shock because I hadn't been this bad for at least a decade. I needed the therapist to help me regain the stability I'd achieved before the depression had engulfed me again.

Over the following seven days nothing changed except that I had the next session to hold on to. To that extent, seeing the therapist had already had an impact. I found myself turning over and over what I wanted to say to her, troubled because I kept coming back to wanting to hurt her. It wasn't really about telling her the facts, more about how to get her to know how bad things felt inside. And, yes, wanting to get what twisted me up most out of the way, to dispose of it.

'I've spent the week working out how to make you suffer.' I paused, aware of just how hateful a wish I'd been nurturing. 'I know that you will care about what has happened to me, that you will be supportive. But what good will that do me? It sounds cruel, but I need to do something more to you. It's not enough that you think about what it would be like to be me, to have lived through the relationship with Jeremy, or to have parents who overlooked things they shouldn't have overlooked. I need you to feel that I am *your* son, that *your* son has been touched and messed up, and *you* have to deal with the guilt and the pain of knowing that *you* were responsible. That *you* should have stopped it. I want to push that into you and hold it there. I don't know how that would help me, but that's what's been going on in my head since I saw you.'

I was crying again. Now that I was telling her, it seemed pointless. With her there in the flesh, I no longer wanted her to suffer. But if I couldn't break through and get her to face the full horror of it all, the overwhelming sense of failure and hopelessness, what was the point? 'I don't understand. Why don't I have any skin, any protection, against this?' Now I felt like I was whining. But this was how I looked at things. 'And why has it come back like this? Everything was going all right. And then suddenly it isn't.'

The therapist finally spoke. 'I wonder if you've any thoughts about that? About why things have gone so terribly wrong again now?'

I'd gone back over it a hundred times: what had changed? 'I went swimming a while ago. I was feeling unfit and thought that maybe if I could do some regular exercise I'd feel better about myself.' I stopped again. Whatever I started to say went back to the same subject.

'You went swimming?'

'Yeah.' The muscles in my throat seemed swollen, and talking was difficult. 'I was up one end when a class of schoolchildren came in to use the pool. They stayed in the shallow end. I started playing these silly mind games – I do that a lot. I felt the eyes of the pool attendants on me, thinking, We know why he's come swimming at this time, it's so that he can gawp at these children. It was horrible.'

'You're burdened with a great sense of shame, I think. You come to me because you hope that I'll be shocked at what was done to you. But at the same time you must be worried that it's *you* I'll be disgusted by. That I won't be able to make a distinction between you and what was done *to* you.'

'When I was younger I was always having dreams where I was covered in shit.' I found myself thinking about the war in Iraq. To be implicated in such carnage was unbearable. The anti-war marches had been great: they'd lifted my spirits. I'd been at one with people from all walks of life, agreeing that the war would be wrong, counter-productive, a terrible crime. But at the end of the day we'd all gone home and left the politicians to carry on their murderous way. Far from feeling connected to the peace-loving side of humanity, I felt isolated in a world dominated by powerful men, exploiting their power to ignore the weak and trample on everything decent. The questions went round and round in my head. Who did they think they were? The world wasn't theirs to fuck up as they pleased. I loathed these jumped-up Jeremys trampling the world with their bombers and tanks, and loathed myself for being powerless to do anything about it.

The war wasn't the only thing on my mind. Carmen had been my rock. It had been a shock to us both when after several bouts of extreme pain, it was found that she had a tumour that required surgery. We went to the doctor's and hospital appointments together, and I tried to stay realistic and useful, to be there for her in her moments of darkest fear. Privately I was terrified: what if it was cancer? What if there were already secondaries? What if she died?

I described these events to the therapist. I tried to hide how upset I felt. Even before she replied, I knew what kind of impression I was making: that of an insecure, over-dependent male who, faced with a wife who was seriously ill, could think only about himself. I hated myself for it, but there was no point in denying the truth.

'You rely on her a great deal.'

'I think I'm one of those men who will drop dead days after their wife dies. You hear stories about that. I can't imagine surviving on my own. It's pathetic.'

There was another silence.

'I was just remembering how in the past I'd hate being at home on my own. I'd stay at work late just to make sure that Carmen would get back before me. And I thought about the state of panic I'd get into if we rowed and Carmen went cold on me, or talked about leaving. I've never felt any good on my own. There haven't been many times when I've been on my own, and then I've just been a mess. Though recently I've been seeking out opportunities to be alone, so that I don't need to hide how I'm feeling.'

'You seem to have no confidence that there'll be someone there for you whatever, unconditionally, as they say. You're not sure that your wife's love for you could survive exposure to the nasty stuff in your head, so you have to protect her from it. And you told me last time how you kept the abuse a secret from your mother, as if you couldn't rely on her being there for you either.'

During that first meeting the therapist had made only one suggestion: that I said whatever came into my mind, however embarrassing or trivial it seemed to me. What came into my mind at this point was a picture, or a series of pictures, of my mum.

The overall impression was confusing. Something cold and brittle, something warm and loving. Mum was tough and reliable – 'tough as old boots' was one of her favourite expressions, and in many ways it summed her up well. But she had also seemed remote, cut off from me.

I wasn't sure what time it was, but I knew it must be getting close to the end of the session. I didn't want to embark on something important and get cut off in the middle, so I disobeyed the therapist's advice and pushed these images out of my mind. But while I'd been thinking about my mother I'd become more conscious of another symptom, so I talked about that. 'One of the worst things at the moment is this feeling I carry around in my stomach. It's another thing I used to have years and years ago. Like a stone, a solid lump of something that's stuck in my gut. It's there when I go to bed each night, and I hope it'll disappear while I'm asleep, but it's always there, the first thing I'm aware of when I wake up. I want to vomit it up, or shit it out. But I can't. It feels heavy, and cold, and its coldness gets into everything.'

'There's something alien lodged inside you?'

My mind immediately switched back to my primary obsession: Jeremy. When I'd shouted at my colleagues at work and run from the room, what had been most shaming was that I'd longed to go back and tell them about Jeremy, to get them to understand, to make them look after me. They'd have thought I'd gone mad, of course. It was so strange – you couldn't open a paper or turn on the television without hearing about abuse, particularly sexual abuse, and yet there still seemed to be a taboo against talking about one's own experience of it. I've always had the fear that if people knew they'd see me as twisted, that they'd be forever imagining me being molested, and that they'd be embarrassed and annoyed that I'd confronted them with some-thing so distasteful.

Since the depression had returned, Jeremy had been a constant presence in my mind once again. I tried to deal with it, but I just went round in circles. I dwelt on each impingement, each humiliation; all the shame and self-deprecation sloshed around in my head. The hatred for what had happened to me, for the mess I'd made of my life, for him – all the bitterness surged and spilt, but what could I do with it? I tormented myself with images of a child at peace with himself, an adolescent without nightmares, an adult who felt free and alive. There seemed no escape from the bleakness, the unnecessary, unending waste.

'It seems to make sense to connect this stone-like thing with Jeremy.'

'Mmmm. I want to get rid of him, but I can't.'

'We're unsure at the moment why you seem to cling to him.'

I wasn't happy at that. Although I blamed myself for so much, I was also very touchy about being held responsible for even trivial things, let alone for holding on to Jeremy. 'Maybe. You're suggesting that we think about why. But that means talk-ing about what happened in more detail. And I'm sure you're about to tell me to leave.'

'You're right. It *is* time for us to stop now.'

I got up without looking back at her, muttered 'Thank you,' and let myself out. My legs were unsteady again, and I sat for a couple of minutes in the car before driving away.

*

As the weeks passed, my therapist began to put forward views of her own about my situation. She thought I should see her more than once a week. She suggested that I was holding back out of fear, and that this was also limiting the potential benefit of our work together. I protested that once a week was all I could afford, which wasn't strictly true. It would have been a bind finding the additional time but not impossible. Deep down I agreed with her absolutely, but still refused to come more often. I knew why this was. She'd become important enough to me already. Being depressed, I was feeling horribly insecure and very dependent. It suited me to divide my neediness between Carmen and my therapist, and wait and see how things turned out.

In therapy I rehearsed the reasons why a little boy might not have told anybody about what was happening to him, but the 45-year-old on the couch continued to rage and rant against his failure to look after himself. I couldn't tolerate contemplating my own lack of action. 'There's something I'll never get over. We can sit here and "understand" why I didn't tell anyone. I know how emotionally dependent I was on Jeremy. I can see it clearly. It was like somehow I'd got myself exiled from earth and found myself on the moon unable to get back, so I had to make do with the Man in the Moon. The gap was too great. And the mad thing was that the link with Jeremy somehow *was* the gap and I didn't realise it: I was dependent on him for help with the stress and strain when he was in large part its cause. Mad. But however we explain it, I can't get away from the fact that at any point I could have walked into my parents' bedroom and stopped it, there and then, dead. At the start I could have said, "Mummy, I don't like Jeremy touching my bottom." It would have been just as good if I'd said, "Mummy, I like it when Jeremy touches my bottom." She would have known and I've no doubt that she would have stopped it, just like that. When I was older I could just have said, "I don't want to spend time with Jeremy any more, so if he phones me I'm not in." I could have just stopped going down to see him. And it all comes back, somehow, to my having chosen my own fate. So who am I to go on whingeing about it now?' I was getting worked up. 'Do you know, once, Alex Jeffreys more or less asked me what was going on with Jeremy.'

The therapist interrupted me: 'I'm afraid it's time for us to stop now.'

'No – I've got to say this last thing. I was about twelve, I think. He asked me what was going on with Jeremy. He said that his mother thought it was odd. He'd been my friend since I was four and a half. And just for that, I cut him out. I pushed him away. I did it.' I heaved myself off the couch, unable to give my usual 'goodbye' or 'thank you'. I let out my first deep sob as I walked down the corridor towards the door, then sat with my arms hugging the steering wheel until the storm had passed.

*

I reread Jeremy's e-mails and decided that I'd been stupid to accept his assurances of being a reformed character. I felt the guilt now more strongly, and images of other children struggling with the devastation wrought by people like him plagued my mind. More, I loathed my passivity for what it said about me. A TV programme in which a crime was reported to the police by e-mail suggested a new avenue. In April 2004 I went to the computer and contacted the US police – I was sure Jeremy had followed his sister and mother, who'd emigrated to the States. The police replied that I should report the crime to my local law-enforcement agency, who would involve them if necessary.

I did a search under 'Metropolitan Police Sexual Abuse' and found a link to the Sapphire Team. I e-mailed, saying that I was contacting them in regard to a crime that had been committed so long before that there probably wasn't any point in reporting it. I said that it was to do with sexual abuse and that I was concerned I hadn't done enough to protect other children who might be harmed. I asked for advice on what I should do next. An unsigned e-mail came back within a few hours, urging me to report the abuse to my local police station. I baulked at this. In my response I said that the idea of standing in a queue, explaining myself over a desk and then filling in a form with the duty sergeant didn't appeal to me. I preferred to leave it to the Sapphire Team to decide whether to pursue the issue or not. I described Jeremy's method of infiltrating mainly poor families in Third World countries, and provided what information I could that might help to trace him. I was, however, concerned to distance myself from the hysterical denunciations of paedophilia that were then a recurrent feature of newspaper coverage of child abuse. Despite the impact Jeremy had had on my life, I didn't feel any great need for vengeance, I said. The only point in pursuing him would be to ensure that he was not harming children any more.

I left it at that, relieved that I'd finally broken my silence.

*

I continued with my once weekly therapy sessions, having no wish to stop this time around. They were proving immensely helpful, draining away the poison that built up in the days between meetings. It was tough, very tough, and at the end of each session I felt bruised and limp. I told my therapist once that I felt like a car being driven at top speed but in second gear. 'It's moving, but you know the parts are wearing themselves out.' However, I did seem more able to manage my normal responsibilities.

It was strange for me that details of my past still had the capacity to shock. I was telling her about the family holiday in Yugoslavia that Jeremy had also been part of, about being put in a room together at the hotel and then leaving with him to go to Rome.

'And you were *ten*?' She was incredulous.

'Ten. It's only strange to me when I see it in terms of someone else's ten-year-old. Difficult to imagine what was in my
parents' minds, really. I've thought so much about that. They
thought it was all good for me, I think. Things were different
then. I'd never heard the expression "child abuse", it just wasn't
around. I don't think it occurred to anyone.'

'I wonder about your rage, where it is.'

'Rage? You've no idea how much rage I feel. I spend all my
time hating what's going on in the world. If Tony Blair came
into the room now, I'd rip his eyes out, I'd tear his limbs off.
I'd like to do it in front of his family. I can't read the news any
more. I feel good inside every time I hear they've killed an
American soldier in Iraq. We've behaved disgustingly, and it's a
good thing if we don't get away with it. We've just gone right
back to the 1880s, and we're all pretending that imperialism is
a thing of the past. It makes me sick. Completely sick.' I
paused, then carried on more calmly. 'I had a dream about Blair
a couple of nights ago. I was screaming at him in some public
place, about how he'd destroyed people's lives, how he'd lied
to everyone, and I was just ripping him apart – verbally this
time – so everyone could see how vile he is – and he is vile –
but I know that all that venom is about Jeremy, and knowing
that I can't exorcise him. And then – just to prove it – I find
myself worrying about him again. You know, if I ever did
expose him, how he might kill himself and how I'd have
destroyed him! And I'm back where I was fifteen years ago. I'm
forty-five years old, for Christ's sake, and still going on about
this stuff. It must make you sick. It makes me sick. Why can't I
just vomit it all up once and for all?'

The rage remained but trapped or displaced. None for my parents, none for my therapist, some for Jeremy – but then accompanied by anxiety. Safer to keep it for myself; or the politicians.

*

'You know, what I come here yearning for most of all is just to be – that you can see me, warts and all, and still stay there. Without the need to make me feel better. Just for me not to protect you from what I'm really like. I've got a wonderful family, who make life worth living, but I'm looking after them all the time. *All the time*. I found myself daydreaming the other day, that you had a son in real life that you had called Matt. Obvious what that's about.'

The therapist didn't speak, but I knew she was listening. I knew too that I was putting off telling her something important.

'Last week I went with Carmen to see *Bad Education*, the new film by Almodóvar. I don't know what to say about it, why it was so extraordinary to watch it. I came out and Carmen asked if I was all right – she knows that watching films about abuse can upset me sometimes – and I could hardly talk about how I felt. There were no women in the film, none at all. It drew an absolutely clear line – there was love between men, and love between boys, both of which were beautifully portrayed – and then there were the destructive intrusions of an adult's lust into a child's life. And the consequences. Going on and on.' I paused. 'The next morning I called the police. The film just made my mind up. I don't feel so comfortable telling you that – what you'll think about it.'

'You think I'll disapprove that you went to the police?'

'I don't know. Maybe. You know how therapy is so much about seeing the problem as happening inside, sorting out one's internal conflicts. So, in some way, I suppose you might have thought it was a cop-out. Anyway, they sent this boy around. The bell rang, I opened the door, and there was a boy in uniform. Turned out he was twenty-two. But good for him; think where I was when I was twenty-two! And he was lovely, really. We sat at the dining table, and he went through a kind of spiel, you could tell that he meant it, but also that he'd learnt it on a course, about what he was there to do, how he would write a report and pass it on to someone in the Child Protection Team who would take it further. And then to say in my own time what it was I wanted to report. Carmen was there too. And I talked. I felt very fragile and had to stop a couple of times. Carmen brought a box of tissues. She was lovely: I really felt her strong presence, but she didn't say a word. I had to look away from her, to say things that I still think are going to disgust her. She held my hand when I cried. Afterwards we were all standing up and talking, I was asking about his work, and suddenly he was crying. The bloody policeman was crying! Unbelievable. He was lovely. I don't know why he's asked to specialise in that work, I dread to think, but he was a lovely man. I'd worried about talking to a male officer, but he was good.

'I said that I didn't expect much to come of it, because of how long ago it all took place. But I would like Jeremy to be interviewed. I'd like a policeman to go up to him and say, "We're arresting you on suspicion of having sexually abused children," and take him in and question him. And push the letters he wrote to me at him and ask him to explain them. "What did you mean by this, what was going on then?" That sort of thing. Make him explain himself. Even if at the end of it all he walked out and nothing more happened. I'd like him to be scared, to know that the world was onto him. Like they did with Pinochet. Because I really think he feels above it all, like he can't be touched. That he's got away with it for all these years, and no one is clever enough to stop him.

'At the same time I'm worried about him. It sounds weird, but I've spent so long looking after this guy that I'm worried how he might not be able to manage it. I sometimes worry about being unfair to him. Especially reading all this hysterical crap in the newspapers. You wonder if the people who write the headlines would have done any better if they'd woken up one morning to find they were only attracted to children. What would *I* have done?'

*

A few days after that session I received a call from the local Child Protection Team, a female officer this time, asking to make an appointment. Stella arrived exactly on time. Carmen was at work, and I saw her alone. We went over the same material in more detail. For me it could only be an emotional experience, and I could see that Stella was not unaffected. She was touched, but she was also strong and professional, and had a job to do.

Stella explained the process. She would need to meet with me again, and after that she would discuss the case with her senior, and between them a decision would be reached about whether there were grounds to prosecute. If they thought there were, a report would go to the Crown Prosecution Service. If not, she would write up a fuller report and trace Jeremy, wherever he was in the world. Then she would send the report to the social services and police departments in that area. Did I understand, and did I want to proceed?

Yes, I did.

The second meeting with Stella was more difficult. I had to describe in more detail the nature of the abuse, who did what to whom, where, at what age. Did anyone else know? Did it happen to my brother or sisters? I didn't think so but couldn't be sure. What other evidence might there be? The questions took me further and faster than I would ever have been able to go on my own. Stella became another person who clearly didn't blame me and wasn't disgusted at what she heard. She was disgusted, and angry, but not with me.

After the meeting I felt good, and wondered why. I realised that a by-product – or perhaps the primary purpose – of contacting the police was to reinforce the efforts I was making in therapy to locate the abuse in time and space. 'It' – the indefinable thing that it seemed best to file under the catch-all 'sexual abuse' – was not going on inside me now. It had happened then, there, to that child. The Jeremy everyone was concerned about was still out there, somewhere, possibly still a danger to the public.

Stella's questions made it necessary to talk to my family again, properly, and also provided me with the confidence to do it.

*

It was the first time I'd mentioned Jeremy to any member of my family for 15 years. I hadn't talked to my brother Peter or my youngest sister Jenny even then.

I phoned Peter. After some small talk I came round to my reason for phoning. 'Peter – well, it's difficult. I don't know if you are aware that a long time ago I told Mum and Dad that Jeremy had not been such a helpful influence … ?'

'I knew something went on. I went round the house one day, and they were really upset and I made them tell me. Nothing was very clear, though.'

'No, I couldn't be specific with them then. Jeremy's a paedophile, and he sexually abused me for a long time. I've recently reported it to the police, and that's why I'm contacting you. They've asked me if anything happened to anyone else in the family, or if anyone else saw anything, if there's any support-ing evidence.'

Peter interrupted me. He sounded shaken. 'Can I think about it? Talk to you later on? Would that be OK? I'll phone you back tomorrow.'

When he phoned back, Peter was his usual self again.

'I've been wracking my brains, Matt, but I can't remember anything. I can remember him doing things that in hindsight were a bit weird, like drying me with a towel after a bath. Things like that. But nothing that could be called abuse. On the other hand,' he added, 'I'm happy to make something up if it'll help us nail the bastard.'

I laughed, relieved to have some humour injected into the conversation, and hearing the solidarity underlying the joke.

I arranged for Carmen and me to have a meal with Ella, who lived close by. Together we went back over the past. Ella was hugely supportive but upset too.

'It's my image of my childhood too, Matt, that's all messed up. I'm so angry: angry with Jeremy for what he did to you but also angry that he fooled our parents, that he convinced me that he was something special. Whenever I've talked to people about my past, I've described this idyllic childhood by the seaside and included Jeremy in that: and the specialness of our trips to Claystone Bay. And all that *crap*.' She was fighting back tears.

I cleared up another issue that had bothered me from the past. 'You remember ages ago, when I talked to Mum and Dad, and you and Joanna, about Jeremy abusing me. I don't think I was very explicit. But it's been weird. Up until that day Jeremy was mentioned all the time. Everyone linked our names constantly. And since that day no one has ever mentioned him to me. And I had the distinct feeling that you were all angry with me because I'd upset Mum and Dad, that I should have kept my mouth shut.'

'It wasn't like that, Matt. Not really. We *were* worried about them; I remember that Dad was ill then. And it was a shock hearing what you were saying, and confusing too because it was like a single conversation and then nothing more. It was difficult to know how to handle it. And you were in a terrible state at the time. Really, I don't know if you remember. There were times when you seemed really ill. It was difficult to know who to worry about and how to look after them. It seemed easier, I suppose, when it all went away again. And then you seemed to get better too. But it's not that I've forgotten.' Later she added, 'I'm really proud of you, Matt. It's a big deal, going to the police. Have you thought about what it could mean: publicity, a court case, cross-examination?'

I'd discussed this with Carmen, but it seemed such a remote possibility. I felt driven along my current course regardless of what it might mean in the distant future.

Approaching Joanna was more difficult. She lived in the West Country, but, more than that, she and I did not get on well. We hadn't spoken properly for years. She agreed to a meeting at a town midway between our homes. We spent the day drinking coffee, walking, eating in a restaurant and talking. Like Ella, Joanna confirmed that Jeremy had never abused her. And, also like her sister, that in the absence of any clear information she had minimised what she imagined had happened to me when I had talked of being abused 15 years earlier.

We talked about the bad blood that existed between us, which, it seemed, sprang from Joanna's perception of me as selfish and spoilt. The way she spoke, conveyed strongly the message that something about me made it impossible for her to like me, that I ruined things, and that it was up to me to make it up to her in some way. It was hard for her then, when I told her more of the truth about Jeremy; it wasn't easy for her to be confronted with information that presented me more as victim than perpetrator. I attempted to reconcile these feelings by suggesting that she had been as much abused by him as I had been: she was always on the outside, never sharing in the treats and the travelling. We should be equally angry with him, and perhaps equally forgiving of one another. It worked, up to a point.

Back home, I wondered what further evidence might be available. I went to the bags of correspondence that I'd lodged up in the attic – I'd always been a hoarder – and was amazed to find dozens of letters from Jeremy. It was uncomfortable rereading them, setting aside those that might be useful to the police. It occurred to me that there was another of Jeremy's protégé's whom I might be able to contact. By means of an internet search I contacted Mikis, now a man with a family and director of a theatre company in Perth, Australia. In contrast to the rather arrogant child I'd remembered, his messages conveyed real warmth. It was amazing to read his description of how Jeremy had adopted the same techniques to get close to him as he had with me. Having been taken in, just like a member of the family, Jeremy had started to touch and kiss Mikis, who had rebelled the first time Jeremy had tried to get into bed with him. It had happened, Mikis wrote, on the visit he had made to London – while I was working on Jeremy's films. Mikis, then 11, had got up and left, making his own way to Heathrow and finding a plane back home. 'I kept matters to myself,' he wrote, 'and eventually told my mother but in a different way.' He gave me permission to share this information with the police.

I posted copies of these e-mails to Stella. The case passed the first hurdle, and her report was sent to the CPS.

After what felt like weeks I had a call from her. 'Matt, I'm sorry to have to tell you that the CPS have decided that we cannot proceed against Jeremy. They've given two reasons. The first is that the offences were committed such a long time ago that Mr Rushton would be able to argue that it was unreasonable to expect him to be able to construct a defence against your allegations. A judge would have to quash any legal procedure on those grounds alone. Second, they're saying that the cost of extradition, with so little chance of a successful prosecution, would be against the public interest. I'm sorry, Matt.'

'Oh, right.' I was trying to sort out my thoughts. 'What would happen if he came back to England? If I told you he was arriving on a particular flight at Heathrow, would you go and arrest him?'

'Because the CPS has declared that it is outside the period when we could prosecute, I wouldn't be able to do that.'

'But if I contacted another police force and made the allegation, they would have to, wouldn't they? Even if in the long run he was released? Because I've had mixed feelings about the case going forward. It might have run on for years, and I don't know what it would have been like standing up and being cross-examined in court, and all that. But I really want him to be arrested. I want someone to turn up at his workplace and take him off in handcuffs, just to feel the consequences, to feel that I had done something and he had felt it.'

'I understand that. If you chose to call another police force, I think they'd have to follow it up. Of course they would. I'm sorry we couldn't do more. But I'm now going to write the report, as I explained before, and we'll track down his whereabouts, and if it turns out there are any children at risk from him, action will be taken to protect them.'

'Good. Good. Thanks.'

Stella had called an hour before one of my therapy sessions. I sank onto the therapist's couch and bellowed my grief and anger, and disappointment and sense of failure. Then I calmed down. 'What's clear to me now is that I was using the police to get revenge. Not just for me but for what Jeremy did to my family. I feel so guilty about what I allowed him to do to us all, and what it has done now to the family's view of itself, and this was the way I had of showing that we weren't just passive victims. That we could say "Fuck off" and make something happen to show that however much we were taken in as children, we're not taken in any more. It was my way of making it up to them.'

I paused, deeply sad.

'But I'm also relieved about the decision. If there was a prosecution, this whole horrible business might have gone on dominating my life for years. Going to the police did help establish that Jeremy is outside of myself, that he's someone I can stand up to and fight. That I'm separate from him. What I'm afraid about now is that it will all flood back inside me, that I'll go back to how I was when I first came here. That's what talking to the police has been about: it's really felt that something that had been at war inside me is not now a private matter. It's about a public crime. Do you know that in all my years of therapy no one ever suggested going to the police, or wondered why I hadn't done that? They always explored the reasons I couldn't talk to my parents as a child, why I hadn't acted on my own behalf then, but not why I hadn't done so as an adult. And while therapy has been a lifeline, and I've changed so much because of it, I've also had the feeling that there's been more of an interest in what it is about me that made Jeremy go for me, you know, figuring out why was I so vulnerable to him. I know that's important, but at times it did feel as if I was to blame after all, that I had this greed for more than I deserved, for an exclusive relationship with one person, and that it was my failing that I hadn't accommodated to being one amongst others in a large family. Perhaps that's right, I don't know. But it has been different and important to talk to people who know it's a crime and who don't demand that I account for my own actions.'

*

Through work and reading I was reasonably well informed about theories of personality development, and I'd become accustomed to hearing and using terms like 'the internal world' in therapy. What I understood this phrase to mean was the way our unconscious mind is elaborated, especially during childhood, taking in important experiences with other people. This was why we were each unique, because we didn't pop out of shells fully formed and relying on instinct to show us how to be. We lived through years of immaturity, in a state of extreme dependence, in order to learn what it meant to be a person. This is the truth that we seem to want to get away from when we give so much attention to DNA and genes as the way to explain emotional and personality disturbances. So much easier, if relief can be found in a packet of pills.

One aspect of my own childhood that this period of therapy had brought alive was the realisation of how split I had been. This was different, I thought, from a rich variety of experience that could be integrated to form a coherent whole. The parts I'd played were mutually incompatible. There was a me who remained hopelessly immature, dependent beyond its time – and therefore hating whoever I felt dependent upon. This was what had poisoned my relationships with various girlfriends. It was still there, but it wasn't always in control. Fortunately there was another side, which I supposed I'd taken in from my life with a loving and wholesome, if also naïve and wrong-headed, family. And school. The parts that Jeremy had been partly or wholly sealed off from.

These two parts were not simply different. The second was without much doubt the basis of all that was wholesome and substantial in my life now, the part that could work well with others who needed consistency and thoughtfulness, that could provide Carmen and Jack with something solid and reliable too. The part that remained stagnant – narcissistic – in Jeremy's care was the part I had to be wary of, the part that wrecked my life when it took over, when somehow 'I' became one with this single sick part of my psyche.

I had a question for my therapist. 'What is it that determines which bit feels like *me*? I know I've got a Jeremy inside me still. I wonder if that's something to do with this stone thing that I get in my stomach.'

'We've speculated that you might have turned to Jeremy as a refuge in the aftermath of your mother leaving,' she said. 'Recently you were afraid that you were going to be abandoned again, by Carmen. I wonder if there's a repetition there, that when you feel in danger of being abandoned you resurrect Jeremy as a protective figure, only to find that his embrace isn't so safe at all.'

'Maybe.' It seemed to make sense. Yet as I lay thinking it over, I realised how distasteful I found it.

In the following days I had a number of dreams that seemed to say something about this moment of falling under Jeremy's influence. In one I was at a party with Carmen and we were talk-ing to another couple. The couple showed no interest in me whatsoever, and eventually I decided to wander off by myself. I walked around and then sat by myself on a sofa. Then I realised I needed to go to the toilet. When I pushed open the bathroom door there was a naked boy in the sink, with a man standing beside him. Could Carmen have represented Joanna, and the couple my parents? And who was the man?

In another dream I was working in a school. I walked into my office and was surprised to find a man in a white uniform and two schoolboys there. I waited until they had finished, and the boys walked out. The man said, 'I work for Save the Children.' I said, 'Where have you worked before?' by which I meant, 'Which countries have you done relief work in?' I said that I had a chest problem I was worried about, and he replied apologetically that he didn't have any X-ray equipment and couldn't help. He left. Then I walked towards the toilets. I saw then that I was dressed in pyjamas, and that I had a heavy object weighing down my pyjama bottoms – I had crapped in my pants. The toilets seemed dirty and wet. Then I belched and an object came up into my mouth. I took it out in my hand and looked at it: it was a slimy lump of shit. I woke up. It was ages before I could relax and get back to sleep again.

'What do you make of this?'

'That nothing can make me clean. That all I do is produce shit, from both ends. I don't know.'

'You do seem to conclude that it's too late for the Save the Children people to help.'

'When I first had therapy, fifteen years ago, it was such a shock to be made aware of the distorted way in which I'd thought about my own life. For a long time I wanted to write a play with a split stage. On one you'd have scenes from childhood, the way things really were, and on the other would be an adult me lying on a couch in dialogue with a therapist. I wanted to be the audience watching the two versions and observing how they differed from one another. If it had been well written, I'd have been able to see how the past gets distorted and how over time the two versions come closer together, perhaps not exactly the same but recognisably the same life. I knew I didn't have the skill to do it. That was one of the first things I was angry with Jeremy about. He tried to teach me so many things that I couldn't learn – even Chinese at one point – and he never taught me to do something he did well, which was write. He always criticised me when I wrote letters, saying that there was something artificial about them, that I hid the "real me". I know I can't write as powerfully as I would like, but so what? What I'm trying to say is that I've been thinking of writing it all down. More than think-ing about it, I've started doing it. Writing a book.'

'An autobiography?'

'Kind of. Trying to trace what it all amounted to. It's been changing shape in my mind. At first it was just about my child-hood, what happened with Jeremy. Then it seemed it had to include the consequences. Its theme is invasion, occupation, corruption and lies. Deception and self-deception. And the long, perhaps unending, striving towards liberation, whatever that means.

'A while back someone was speaking on the radio about why people don't write. He said that it's not helpful to sit down in front of a blank sheet of paper feeling that you've got to produce a masterpiece. It would be better to say to yourself, "Here, I think there's something that might interest you."'

After a pause the therapist said, 'You internalised the abusive relationship with Jeremy, and the police investigation certainly helped you to externalise it again. That was important. You're afraid that it might force its way back inside you, and now you have a project to try to keep it on the outside. I wonder what will happen when you've finished writing this book?'

The long silence that followed was broken with her quiet amen: 'It's time for us to stop now.'

MY 'TRUEST' FRIEND

~ Epilogue ~

I'm sitting with Carmen in what passes for a café in a remote cove in northern Tenerife. It's not so warm, so we've kept our coats on. Out to sea the sky is blue and the sunshine brightens the horizon, making beautiful an old cargo ship moored offshore. There's no silence: like pilgrims, an endless succession of rollers break in supplication, relinquishing their power before the cathedral cliffs that rise ridged and crenulated out of the black volcanic sand.

We talk of this and that. It's a beautiful spot, and we'll come back again, hopefully when it's warmer. Then we're quiet, just taking in the scene.

I've spent the last few days going over this book, and I'm wondering what to make of the versions of myself it contains, some of which, today, I cannot connect with. Yet I recognise them all. In Pullman's *His Dark Materials*, Lyra finds the secret doors – or rather rents – in reality that enable her to slip from one parallel universe to another. Some of these 'places' are entirely separate from one another; some share the same geographical location but exist in different historical times. The openings are dangerous. They make me think of these various people I seem to have been, that I still am, as if there's some way I slide from one edition of myself to another without realising it, and without knowing the way back.

The book belongs to a genre of childhood recollections, of lives whose beginnings were blighted by violence and neglect of one kind or another. Typically, they end on a comforting note: of hardships overcome, of love found at last, of cures for addictions, and of despair and self-loathing giving way to hope and self-respect. I don't know if readers look forward to such resolution, but I have to end more equivocally.

At the moment I feel OK. Inside and out I find value, meaning, significance, connection, proportion, cause and effect, colour, potential. Happiness, certainly, but also sadness, and grief. It's not all pleasure and joy, but here even the difficult parts seem to be about movement, about acceptance and adjustment to what's real. Yesterday, today and hopefully tomorrow – it's good to be alive.

But I've learnt not to be complacent. It's like living in an earthquake zone, over a geological fault. You don't think about the danger all the time, but every now and then there's a discernible tremor, a reminder that mean and destructive forces lurk somewhere within, subdued but not eliminated.

Today, though, it's good to be alive, and there's so much to live for. I've a new and deeply satisfying job. And a wonderful family. Jack's growing too fast – too fast for me, that is. The focus of his world is now his friends and his music, out there somewhere. Which is just as it ought to be. But I can't say that I don't look back at the old photos of him as a little boy, asleep on the back seat of the car or splashing in the sea, without a pang or three. Being Dad to Jack has meant taking a crash course in mourning. From the very start, there was only just time to appreciate what he was and then he wouldn't be that any more. What came next was always more than compensation. But there's only so much loss one should have to take! It seems that Jack's life represents the kind of childhood and adolescence I might have had, and that thought both brings immense joy and opens up a vent of hurt. At the same time I whisper a warning to myself: my parents no doubt had the same thoughts watching me, as I made my apparently gilded way through life.

Of course the depressions have had an impact on Jack. During one difficult time, when he was very small, he told Jayne that I was the most serious person he knew. Sometimes I'm not aware of how negative I might sound – how depressed my thinking is even when I'm not feeling down. We were in a remote area of lakes and volcanoes in South America – we'd gone there to meet Carmen's family – and I felt inspired, as I always am in places where nature still seems to hold its own against the human onslaught. I was holding forth on the wonders of Stone Age culture and hunter-gatherer societies, comparing my romanticised image of them with the horrors of city life.

Jack interrupted me. 'You don't like people very much, do you, Dad?'

I was taken aback and forced to consider my position. 'I'm not sure that being in large numbers brings out the best in us,' I replied. Still, though he's aware that my thinking can get a bit warped, he shows no sign of feeling that he has to have the same outlook on the world.

And I look across at Carmen. These many years on, we're still disagreeing about our favourite music, still upholding related but distinct views on the world and how it works, still together. I smile, thinking of what Jeremy would have made of the person I've turned out to be: driving a car (no longer cycling!); paying off a mortgage; married to Carmen, with a love that has survived not just body hair but greying temples, and bodies no longer toned and beautiful. Total capitulation!

And it feels just right, the two of us sitting beside the sea, doing nothing in particular. Being lazy. We sometimes wonder about the chance factors that led us – a bookseller's son from an English resort and a teacher's daughter from a mining village in the Atacama Desert – to find peace together. It's odd to think that the Jeremys and the Pinochets of this world had their part to play.